Basics of Language for Language Learners

Basics of Language for Language Learners

Peter W. Culicover and Elizabeth V. Hume

 THE OHIO STATE UNIVERSITY PRESS / COLUMBUS

Library of Congress Cataloging-in-Publication Data
Culicover, Peter W.
Basics of language for language learners / Peter W. Culicover and Elizabeth Hume.
    p. cm.
Includes bibliographical references and index.
ISBN 978-0-8142-5172-0 (pbk. : alk. paper)—ISBN 978-0-8142-1120-5 (cloth : alk. paper)—ISBN 978-0-8142-9128-3 (cd-rom) 1. Language and languages—Study and teaching. I. Hume, Elizabeth V., 1956– II. Title.
P51.C78 2010
418.0071—dc22
                              2009045071

This book is available in the following editions:
Cloth (ISBN 978-0-8142-1120-5)
Paper (ISBN 978-0-8142-5172-0)
CD-ROM (ISBN 978-0-8142-9128-3)

Cover design by Laurence Nozik.
Text design by Jennifer Shoffey Forsythe.
Type set in Adobe Minion Pro.
Printed by Thomson-Shore, Inc.

♾ The paper used in this publication meets the minimum requirements of the American National Standard for Information Sciences—Permanence of Paper for Printed Library Materials. ANSI Z39.48-1992.

9 8 7 6 5 4 3 2 1

Contents

Acknowledgments ix
To the Language Learner xi

CHAPTER 1 **Preliminaries** **1**
Overview of the Book 1
First Language Learning 4
Second Language Learning 13
Exercises 18
References 18

SECTION I **SOUNDING LIKE A NATIVE SPEAKER** **19**

CHAPTER 2 **Foreign Accents** **21**
Knowing How to Speak a Language 21
Dealing with Unfamiliar Sounds 22
Dealing with Unfamiliar Sequences of Sounds 25
Dealing with Unfamiliar Syllable-, Word-, and Sentence-Level
  Properties 27
Summary 29
Reference 30

CHAPTER 3 **How to Make a Consonant** **31**
Introduction 31
Creating Speech Sounds 34
Parts of the Vocal Tract Involved in Making Sounds 35

	Places Where the Air Passage Is Narrowed for Consonants	36
	Narrowness of the Air Passage	41
	Air Flow through the Nose and Mouth	44
	Position of the Vocal Folds	45
	Length of the Consonant	47
	Summary	48
	Additional Exercise: Comparing Consonants	49
	References	50
Chapter 4	**How to Make a Vowel**	**51**
	Introduction	51
	Parts of the Vocal Tract Involved in Making Vowels	51
	Places Where the Air Passage Is Narrowed for Vowels	52
	Narrowness of the Air Passage	54
	The Shape of the Lips	56
	Changing Vowel Quality from Start to Finish: Diphthongs	57
	Air Flow through the Mouth and Nose	58
	Length of the Vowel	59
	Summary	60
	Additional Exercise: Comparing Vowels	61
	Reference	61
Chapter 5	**Putting Sounds Together**	**62**
	Introduction	62
	Sound Sequences in English and Other Languages	64
	Summary	70
	Exercises	70
	References	72
Chapter 6	**Common Pronunciation Errors**	**73**
	Interpreting Unfamiliar Symbols	73
	Aspiration	74
	Alveolar vs. Dental Consonants	77
	Flapping	80
	Released and Unreleased Stop Consonants	81
	Full and Reduced Vowels	82
	Monophthongs vs. Diphthongs	83
	Unrounded Back Vowels	84
	Summary	85
SECTION II	**THINKING LIKE A NATIVE SPEAKER**	**87**
Chapter 7	**The Work That Language Does**	**89**
	Accent: A Feeling for Form	89

An Example: Communicating an Idea   90
Form, Content, Function, and Force   93
Grammar: The Role of Form in Language   95
What Is Structure?   97
Categories   98
Summary   102
Additional Exercises   103
References   103

Chapter 8   Talking about Things   104
Introduction   104
Nouns   105
Do Other Languages Have Nouns?   107
Determiners   109
Adjectives   118
Relative Clauses   126
Summary   130
Additional Exercise   131
References   131

Chapter 9   Expressing Meaning   132
Some Errors in English   132
Verbs and Verb Phrases   134
Identifying the Participants in an Event or State   138
Subject and Object across Languages   142
Actives and Passives   148
Time and Truth   152
English Auxiliary Verbs   161
Expressing Sentence Function   162
Summary   169
Additional Exercises   170
References   171

SECTION III   ACTING LIKE A NATIVE SPEAKER   173

Chapter 10   The Link between Language and Culture   175
Introduction   175
Language and Culture   177
Language Varieties   180
Language Attitudes   181
Gesture   187
Summary   193
References   193

Chapter 11	**Politeness**	194
	Introduction	194
	Solidarity and Deference	195
	Expressing Politeness in English	196
	Politeness across Cultures	198
	The Expression of Politeness in Grammar	202
	Summary	207
	References	207
Chapter 12	**Swearing, Insults, and Taboos**	**209**
	Introduction	209
	Swearing, Insults, and Language Learning	210
	Common Bases for Swearing and Insults across Cultures	211
	Summary	215
	References	215
Chapter 13	**Conclusion**	**216**
	Language Is a Human Phenomenon	216
	Language Is a Skill, and Practice Is Essential	216
	There Is a Social Aspect to Language	217
	Look at Your Own Language	217
	How to Use This Knowledge	218
Subject Index		219
Language Index		225

Acknowledgments

We would like to express our appreciation to a number of individuals who played a role in the development of this book: Dan Culicover, Hope Dawson, Kathleen Currie Hall, Dan Humphries, Julie McGory, Jeff Mielke, Sharon Ross, and Bridget Smith. We are grateful to Malcolm Litchfield at The Ohio State University Press for his input and enthusiastic support of this project. And we are grateful to the many students who worked with these materials over the years and provided us with their invaluable feedback.

To the Language Learner

Who This Book Is For

We wrote this book for the student of language who wants to better understand how language works. We assume that the student is a speaker of English, either a native speaker or someone who has learned English as a second language. The challenge for this student is to learn how to become a successful learner of other languages.

Our view is that you (the student) have had a reasonable amount of exposure to learning a language. You have found certain parts of the activity to be relatively easy and others to be very challenging, perhaps almost impossible. Our goal is to help you take advantage of the parts that you find easy and build on them, and find ways to deal more effectively with the parts that you find more challenging.

Language learning, like many other skilled activities that people engage in, does not come easily for the average person. Think of playing a sport at a very competitive level, or a musical instrument. Success in these activities, and in language learning, requires perseverance and practice for the average person (and that's most of us!). The truth is that there is no silver bullet, no magic potion, no super pill that will get us where we want to go without exerting the effort.

How Language Works

"OK," you say, "I understand that this is going to take work, and I am willing to put in the effort." The approach that we are taking in this book is that the effort will pay off much more if you have an understanding of how language works. In learning a second language, you have a tremendous advantage, which is that you have already learned at least one other language, your native language. You already have an **intuitive** understanding of how language works, so that you will very likely recognize a lot about language if we illustrate it using your own language.

But most people have a very imperfect and sometimes mistaken **explicit** understanding of how language works. That is, they are not able to recognize aspects of language, such as what the possible sounds are and how they are produced in a given language, and explain them to themselves and others. What we are aiming for in this book is a basic **explicit** understanding of how language works that is **based on** one's own language and that can be **applied to** thinking about the language to be learned. It is our belief that a conscious understanding of the workings of language is a very important tool in dealing with the challenge of learning another language. It does not substitute for perseverance and practice, but it should help you make the best use of the effort that you are willing to put forth.

Here is one illustration. In order to be able to speak a language, you need to be able to make the sounds. You can try to imitate the sounds and get correction from an instructor, you can hire a tutor, you can work with tapes and software, and you can even go live in a country where the language is spoken. All of this is helpful, and if you work at it long enough, your skills will improve.

What this book contributes is an understanding of how the various parts of the mouth are used to make different sounds and how the sounds differ depending on how the parts of the mouth are used. It does not substitute for imitation and correction, practice with tapes, working with a native speaker, and so on. Its goal is to provide you with a **conscious understanding** of what is going on in your mouth and in your mind as you are trying to produce the sounds of a language. We want you to understand why some sounds are easy for you and some are hard, what kinds of mistakes you make and why those, and how you can fix your mistakes most efficiently.

We have the same kinds of goals in your understanding of grammar, of how language is used in social settings, and of how language can be inadvertently misused. This book is not about theory; it is about practical understanding. Of course, there is a lot of theory behind what we have put in this book—we are not making it up. But your concern is not with understanding the theory of how language works; it is with understanding how language works.

So, with this in mind, we keep the technical terminology to a minimum. We introduce terms for things so that we can refer to them—the first sound in *boy* is a bilabial stop (we'll explain what that is soon), the word *boy* is a noun, and so on. Some of these terms are familiar to some readers, but not all are familiar to all. So check off what you already know, and pay close attention to what is new to you. Most importantly, the things that are most familiar to us in our own language reemerge in other languages in many different ways, some of which are familiar, and some of which are not. We are using the native language—English—and the terminology for main features of the native language as a platform for looking at other languages that differ from it.

Preliminaries

Overview of the Book

*T*his book is intended to help you become a more effective and efficient student of a foreign language. If you have studied another language in the past, you know that the task of language learning is exciting but it can also be very challenging. The challenge stems in part from the basic fact that to become proficient in another language, you need to learn how to combine potentially new sounds and words in novel ways to create what are most likely unfamiliar structures. Learning how to do this, and practicing it, take time and effort.

Pal franse pa ki lespri pou sa.
'To speak French doesn't mean you are smart.'

HAITIAN PROVERB

Learning a second language is a very different experience from when you learned your first language! Children learn their first language completely naturally, apparently effortlessly and without formal instruction. If they are exposed to more than one language, they learn each language without difficulty. Moreover, they become competent native speakers in just a few years, in full command of the sounds and structures of their language, although they continue to acquire vocabulary over many years as their understanding of the world develops. And children are indistinguishable from other native speakers in their ability to interact socially with the language. They **are** native speakers.

Contrast this situation with that of an adult learning a second language. For the vast majority of us, this learning does not feel entirely natural, it is certainly not effortless, and formal instruction appears to be helpful for most of us (although it is typically not sufficient). The adult second language learner typically has a foreign accent, makes grammatical errors, does not have active control over the full vocabulary, sometimes has difficulty figuring out how to say even the most mundane things, and often does not understand what is being said. In many respects, the linguistic abilities of a second language learner are comparable to those of a very young child (say, 2 or 3 years old) who is learning a first language.

These observations certainly do not come as news to anyone who has tried to learn a second language. Further below, we focus on some of the differences between first and second language learning, and on why first language learning appears to be so easy. This will help us understand what we have to do to facilitate our approach to learning a second language (although it will never be totally effortless).

It is important to be clear at the outset about how the information that is conveyed in this book can be useful to the language learner. There is little evidence that explicit knowledge about the structure of a language leads directly and automatically to improvement in the ability to speak and understand that language. It is no substitute for extensive and well-structured practice in pronunciation, conversation, reading, and writing.

However, even a casual glance at any introductory textbook will show that the teaching of second languages appeals to familiarity with concepts about how languages work, how the sounds of language are produced, and how the sentences of a language are structured. You may be familiar with some of these concepts. However, our experience with students whose native language is English is that many of them have less knowledge than they would like to have about how their own language works, how its sounds are produced, and how its sentences are structured. Thus there is an added challenge involved in learning a second language, when these concepts are appealed to as a way of explaining how the second language works, how its sounds are produced, and how its sentences are structured.

Consider the problem of learning the sounds of another language. Because languages use different sounds, it is not possible to simply transfer the sounds of your own language into the language you are learning. This is true even if your language and the language you are learning use the same alphabet.

For example, instruction in English for German will try to relate the German sounds to English sounds. Here is a typical description of the German "long *o*" sound:[1] "Long *o*. Spelling: oh, o, oo. Pronunciation: Like the vowel in English 'so,' but with lips extremely rounded and no offglide into an 'ooh'-sound."

Such descriptions raise lots of questions. You might know the answer to some of them, but not to all of them. What is a vowel? What is an offglide? What is the difference between a "long" and a "short" vowel? What is lip rounding?

And what about that strange letter *ö*? "Long *ö*. Spelling: öh, ö. Pronunciation: Somewhat like the vowel in English 'burn.' To produce it, say the German long *e*, then round the lips as for the long *o*. Do not allow your tongue to move toward the back of your mouth as you round your lips. Note the difference between the long rounded back vowel *o* and the long rounded front vowel *ö*." Whew! How do I control my tongue so it doesn't

---

1. Adapted from the website http://www.wm.edu/modlang/gasmit/pronunciation/.

move toward the back of my mouth? What happens if I don't?

All languages have sounds that are similar to some extent to English sounds, but different from them in how they are produced in the mouth. One of our goals is to help you understand the common terminology that is used to describe these sounds. Such terminology includes concepts such as "vowel," "lip rounding," and so on. Another is to help you understand the ways in which sounds can differ from one another, and how these differences correspond to the way different types of sounds are produced in the mouth. Such understanding requires study of how the mouth is structured and how the vocal cords, the tongue, and the teeth are used to produce different sounds.

Of course there is another part to knowing a language: knowing how to make sentences. Again, typical second language instruction uses concepts and terminology that can be very useful. In learning a language such as Spanish, you will be taught about "nouns" that have "masculine" or "feminine" "gender." What is a noun? How can a *table* be feminine? "Verbs" have "conjugations," with forms in the "present," "past," and "future" "tense." But what is a verb, what is a conjugation, what is future tense? Does English have future tense? And so on.

In summary, our goal is to help you understand these terms and concepts so that you can put them to use most effectively. We want to help make the task of learning a language more manageable. One of the ways that we'll achieve this is to help you develop the ability to think analytically about language so that you are tuned into the structures of language and how they work. Understanding the task better will not automatically improve your memory or the speed at which you learn, but it may help you focus on the parts of the task that are most challenging for you.

You will also become familiar with the various dimensions along which languages can differ, such as sounds, words, sentence structure, and culture. Being aware of the ways in which the language you are learning differs from your own language may help you appreciate why you make particular errors in the pronunciation of sounds or the ordering of words within a sentence, for example.

Just below we provide a more detailed overview of the three sections that make up this book:

Section I: Sounding like a Native Speaker
Section II: Thinking like a Native Speaker
Section III: Acting like a Native Speaker

Foreign accent, one of the most noticeable aspects of foreign language learning, is the topic of Section I, "Sounding like a Native Speaker." It is easy enough to spot a foreign accent in someone speaking English, but what does an "American" accent sound like in Spanish or Japanese? What do you do when you speak foreign words that make you sound, well, like a foreigner? Can you do anything to sound more like a native speaker of the language? In addressing these questions, you will learn about making so-called exotic sounds as well as combining them to form new words. You will also learn how to avoid making the typical mistakes that may interfere with communication.

Section II, "Thinking like a Native Speaker," delves further into language structure, focusing on how words combine to form sentences. Every language has to provide its speakers with ways of carrying out the same basic human activities of expressing and communicating ideas, intentions, and desires. The way languages do this is by combining words and other linguistic elements into phrases and sentences in particular and systematic ways. How a given language forms phrases and sentences is called its **structure** or its **grammar.**

But languages differ, sometimes subtly and sometimes dramatically. The structure of a language may be identical or very similar to English in certain respects and very different in others. Being able to deal effectively with learning the grammar of another language involves having an understanding of how one's own language works and recognizing the similarities and differences.

As will become clear in Section III, "Acting like a Native Speaker," there is much more to learning a language than learning its structure. Language is a human phenomenon, and since an important part of how people define themselves is through culture, it is not surprising that language and culture are necessarily interwoven. In this section, we explore the link between language and culture in two ways. On the one hand, we introduce some of the roles that language plays in social interaction and examine how these roles can differ from one culture to another. One example relates to expressing emotions. Do all cultures express anger or insults in the same way? How about politeness? We will see that they do not. We'll also explore ways in which cultural ideas are reflected in language. One topic treated in relation to this concerns potential differences in how language is used by men and women in English as well as in other languages.

Before delving into these topics, however, we begin by giving you some information on some the most salient characteristics of language learning. We survey what particular tools children bring to the task of language learning that make them so successful. We also look at the learning environment in which the child typically acquires a first language. We sample some of the errors that children make in learning their first language, and we take note of the major stages in first language development.

We then turn to second language learners (that is, us) and compare our situation to that of a first language learner. On the basis of this comparison, we make some observations about where we have to focus our attention and energies in learning a second language. We also discuss the ways in which we as adults have certain advantages over a first language learner that we should try to make use of when possible.

First Language Learning

THE BASICS OF FIRST LANGUAGE LEARNING

From the study of first language learning by children, we have learned a number of interesting and sometimes surprising things. (For a comprehensive linguistic survey, see Guasti 2002, and for an important psychological perspective, see Tomasello 2003.) It is of course quite obvious that very young children are not exposed to formal language instruction of the sort that we experience in school. Yet by the time they begin formal schooling, they are already competent speakers of their language(s). And this fact raises a number of puzzling questions: Who taught them and how was it done? Where were the language lessons? How were their mistakes identified and corrected? And, come to think of it, who trained the teachers?

The answers to these questions are surprising. No one teaches children language. There are no language lessons. In general, and contrary to popular belief, children do not acquire their language as a consequence of correction of mistakes by their parents and other adults (and older children) whom they interact with. Most of the mistakes that children make are not corrected by adults. When they are corrected, the children generally persist in making the errors in spite of the correction, sometimes for years. And, of course, since there are no language teachers for first language learners, there is no teacher training for first language acquisition. So even if we wanted to correct our children's mistakes, except for the most obvious errors we would have a difficult time figuring out what the errors actually consist of and how to correct them.

It is true that when people speak to young children, they speak very simply and tend to repeat themselves. An early hypothesis was that adults organize their speech to children into language lessons, using a simplified version of the language called "Motherese." However, it appears that this simplified speech simply reflects an under-standing on the part of adults that children do not understand more complex speech. In fact, not all children are exposed to simplified speech, yet they all acquire language. (See Pinker 1994.)

Much of the evidence about what goes on in first language learning comes from detailed diary studies of children's language development and the analysis of transcripts of interactions between adults and children. Many of the materials are available to all researchers on the CHILDES database (the **Chi**ld **L**anguage **D**ata **E**xchange **S**ystem at http://childes.psy.cmu.edu/; see also MacWhinney 1995).

As we think about the difference between first language learning by children and second language learning by adults, the disparities become ever more astonishing. How can it be that adults, who are so much more educated and knowledgeable about the world, have so much more difficulty in learning a language? There is an old joke about an American who goes to Paris, comes back to the United States, and says to his friends that the French kids must all be geniuses—they can all speak French like natives!

But obviously, the reason that they can all speak French is that they **are** all natives. Learning a first language is what it means to be a native speaker. There is something special about the tools that the child brings to the task of language learning and about the language learning environment that makes acquisition of native competence by the child the norm. And in the adult, there are critical differences that make the task much different, and in general more formidable.

WHAT ARE THE CAPACITIES OF THE FIRST LANGUAGE LEARNER?

All scientists who specialize in the study of learning believe that human beings are born with powerful abilities for extracting patterns from the world around them, associating patterns with one another, and generalizing from particular instances to general rules. Many, but not all, believe that humans are born with specialized tools for learning language, exclusive of their ability to acquire other complex skills (like driving a car or playing a musical instrument or a sport such as basketball) and complex systems of knowledge (like chess or mathematics). We do not take a position on this issue here, but simply note that whatever capacities humans are born with, these capacities make them extraordinarily adept at learning a first language. Other creatures, regardless of what capacities they may have, cannot learn a language (nor for that matter can they drive a car, play a musical instrument, play basketball, play chess, or do mathematics).

But other creatures, especially highly evolved creatures, are capable of communicating with one another, and they are also capable of some extraordinary feats by virtue of their biological makeup. And many are capable of acquiring certain simple aspects of very complex tasks. For example, some primates and birds can count to as high as 6 or 7, some dogs have been taught to distinguish between "left" and "right," some primates can do very simple arithmetic (addition and subtraction), and some primates have been able to acquire hand gestures that stand for objects and relations between objects. These species have impressive cognitive capacities, and the extent of these capacities has yet to be fully understood. But it is fair to say that they do not have the capacities that humans have, and they do not have language in the sense that humans have language.

The first language learner is exposed to spoken language from the moment she achieves consciousness in her mother's womb, prior to birth. The sounds of language can be perceived by the prenatal language learner, and experimental evidence shows that the prenatal learner has already developed a certain sensitivity to the sounds and rhythmic patterns of the language that she will be learning. The ear develops in the 3rd week after conception and becomes functional in the 16th week; the fetus begins active listening in the 24th week. Prior to birth, while still in the womb, the fetus responds distinctively to her mother's voice. Lecanuet et al. (1995) found that just prior to birth the fetus is able to discriminate reversals of vowel sounds, such as "bobi" versus "biba." When the fetus hears the same sequence over a period of time, she becomes habituated to it (as measured by heart rate); when the sequence changes, the heart rate decelerates briefly, indicating recognition of the distinctive properties of speech. Other experiments have shown the sensitivity of the fetus to music.

Adults talk to the newborn child even though it is clear that the child cannot possibly understand what is being said. As the child gets older, but still cannot speak the language, adults continue to interact with him. Figure 1.1 is a sample of an interaction between Stefan, aged 14 months, and his mother and father (Feldman, CHILDES database). The child's utterances are notated as *STV, the mother's as *MOT, and the father's as *FAT. We've highlighted the child's utterances in boldface. Notice that the child is exposed to a considerable amount of talk, although he is very limited in his ability to

```
*FAT:  hi there.                      *FAT:  it's not a bottle.
*FAT:  woh.                           *FAT:  it's a badada?
*FAT:  yes.                           *STV:  badada.
*STV:  gee.                           *FAT:  ok.
*FAT:  uh huh.                        *FAT:  absolutely sure.
*FAT:  is that your badada           *MOT:  and what's this?
       down there?                    *FAT:  no uncertainties.
*FAT:  badada and your red           *STV:  badada [x 4].
       balloon.                       *MOT:  is this a badada or is
*FAT:  oh did you like that                 this a bottle?
       last night.                    *FAT:  this is a bottle,
*MOT:  the body lotion?                      right?
*FAT:  oh, you wouldn't, when        *STV:  badada.
       you were going down?           *MOT:  there's an overlap
*MOT:  you know what?                        there.
*MOT:  you know why he likes         *FAT:  I guess there is !
       this all of a sudden?          *MOT:  clearly this has milk
*FAT:  why's that?                           in it.
*MOT:  because I take the lid        *FAT:  ah.
       off for him.                   *STV:  baba.
*FAT:  yeah, last night I            *FAT:  yeah.
       opened it up.                  *MOT:  now he said baba for
*MOT:  right.                                the body lotion.
*FAT:  and he is just fasci-         *FAT:  yeah.
       nated with that.               *MOT:  the empty one.
*FAT:  do you like that bada-        *FAT:  right.
       da?                            *STV:  badada baba.
*FAT:  now, tell me Stef, is         *MOT:  ok, thank you for clar-
       this a badada or is it                ifying things.
       a bottle?
*STV:  badada.
*FAT:  it's a badada.
*MOT:  it had Stef's body
       lotion in it.
*MOT:  right?
*MOT:  at one time.
*STV:  Dada.
*FAT:  yes, Stefan?
*MOT:  body lotion.
```

Figure 1.1

contribute to the conversation at this point.

For purposes of comparison, Figure 1.2 is a brief excerpt from an interaction between Stefan and his parents about 13 months later. At this stage, the child gives the impression of being a more or less fully competent speaker of the language, although there are still childlike mannerisms, like *budleyley stuck* instead of *budleyley's stuck*. Particularly striking is the transition from being limited to producing utterances like *badada* at 14 months to saying things like *I don't like you sitting there* just 13 months later.

```
*FAT:   you got a budleyley        *FAT:   got it, what does this
        with ya there, huh?                say Tadi, m o m mom?
*MOT:   oh boy.                     *MOT:   what's m o m mom?
*MOT:   the budleyley's goin(g)     *MOT:   oh, it does.
        kaboomps too?               *FAT:   m o m mom!
*STV:   no.                         *FAT:   and with d a d.
*STV:   budleyley stuck.            *STV:   and Derek.
*FAT:   oh.                         *FAT:   yeah, here's Derek.
*STV:   budleyley stuck.            *FAT:   and Derek.
*FAT:   yeah.                       *STV:   Derek.
*FAT:   whoops !                    *MOT:   oh, and Bobbie.
*STV:   <xxx> [>].                  *FAT:   here's Bobbie !
*MOT:   do you <you want> [<]       *FAT:   oh, hi Bobbie !
        Bob the puppet or not,      *FAT:   oh, give Bobbie a
        Stefan?                            big hug.
*FAT:   you want Bob the pup-       *FAT:   oh.
        pet?                        *MOT:   your friend, huh?
*MOT:   do you wanna see Bob        *FAT:   yeah.
        the puppet?                 *MOT:   can I sit here?
*STV:   yeah.                       *STV:   I don't like you
*MOT:   yeah, ok.                           sitting there.
*FAT:   mama is gonna bring         *MOT:   in the car?
        that out.                   *STV:   yeah.
*MOT:   I am.                       *MOT:   ok
*MOT:   and maybe Bob would
        like to read the book
        too.
*FAT:   yeah.
*FAT:   wanna read this bookie?
*MOT:   wake up Bob the puppet.
```

Figure 1.2

In order to be able to achieve native competence in the target language, the learner must be able to carry out the following tasks, among others.

Distinguish speech sounds. As a preliminary to learning words, the learner must be able to distinguish the sounds of a language from one another. These sounds may be very similar to one another, like 'th' and 's' in English, but distinguishing them is critical to understanding and being understood (consider the difference between *I thank my friends* and *I sank my friends*).

Correlate sound differences with meaning differences. Different languages distinguish different sounds, as we will discuss in Chapters 2, 3, and 4. Sound differences that are meaningful in one language may not be in another. So it is not simply a matter of hearing that two sounds are different; it is a matter of relating this difference to a difference in meaning. Being able to do this presupposes that the learner can link the sounds of the language to the meanings that are expressed. Of course, the sounds are not produced in isolation, but are produced in words, and it is the words, with their particular forms, that have meaning and may differ in meaning.

Understand the intentions of other speakers. The learner must understand why other people are making sounds. It is possible that the learner figures this out from the fact that the same sounds (that is, words and phrases) are being produced by others in the same kinds of contexts. For example, when there is a dog, parents may say *dog* and point to the dog. But then the learner must be able to understand what communicative function the pointing is intended to perform. Tomasello (2003) argues that in general, other animals, even higher primates, are not able to link the production of a symbol, such as a word, with pointing to an object and understand that the speaker intends the symbol to be treated as the name or description of the object. Understanding these complex intentions, Tomasello argues, is an essential prerequisite to acquiring a language, and only humans have this capacity.[2]

Understand what language is about. A word or a phrase may refer to an object, such as *book*. A word or phrase may also refer to an object with a certain property, such as *big book,* to an event, such as *the World Series* or *We ate the cake,* to a time, to a place, to an emotion, to an idea, and so on. In order to be able to understand what language is about, a learner must have an understanding of the world that the language refers to. The learner must have an understanding of things, properties, times, places, events, and so on, that may be guided by language but that must at least in some respects precede language. In order to be able to learn that a linguistic expression has a particular meaning, the learner must already have the meaning in some form as a consequence of experience in the world.

Put words together. The learner must have both the capacity to put words together to express complex ideas and the understanding that this is what other speakers are doing when they speak. Again, it is not clear whether this is a specific capacity of human beings when they come into the world or whether it is something that we all learn to do through experience.

With this background in place, let's consider in a little more detail the course of first language development.

WHAT IS THE COURSE OF DEVELOPMENT?

There are traditionally four stages of language development. These stages do not have sharp boundaries; that is, we cannot see dramatic transitions between them from one day or week to the next. But if we step back and look at the entire course of language development, we can see that things occur early in development that are subsequently lost, and things do not occur early that are fully in place at some later point.

Babbling. When children begin to produce speech sounds, they "babble." That is, they do not produce words of the target language, or even nonsense that sounds like the target language, or even exclusively sounds of the target language. The babbling stage

---

2. Experiments suggest that a dog is able to recognize that when a human points to an object in the environment, the human intends for the dog to attend to the object also. See Hare and Tomasello, 2005, pp. 439–44.

lasts until 8 to 10 months of age. Toward the end of the babbling stage, children's babbling begins to take on qualities of the target language. That is, the sounds are those of
the target language, but the babbling is still nonsense.

The one-word stage. At about 1 year of age, children begin to produce single word
utterances. During this one-word stage children's vocabulary grows slowly. Comprehen-
sion typically exceeds production by a factor of about 10 to 1. A child typically produces
on the order of 20 distinct words at 1 year of age, and about 50 at one and a half years.

The two-word stage. At around 2 years of age children begin to produce phrases. The
first phrases consist by and large of two words; hence this is called the two-word stage. At
around this time, the number of words that a child knows begins to grow significantly, as
does the rate of increase in word learning. It is difficult to measure vocabulary size precisely, but it appears that at 2 years of age and beyond, a child is learning about 10 words
a day. Note that the vocabulary size of the typical high school student is 60,000 words.

Grammatical competence. After the two-word stage, not only is there a significant
growth in vocabulary, but children begin to show evidence that they have acquired or
are in the process of acquiring the rules and constructions of the grammar of a language
(see Stefan's *I don't like you sitting there* at age 27 months).

WHAT KINDS OF INFORMATION ARE CHILDREN EXPOSED TO?

In order to understand the differences between first and second language learning, we
should think a bit about differences in the learning environments for the two types of
learners. There are three main characteristics of the first language learner's environment
to take note of.

Quantity. A first language learner is exposed to an extraordinary quantity of linguistic
experience. In a typical transcript of an interaction between Stefan and his parents, 95
sentences were spoken by the parents in 34 minutes, or about three sentences per minute. Assuming that the child is awake and interacting with his parents ten hours per day
between the ages of 1 and 3, the parents make approximately 650,000 sentences per year.
If sentences spoken to young children average five words per sentence, the child has heard
around 3,250,000 word tokens (that is, individual words) during the first year of linguistic
interaction. Over the first four years this would come to over 2.5 million sentences and 13
million word tokens, even assuming an average of five words per sentence.

Cognition and concreteness. In general, the language spoken to children is about
things that the children understand, especially when we are responding to what a child
says or are trying to get the child to do something. We typically do not talk to very
young children about politics or philosophy, or even about future or possible future
events, at least not with the intent of communicating. Nor do we talk extensively to
children who have only a very minimal understanding, to say the least, of calculus or
theoretical physics. It is very likely that until children have the cognitive development to
understand these matters, what we say to them is effectively meaningless, although they
might assign some interpretation to it.

```
*FAT:  you got a budleyley        *FAT:  you want Bob the pup-
       with ya there, huh?                pet?
*MOT:  oh boy.                     *MOT:  do you wanna see Bob
*MOT:  the budleyley's goin(g)            the puppet?
       kaboomps too?              *STV:  yeah.
*STV:  no.                         *MOT:  yeah, ok.
*STV:  budleyley stuck.            *FAT:  mama is gonna bring
*FAT:  oh.                                that out.
*STV:  budleyley stuck.            *MOT:  I am.
*FAT:  yeah.                       *MOT:  and maybe Bob would
*FAT:  whoops !                           like to read the book
*STV:  <xxx> [>].                         too.
*MOT:  do you <you want> [<]       *FAT:  yeah.
       Bob the puppet or not,
       Stefan?
```

Figure 1.3

What we do talk to young children about most often concerns objects in their experience, such as food, animals, and diapers. The properties that we talk about are more or less concrete: hot, cold, sharp, and pretty. The events that we talk about are also concrete: eating, bodily functions, sleeping, and playing.

At the same time, we talk about other things in the presence of the child, and sometimes to the child, not knowing exactly how much the child knows. When the child's understanding of the world grows, words that we use become meaningful to the child as she becomes connected to the context in which the words are used.

Redundancy. While the number of sentences and words that the first language learner is exposed to is very large, there is much redundancy in this experience. The same words and linguistic constructions are used over and over again, particularly when adults are talking to the child, rather than to one another in the presence of the child. Figure 1.3 is a sample interaction taken from a transcript with Stefan at approximately a year and a half. And for comparison, Figure 1.4 below is a portion of a transcript with another child, Eve, at 18 months, also in the CHILDES database. Here, *CHI is the child.

```
*CHI:  more cookie.              *CHI:  more cookie.
*MOT:  you xxx more cookies?     *MOT:  you have another cookie
*MOT:  how about another gra-            right on the table.
       ham cracker?             *CHI:  more juice?
*MOT:  would that do just as     *MOT:  more juice?
       well?                     *MOT:  would you like more
*MOT:  here.                             grape juice?
*MOT:  here you go.
```

Figure 1.4

Notice that when the parents talk to the child, they repeat what they say and what the child says, and sometimes add elaborations. Typically the contexts for young children are very concrete, involving such things as food and drink.

WHAT KINDS OF MISTAKES DO CHILDREN MAKE, AND WHY?

Our intuition tells us that children learn language by imitating the language spoken around them. Examination of the transcripts shows that the adults speak like adults (unsurprisingly), while the children speak like children. In a way this is a puzzle: if children imitate adults, why don't they speak just like adults do?

A number of answers have been offered to explain this puzzle. They are not mutually incompatible, so they may all be right, at least to some extent. Here are some of the most plausible answers:

- **Memory:** Young children have limited memory. As a consequence, they are unable to remember the full form of a word and so they truncate it. Similarly, they are unable to process long sentences and thus cannot learn complex linguistic constructions at the early stages of language learning.
- **Articulation:** Young children are unable to produce the more complex sounds and sound combinations that they hear, and therefore they produce approximations, such as *baba* instead of *bottle*.
- **Structure:** Young children do not have immediate access to the full range of grammatical structures that occur in human languages and therefore are able to acquire and produce only a limited subset.
- **Generalization:** Young children do not have enough experience to recognize that certain forms are exceptional and have to be learned separately, so after they have learned a general rule, they tend to use it even when it should not apply. Hence we get children's forms such as *goed* instead of *went*.
- **Cognition:** Young children have a very restricted mental representation of the world and little or no understanding of abstractions like time, emotion, and opinion. Therefore they are unable to understand talk about these things and are unable to acquire the words and constructions that are used to express ideas about them.

SUMMARY: THE ESSENTIAL CHARACTERISTICS OF FIRST LANGUAGE LEARNING

To summarize to this point, we have seen that young children are very good at learning language. While they make mistakes, they are presented with an overwhelming amount of redundant information about how the language is supposed to be used, and they therefore have a very good basis for correcting their mistakes. The amount of linguistic experience that children are exposed to may well make up for memory limitations that children may have, since repetition relieves the child of the burden of having to remember what was said. Moreover, since language is a crucial aspect of the interactions between children and adults, it allows for children to get their basic needs met.

Second Language Learning

Let's turn now to the situation of an adult second language learner by comparing it to that of the first language learner.

CRITICAL PERIOD

There are two very salient properties of first language learning. One is that it is accomplished naturally and quickly by all typical children without formal instruction. The second is that as a person approaches adulthood, he or she loses the ability to naturally and quickly acquire a language. Some scientists have proposed that there is a "critical period" for language learning during which the parts of the brain devoted to language acquisition remain active and after which they turn off. It has been suggested that the end of the critical period correlates with the onset of puberty, which is one mark of the transition to adulthood.

Others have suggested that there is no critical period specific to language, but that as we age there is a gradual falling off of the capacity to learn complex skills naturally and accurately. In this view, the loss in our ability to acquire native competency in a language is paralleled by a loss in our ability to acquire expert facility in playing a musical instrument or a sport. As is the case with language, we are able to learn to do these things as adults, but lack the deep intuitions and instinctiveness that we develop when we begin to learn them as children.

There is evidence that some aspects of a language are more difficult for second learners to acquire than others. While some adult learners are able to acquire the sounds of a second language without an accent, the older a learner is—the further beyond very early childhood—the more likely he will have an accent. On the other hand, it has been argued that the acquisition of vocabulary does not get more difficult with age.

Finally, the ability to acquire native-like facility with the grammatical rules of a second language appears to diminish with age. Whether there is a particular critical period for language in general, or different critical periods for different aspects of language, or no critical period at all is an open question that is actively debated. (See, for example, the references at the end of this chapter.)

Whatever the case may be for a specialized critical period for language, the fact remains that adults are not as adept at language learning as children. And we do not have the advantages that the child has. This means that we have to approach the task in a very different way than the child approaches it.

DISADVANTAGES

In addition to the fact that they have passed out of the critical period, adults are at a disadvantage in learning a second language in other ways.

Motivation. The first language learner has an extremely strong motivation to learn the language. This motivation may be in part biological and in part social. In any case, there is no conscious decision on the part of the child about whether to learn the language or what language to learn. The child simply **must** learn the language of the surrounding environment.

In order to be successful in learning a second language, an adult must seek the strongest possible motivation. In an academic setting, the motivation is in part external—there is a requirement to be satisfied, there is a grade to be assigned, and so on. But what would be far stronger is a genuine desire to learn the language and a sense of enjoyment in doing so since the work involved is considerable and can be very tedious. In order for the effort to be successful, the learner must find a language to learn that is so attractive to study that putting in the effort is itself appealing. A book cannot tell you what **your** motivation might be, but we strongly urge you to find a language to study where your motivation is as strong as possible.

Strong first language. As a consequence of having spent many years hearing and speaking our native language, we have developed very rapid mental computations for translating between sounds and meaning. When we hear something in our language, we know immediately what it means, and we typically understand the words and the intentions of the speaker as reflected in her use of particular phrasings, intonation, and style. We may have a good idea of the social group or groups that the speaker belongs to.

Similarly, when we want to say something, typically the words spring to our tongue to express the thoughts that we have. We do not have to remember the words or figure out how to pronounce them. We have been practicing the articulatory gestures that are necessary for us to be able to sound like a native speaker for years, perhaps dozens of years. No wonder that we are able to sound "just like" native speakers! This level of competence and this amount of practice make up a good part of what it means **to be** a native speaker.

And we know exactly where to put the words in order to make our sentences grammatical. In English, the subject usually comes first, and when the subject is finished, we add the verb or sequence of verbs, followed by the object and perhaps adverbs and other similar expressions. The ordering of words is different in other languages, but in each language, the speakers have been practicing their entire lives putting the words where they are supposed to go.

Thus, the habits connected with the first language are very strong in the adult. In order to develop some level of competence in a second language, the habits of the first language must be identified and controlled, even suppressed, when they differ from those of the second language. The situation is very similar to that in which American drivers and pedestrians find themselves when they go to Great Britain (and when the British go to parts of Europe or to the United States). In the U.S., cars must be driven on the right side of the road; in England, cars must be driven on the left. After driving for many years in the U.S., we have the habit of making a left turn into the right-hand lane of the road we are turning on, as shown in Figure 1.5.

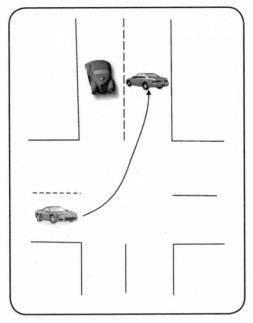

Figure 1.5
U.S. left turn.

But in Great Britain, the left turn must be made as in Figure 1.6.

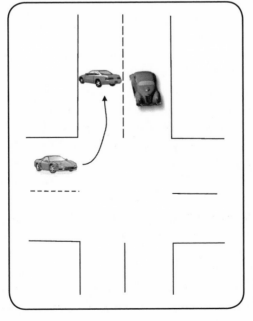

Figure 1.6
G.B. left turn.

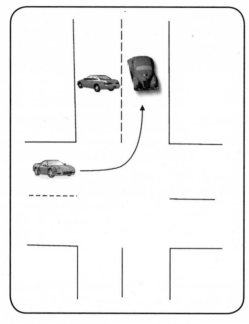

Figure 1.7
U.S. left turn in
G.B.

It is very natural for someone with U.S. driving habits to make a left turn into the right lane, something that can be quite dangerous if there is oncoming traffic, as in Figure 1.7.

The solution here is to control U.S. driving habits by putting them aside while creating an equivalent British driving habit. Creating the British driving habit does not mean forgetting how to drive in the U.S.; it simply means becoming conscious of the old habit and learning how to suspend it while the new habit is being implemented. Learning a second language requires the same type of suspension of an old and very well learned habit.

Perceptual biases. Adults can have similar difficulty in distinguishing the sounds of a foreign language. Yet, a very young child is more or less neutral with respect to the sounds of language, although he already has some preference for the sounds of the language in the environment. After 10 or 20 years of being exposed only to the sounds of this language, the first language learner has become extremely adept at picking out very fine distinctions among sounds that signify differences in meaning. When an adult is exposed to the sounds of a new language, he naturally imposes the habits of hearing on the new language, even though the new language may have very different sounds and very different distinctions than does the old language.

Limited input; limited redundancy. The young child is exposed to a vast amount of information about a first language. In general, the adult second language learner, particularly in an academic setting, is exposed to dramatically less information. Moreover, the adult second language learner is an adult and is therefore not being spoken to patiently and redundantly for 10 to 15 hours per day by attentive parents about a limited range of topics such as food and basic bodily functions. In contrast, the adult second language learner is talking to other adults and wants to talk about the wide range of topics that interest adults, which certainly go far beyond food and basic bodily functions. Finally, the child has basically nothing else to do besides learn the language (as well as other basic aspects of social interaction), while the adult has many other important things to do.

So, to put the difference in the starkest terms, the environment for first language learning, on the one hand, is perfectly well designed to give the child every opportunity to learn his native language. On the other hand, the environment makes it anything but easy for an adult to learn a second language, and the adult's greater maturity and range of interests may actually work against his being successful. This being said, the adult does have some potential advantages over the first language learner.

ADVANTAGES

There is no question that compared with a young child, an adult has advantages in acquiring certain types of knowledge. We have already noted that young children are incapable of learning complex systems of knowledge such as calculus and physics. They are also incapable of learning **about** grammatical rules, although, of course, they are capable of acquiring these rules unconsciously. An adult, on the other hand, can explicitly or implicitly learn a grammatical rule and then proceed to focus on practicing the particular language patterns relevant to that rule.

The adult also has the ability, in principle at least, to consciously structure the learning environment. The adult can focus on particular difficulties, can talk about problems and identify ways to solve them, and can (again in principle at least) make language learning something that is fun rather than a chore.

We have seen that even with motivation, adults are handicapped by the fact that they do not have as much **useful** experience with the language that they are learning as the child does. We stress "useful" because it is relatively easy for an adult to be exposed to a second language for hours and hours a day, for example, by listening to the radio or watching television. There is a difference between this type of experience and that of the child, however. As the child develops and begins to interact with her parents and other adults, her linguistic experience is not only very extensive but also very redundant and overwhelmingly about things that the child cares about and understands. It is this involvement with and understanding of what the language spoken in the environment is about that makes it relatively easy for the child to correlate the words and phrases with the relevant aspects of the physical, social, and emotional environments. Without such understanding, the language that the child hears is effectively little more than noise, and the child can do nothing useful with it.

It is therefore most effective for the adult learner to enter or create a learning environment where what is being talked about is fully understood by the adult. Moreover, there should be substantial repetition and elaboration, so that the adult, like the child, does not have the opportunity to forget things that are once learned.

With this as a basis, we turn now to the heart of this book and focus on sounding, thinking, and acting like a native speaker.

Exercises

1. Think about your own experiences in trying to learn a second language. If you are studying a language now, keep a diary about what aspects of the language you find most challenging and what aspects you find easiest. For example, are there particular sounds that are very difficult for you? Are there vocabulary items that are hard to remember, no matter how many times you review them? Are there grammatical constructions that you find difficult, while others seem very straight-forward? Are there particular environments where language learning seems to be easiest? Keep track of these things so that it will be productive for you to reflect on them as you proceed through the various topics covered in this book.

2. Another difference between first and second language learning is that children are typically exposed to many different speakers, while adult learners in the classroom are typically exposed only to the speech of the instructor (and possibly speakers on CDs or other media). Do you find it more challenging or less challenging to follow what is being said in another language when you are confronted with a variety of speakers as contrasted with a single speaker?

References

Birdsong, D. (Ed.). (1999). *Second language acquisition and the critical period hypothesis.* Mahwah, NJ: Lawrence Erlbaum Associates.

Cenoz, J., Hufeisen, B., and Jessner, U. (Eds.). (2003). *The multilingual lexicon.* Dordrecht: Kluwer Academic.

Child Language Data Exchange System (CHILDES). Online: http://childes.psy.cmu.edu/.

Ellis, Rod. (1994). *The study of second language acquisition.* New York: Oxford University Press.

Guasti, Maria Teresa. (2002). *Language acquisition: The growth of grammar.* Cambridge, MA: MIT Press.

Hare, Brian, and Tomasello, Michael. (2005). Human-like social skills in dogs? *Trends in Cognitive Sciences* 9(9): 439–44.

Lecanuet, J. P., Granier-Deferre, C., and M. C. Busnel. (1995). Human fetal auditory perception. *Fetal Development: A Psychobiological Perspective,* ed. J. P. Lecanuet, W. P. Fifer, N. A. Krasnegor, and W. P. Smotherman. 239–62. Mahwah, NJ: Lawrence Erlbaum Associates.

MacWhinney, Brian. (1995). *The CHILDES project: Tools for analyzing talk.* Mahwah, NJ: Lawrence Erlbaum Associates.

Pinker, Steven. (1994). *The language instinct. The new science of language and mind.* London: Allen Lane, The Penguin Press.

Tomasello, Michael. (2003). *Constructing a language: A usage-based theory of language acquisition.* Cambridge, MA: Harvard University Press.

I: Sounding like a Native Speaker

Foreign Accents

Knowing How to Speak a Language

Being able to speak a language means that you know how to pronounce and understand the words and sentences of your language. If you are a native speaker of English, for example, you know that the letters 's' and 'sh' both represent sounds of the English language since they occur in distinct words like *sin* and *shin*. As a native speaker you have learned how to pronounce these sounds as well as the many other sounds that are used in your language. You also know the way that sounds combine to make English words. For instance, you know that 's' can be followed by 'l' because of words like *slow*. You are also aware, at a certain level of consciousness, that 'l' cannot be followed by 's' at the beginning of a word—there are no words like *lsow* in English.

One of the things that makes languages so interesting for linguists who study them, but so difficult for those trying to learn a new language, is that languages can differ in terms of how sounds are put together to form words. Of course, the ways that sounds combine in two languages may be similar in some respects, but you can be almost certain that there will also be differences. A challenging aspect about learning another language, then, is that languages differ both in terms of the kinds of sounds that are used and in the ways that the sounds combine to form words. To learn another language therefore means that you will at least need to learn new ways of combining sounds to form words, and possibly new sounds as well.

In the next few chapters you will become familiar with some of the ways in which languages differ in terms of how speech sounds are made and used. You should also gain a clearer understanding of how your own language works. With this knowledge, we hope that you will come away with an appreciation for how your native language and the language(s) that you are learning differ. Being aware of how the languages differ is a huge step toward understanding how you can sound like a native speaker, since it will allow you to identify areas to pay special attention to when trying to master your new languages(s).

We begin by considering foreign accents and what exactly makes an accent sound foreign. We have all heard someone speak English or some other language that we speak natively and have known right away that he is not a native speaker. What is it about the way the person speaks that makes him sound foreign? As you will see, how an individual produces the sounds, words, and sentences of a foreign language is directly influenced by the sounds, sound combinations, and other properties of his native language.

Dealing with Unfamiliar Sounds

One of the most basic reasons why an accent seems foreign relates to the sounds that make up the speaker's native language and those of the language she is speaking non-natively. We will refer to the collection of speech sounds that are used in a particular language to form words and sentences as a language's **sound inventory.**

A Language's Sound Inventory
The collection of speech sounds that are used in a particular language to form words and sentences.

When the sound inventory of your own language differs from that of a language that you are learning, you may be confronted with unfamiliar sounds. In this case, part of learning the new language obviously means learning how to produce and combine new sounds. In attempting to pronounce these new sounds, you may modify your speech in some way to make it more similar to the sound patterns that you are used to. In this chapter, we focus on the various strategies used by language learners to deal with unfamiliar sounds and sequences of sounds. If you use these strategies, your speech will sound different from that of a native speaker, thus giving you a foreign accent.

One common strategy is to **replace an unfamiliar sound** with one that is relatively similar to it from the learner's native sound inventory. This can result in an accent quite noticeable to the native speaker's ears.

Strategy #1
Replace an unfamiliar sound with a similar, more familiar one.

We illustrate this strategy first by considering some examples of non-native English speakers speaking English, and then of English speakers speaking other languages. In each case, a sound that occurs in a word in one language is replaced with some other sound. The reason, of course, is that the particular sound does not occur in the speaker's native language. As a result, the person may not have had experience pronouncing or listening to the sound and therefore may substitute an unfamiliar sound with one that is similar sounding.

Let's begin by considering one aspect of Greek-accented English. The sound inventory of Greek, like that of many languages, including Spanish and Korean, differs from

English in that it does not include the vowel sound [ɪ],[1] which occurs in English words such as *sit, bit, kit*, etc. That is, there are no words in Greek (or Spanish or Korean) that are formed with the sound [ɪ]. On the other hand, the sound inventories of Greek and English are similar in that they both include the sound that we will symbolize as [i]. This stands for the vowel in English words like *seat, beat, feet*. If an English speaker uses the vowel [i] instead of [ɪ] in a word, it can change the meaning of the word: compare *sit* ([ɪ]) vs. *seat* ([i]); *bit* ([ɪ]) vs. *beat/beet* ([i]). Notice that it is only the quality of the vowel that distinguishes the meaning of these pairs of words. We therefore say that the vowels [i] and [ɪ] are **distinctive** in English.

Unlike English, the Greek language does not make use of the distinction between [ɪ] and [i] to change the meaning of words since there are no Greek words with [ɪ]; [i] and [ɪ] are then not distinctive in Greek. This means that Greek speakers may not have had practice producing or listening to the sound [ɪ] and may have difficulty hearing the difference between [i] and [ɪ]. They may also replace the unfamiliar [ɪ] sound in English words with the similar yet more familiar [i]. As a result, both the words *sit* and *seat*, spoken in Greek-accented English, may be pronounced similar to *seat*. Speakers of Greek-accented English have made use of the first strategy for dealing with an unfamiliar sound: replacing an unfamiliar sound with a similar, more familiar one.

Let's look at some common replacements from other languages. Korean, unlike English, does not distinguish between the sounds [p] and [f]. These occur in English words such as the following: [p] *pool, punch, paper, cup*; [f] *fool, photo, caffeine, enough*. The reason for the lack of distinction between [p] and [f] in Korean is that only [p] is part of the language's sound inventory. Therefore, one common trait of Korean-accented English is for the sound [f] to be replaced with a [p] sound in English words.

An Aside
Remember that it is vowel sounds that we are concerned with here, not how these sounds are spelled in words. To illustrate the difference, compare the words *beat* and *beet*. They both have the same vowel sound [i], but the sound is spelled as *ea* in *beat* and as *ee* in *beet*.

Why, you might ask, is the [f] sound replaced with [p] as opposed to some other consonant like [t] or [k]? The answer is that to Korean speakers, [p] and [f] sound fairly similar. One of the reasons for this is that they are both made with the lips. To make the sound [p], the lips close together tightly and then open, letting the air pass through the lips. The lips are also involved in making the sound [f]. In this case, the bottom lip rests gently against the top row of teeth as the air goes out of the mouth. (We will have more to say about making these kinds of sounds in the following chapter.) It is important to keep in mind that sounds like [p] and [f] may seem very different to a speaker of a language like English who uses them to differentiate words like *pool* and *fool*. But for speakers of languages where the sounds are not distinctive, the two sounds can be very difficult to tell apart, and the unfamiliar sound can be difficult to pronounce.

---

1. The symbols used to represent vowel sounds are discussed in Chapter 4; see also the symbol reference chart at the back of the book. To differentiate the symbols used to characterize speech sounds from the letters used to spell words, sound symbols are enclosed in square brackets.

As a final example of foreign-accented English, consider one way in which German and English differ. German lacks a distinction between the sounds [w] and [v] as in *wine* and *vine;* there is no [w] in the German sound inventory. So, in German-accented English, in a phrase such as *Victoria's wine shop,* the first sounds in *Victoria* and *wine* may both be pronounced as [v], a sound very similar to [w].

Now let's reverse the process and consider some of the common pronunciations that make American English speakers sound foreign in other languages. Continuing with German and English, you may be familiar with how the final sound in the German composer's name *Bach* is commonly pronounced in English—with a [k] sound and rhyming with *rock*. In German, however, the last sound in this word is actually pronounced with a sound that, though similar to [k], is nonetheless different. The symbol for the German sound is [x], and it is made, like [k], by raising the back of the tongue up to the back of the mouth. In making [k], the tongue briefly touches the roof of the mouth, and consequently the flow of air is temporarily interrupted as it goes out of the mouth. (At this point you should convince yourself that [k] is made in this way by slowly saying the word *rock* and paying attention to where your tongue touches the roof of your mouth when you make the sound [k].) For the sound [x], the tongue comes close to the roof of the mouth but does not touch it. In this way, the air passes though the narrow opening and creates turbulent noise. Technically speaking, [k] is called a **velar stop** and [x] is a **velar fricative** (see the next chapter for additional discussion). Since the English sound inventory does not include [x], English speakers commonly replace this unfamiliar sound with the more familiar [k], a common trait of English-accented German.

Another characteristic of English-accented German (or French, Swedish, Turkish, and so on) has to do with the way that certain vowels are pronounced. German, like many other languages, makes a distinction between the vowels [i], as in English *beat,* [u], as in English *boot,* and [y], as in the German word *Tuer* 'door.' The last sound does not occur in English's sound inventory. The sound [y] can be thought of as a combination of the sounds [u] (*boot*) and [i] (*beat*): the lips are protruded as in [u], but the position of the tongue is the same as in [i]. We will work on learning how to make sounds like this in later chapters. Since English lacks this sound, English speakers typically replace foreign words containing the sound [y] with [u]. The reason that [y] is replaced with [u] (and not [i]) may be due in part to the fact that, in German at least, the sound [y] is written in words as the letter 'u,' as we saw with the word *Tuer* 'door,' so English speakers unfamiliar with German will equate the letter 'u' with the English sound [u].

Strategy #2
Omit an unfamiliar sound from a word.

In each of these cases, the English speaker sounds noticeably foreign, and once again, the reason is that a sound belonging to some other language's sound inventory does not occur in English. In order to pronounce words like a native speaker, you will obviously need to learn how to pronounce the unfamiliar sound.

A second strategy that non-native speakers use to deal with an unfamiliar sound is to simply **omit the foreign sound** entirely. The omission of a sound is a common trait of French-accented English when dealing with the unfamiliar sound [h], as in English *hello, hat, heavy.* There are at least two reasons why French speakers may omit the [h] from their pronunciations of English words. First, there is no [h] in French, and there is also no sound that is particularly close to [h]. Second, given that the sound [h] is absent from the French sound inventory, French speakers may not be able to hear the sound and thus do not reproduce it. This is because as a child acquires a language, she learns to focus on the parts of the acoustic signal that carry meaning in her language, ignoring others. Thus her perceptual system becomes fine-tuned to the sounds of her own language which in turn influences what she does and does not hear. What characterizes "foreignness" in this case, then, is the **absence** of a sound.

The example from French allows us to emphasize once again the important distinction between **sounds** and the **letters** that we use to spell words. Note that while the letter 'h' is written in some words in French, such as *haricot* 'bean' and *homme* 'man', it is never pronounced as [h]. This fact shows that the spelling used in a language does not always reflect what sounds occur in that language. French is not alone in this regard; it is also true of English and many other languages. Consider the letter 'p' at the beginning of some words in English, e.g. *psychology*: although the letter 'p' is present in written English, it is not pronounced in this word. Similarly, the 'l' in *salmon* is not pronounced, nor is the 'k' in *knife*, nor the second 'b' in *bomb*.

Another aspect of spelling that can be confusing when learning a new language has to do with the fact that languages can differ in the ways in which written words are pronounced. This is especially challenging when the same sequence of letters is pronounced differently. For example, the spelling 'ch' in English is pronounced like the initial or final sounds in <u>church</u>, while in Italian, the spelling 'ch' is pronounced with the sound [k]. As a result, the first sound in the Italian word <u>che</u> 'what' approximates the first consonant in the English word <u>Kay</u>.

All of the examples we have considered above underscore several important points when it comes to learning a new language: Do not assume that the language that you are learning is identical to your native language in terms of the sounds or the rules for spelling. Be aware of the differences with your native language, learn how to pronounce the new sounds, and, of course, practice!

Dealing with Unfamiliar Sequences of Sounds

As we all know, learning another language involves more than just learning new sounds. We also need to learn how to combine them to form new words. Because of this, it is sometimes the particular combination of sounds, not the sounds themselves, that is unfamiliar to a non-native speaker. Part of knowing how to speak a language involves knowing what **sequences of sounds** are possible, that is, a language's **phonotactics.** An English speaker, for example, has learned that a word can begin with sequences like [bl], [pl], [pr], [sn], [tr], and [gl] because there are words in the language like *blue, please, price, snow, truck,* and *glue.* It is likely than an English speaker would say that *plake* is a possible word of English because it contains combinations of sounds found in English, even though, at the present time, it is not an actual word. On the other hand, there are no

English words that begin with the sequences [bn], [pb], [rt], or [gd], and knowing that these are not sequences of English is also part of a native speaker's knowledge of English. As a result, a sequence like *bnark* would sound very strange to an English speaker's ears; in fact, he would probably say that it could not be an English word.

What happens when the language you are learning has unfamiliar combinations of sounds? One strategy often used by native speakers is to omit one of the sounds, as we saw above for French with [h]. A different strategy is to **insert a sound** in order to bring the sequence more in line with the phonotactics of the native language. In other words, inserting a sound gives the sequence a more familiar structure.

Strategy #3

Insert a sound to make a sequence of sounds more familiar.

Consider the effects of this strategy for an English learner of Polish, a language where words can begin with many different kinds of consonant sequences. For example, in Polish the sound [g] (e.g. English *go, dog*) can be immediately followed by [d] (e.g. English *do, bud*) at the beginning of a word. In fact, the name of one of Poland's major cities, *Gdansk*, begins with just this sequence of sounds. Try saying this word. Most native speakers of English unfamiliar with the sequence [gd] will insert a short vowel between the two consonants so that the word is pronounced like *G*ᵉ*dansk*. If you are a native speaker of another language that does not permit [gd] at the beginning of a word, determine whether you use this same strategy or a different one when pronouncing this word.

Inserting a vowel is also a trait of Spanish-accented English. One difference between English and Spanish is that words beginning with the sound [s] followed by another consonant are common in English, while they do not occur in Spanish. As a result,

Exercise: Your Strategies

If you are learning another language, it is almost certain that you will have a foreign accent when you speak. But what makes your own speech sound non-native? How do you deal with unfamiliar aspects of the language that you are learning? Which of the strategies above are you using?

Introspecting about your own accent can be hard, especially if you are trying to do it while speaking. A better approach would be to record yourself saying individual words or small phrases. If you have access to recordings of a native speaker, you could even record yourself repeating what the speaker said. Then listen carefully to each word several times, comparing it to the native speaker's version, if possible. Try to pinpoint parts of the word that differ. What is it that makes them sound different? Are different sounds being used? Are you omitting or inserting sounds in places where the native speaker is not? Having a native speaker of the language help you identify the foreign-sounding aspects of the words will make the task easier.

This is a difficult exercise because how you hear sequences of speech has been strongly influenced by the languages that you learned as a child. Learning to hear in new ways is possible with practice, however, if you work hard at it.

the consonant sequences at the beginning of the following English words simply are not found in Spanish: _speed, stoop, strike, ski_. For Spanish speakers learning to speak English, a vowel is generally inserted at the beginning of the word. In this way, a word like _school_ is pronounced something like _eschool_ with a vowel pronounced before the [s] + consonant sequence.

A similar strategy is used in Korean-accented English. Although English does not have as wide a variety of consonant sequences as Polish, a fair number of different consonant sequences still occur in the language, such as _snow, fifth, strike, fast food_, and so on. These kinds of sequences do not occur in Korean. Consequently, Koreans often make use of the same strategy as English and Spanish speakers: they insert a short vowel to give the sequence a more familiar structure. In this way, the word _strike_ may be pronounced like _s^et^erike_ and _fast food_ as _fas^et^e food_.

Dealing with Unfamiliar Syllable-, Word-, and Sentence-Level Properties

Thus far we have focused on strategies that language learners use when dealing with unfamiliar sound inventories and phonotactics. Yet, languages can also differ in terms of other properties relating to syllables, words, and sentences. In this section we will consider three types of properties relating to these elements: word stress, tone, and intonation. Understanding that your native language may differ from the one that you are learning in terms of any of these properties can help you become aware of how you need to modify your speech if you want to sound more like a native speaker of the language you are learning.

WORD STRESS

In most languages, one part of a word may have greater emphasis or prominence than another part. We use the term **stress** to refer to this property, and the term **syllable** to refer to the various parts of a word that can have stress. For example, speakers of English would probably agree that the word _baby_ has two syllables: _ba-by_. On the other hand, _elephant_ has three: e-le-phant. Which syllable of the word _baby_ has stress? Do you say _BAby_ or _baBY_? Clearly, there is greater prominence on the first syllable. The stress in _elephant_ also falls on the first syllable. In the word _computer_, however, stress falls on the middle syllable: _comPUter_. If you are a native speaker of English, you have learned that certain syllables in English are pronounced with more emphasis than others and, as a result, are louder, are longer, and/or have higher pitch. This is part of your knowledge of English. Since languages differ in terms of where stress occurs in words, one common quality of speech that cues us to an accent as foreign involves the misplacement of stress.

In French, for example, stress typically falls on the last syllable of a word. Thus, one characteristic of French-accented English is the misplacement of stress on the final syllable of a word. A French-speaking politician was commonly heard pronouncing the English word _economic_ as _econoMIC_, with stress on the last syllable, instead of on the third syllable: _ecoNOmic_. In Czech, by contrast, stress systematically occurs on the first syllable of a word. Being aware of differences in stress placement between your native language and your new language, then, is important to keep in mind.

TONE

Another property of syllables that can be challenging to the language learner is tone. In many languages, such as the Chinese language Mandarin, the only difference between two words may be the tone, or the pitch, of the syllable. As a result, tones can distinguish the meaning of otherwise identical words. Four different tones are used to do this in Mandarin. The first is called a level high tone and occurs in the word [mā] 'mother,' for example. The second is called a rising tone, where the pitch starts out low and ends up high, as in the word for 'hemp,' [má]. The third tone is called a falling-rising tone. It starts out high, dips lower, and then ends high. This is the tone that occurs on the word for 'horse,' [mǎ]. Finally, there is the falling tone which starts out high and ends up low, as in 'to scold,' [mà]. Note that all four words have exactly the same consonant and vowel. Only the tone lets you know which word is which. For speakers of languages that do not have tone, learning a language like Mandarin Chinese means that you also need to learn a new property of sounds that carries meaning in the language. Not pronouncing the tones correctly is a typical property of English-accented Mandarin Chinese.

INTONATION

A foreign accent can also involve differences relating to the melody, or intonation, of a phrase or an entire sentence. In standard American English, for example, intonation can distinguish a statement from a question. Say the following two sentences and pay close attention to how the pitch levels at the end of the sentences differ:

Statement: Zach eats pizza for breakfast.

Question: Zach eats pizza for breakfast?

When the pitch falls, as at the end of the first sentence, the utterance is interpreted as a simple statement. When the pitch rises, as in the second sentence, it is a question. Being able to assign the correct interpretation to a sentence according to these different intonation patterns is part of English speakers' knowledge of their language.

But not all languages use different pitch contours to distinguish sentence function. Speakers of Chinese languages, for example, tend to keep the intonation pattern pretty much the same for questions and statements. Instead, they include the marker [ma] in the sentence to indicate that a question interpretation is intended. Finnish is similar in using a marker to indicate the difference between a statement and a question.

It is also interesting to note that even within a single language, intonation patterns can differ depending on dialect. In contrast to the pattern illustrated above for standard American English, African American Vernacular English indicates a yes-no question (e.g. *Did Zach eat pizza for breakfast?*) with a very high, flat pitch pattern.

Intonation patterns can appear to differ quite subtly, particularly in a language that you are learning. Yet, producing an intonation pattern incorrectly, just like mispronouncing a word, can convey a meaning other than what you might have intended. In a study by Hewings (1995), for example, it was observed that Indonesian learners of British English frequently used a falling pitch in inappropriate contexts, which in turn led to their being perceived as contentious.

As a native speaker of English, you are biased to perceive and pronounce utterances with the intonational patterns that you have learned for English. (In fact, you are biased toward all aspects of your language!) This is the case whether you are listening to English or to some other language. Learning to undo these patterns is challenging for an adult learner. You can start, however, by trying to pay attention to the melody that accompanies the words in an utterance when you are listening to a speaker of another language. Does the pitch go up at the end of a sentence? Does it go down? Is it a familiar melody, or is it quite different from what you have learned to expect? Some language learning materials focus on intonational patterns and can thus serve as a valuable resource for determining what part of the utterance to pay attention to when learning to produce the melody. If you are learning a language in a formal language setting, you can also turn to your instructor for information about the melodies used in various contexts.

Summary

We hope to have accomplished three goals in this chapter:

- The first was to help you understand some of the reasons why people speak with a foreign accent.
- The second was to outline what parts of a language's sound system can be affected when speech sounds foreign.
- The third was to identify some of the strategies that non-native speakers use to deal with unfamiliar elements.

As we saw, the reason why people speak with a foreign accent is that they are making an unfamiliar structure more familiar. It is important to stress that familiarity in this context is determined by one's native language. For this reason, the accent of an English speaker learning Russian will be different from that of a Swahili speaker or a Korean speaker learning Russian. Virtually any

(continued on next page)

Summary (continued from previous page)

aspect of a language can be modified to make speech sound foreign, including individual sounds, sequences of sounds, stress, tone, and intonation. In making a language structure more familiar, learners will generally do one of three things:

- replace the unfamiliar element with something familiar,
- omit the unfamiliar element, or
- insert another sound.

Analyzing the sound system of your language as well as the one that you are learning will help you understand the ways in which the two languages differ, and by being aware of these differences, you will have more control over how you speak.

Reference

Hewings, M. (1995). Tone choice in the English intonation of non-native speakers. *International Review of Applied Linguistics* 3: 251–65.

3

How to
Make a Consonant

Introduction

*I*n this chapter, you will learn how to make a consonant. Of course, you already know how to make many consonants, or you would not be able to speak English or any other language! What we are going to do, though, is focus on what making a consonant involves. This, we hope, will give you tools to learn new speech sounds, as well as to undo aspects of English pronunciation that can give you a foreign accent when speaking another language. Let's start with a short exercise to show you just how skillful you already are.

Learning to speak a language is in some ways like learning to juggle: you have to coordinate many different movements in order to produce an intended effect. To see what we mean by this, say the word *punctuate* out loud <u>very</u> slowly. It may be helpful to watch your mouth in a mirror as you pronounce the word. Pay attention to what you are doing with your lips and tongue as you say the word. You may need to say it a few times in order to get a feel for what you are doing. Notice that you start out with your lips brought closely together. Feel where your tongue is positioned while your lips are closed. Is it toward the front of your mouth or closer to the back?

Now open your lips and continue saying the word. Notice that by the time you say the 'unc' part of the word, your tongue is bunched up toward the back part of the roof of your mouth. What happens when you continue to pronounce the word? Your tongue is on the move again. This time the front of your tongue should be touching the center of the roof of your mouth. Your lips are probably also protruded.

To complete the word, your lips will spread apart, showing your teeth, and your tongue will end up close to the front of the roof of your mouth. And these are only the gestures involving your tongue and lips! Another gesture was needed to allow air to pass through your nose during part of the word, and another gesture was involved to make the air vibrate when you made the vowels and a consonant. How did you get so good at moving the various parts of your mouth around to make these sounds? Much of it has to do with practice, and since you have probably been speaking English for many years, you have had years of practice!

In any activity that requires precise, coordinated gestures—whether it be juggling, playing the violin, driving a manual transmission car, or playing soccer—the more you practice, the better you get. Learning how to speak a new language is no different. You have to learn how to coordinate gestures in ways that may at first be unfamiliar to you. Learning to speak another language may seem very complicated at first. However, if you break words and sounds down into their basic components, the task will likely be more manageable. In fact, it may even be easier than you think since you are already familiar with many of the movements required to make speech sounds in other languages. You just may not have had the experience of putting the movements together in the necessary way. But you **can** make new sounds based on what you already know.

To illustrate, let's try pronouncing some sounds that may be new to you. We will start by making a vowel that does not occur in the English sound inventory but is found in many other languages, including Chinese, German, French, Turkish, Hungarian, and Swedish. (You saw this vowel in the previous chapter in the German word *Tuer* 'door.') The symbol that linguists use to describe this vowel is [y], which is part of the International Phonetic Alphabet (IPA), displayed on the back inside cover of this book. (A common alternative symbol for this sound is 'ü'; in fact this is the symbol used in German to spell words with this sound.) Technically speaking, [y] is referred to as a front rounded vowel. The **rounded** part of the vowel means that the person's lips are protruded when making the vowel, as in the English vowel [u] (*boot*, *coupe*). By referring to a vowel as **front,** we are making reference to the position of the tongue in the mouth; that is, the tongue is bunched toward the front of the mouth. You can feel this for yourself by pronouncing the front vowel [i] in words like *beet* and *sea*. We will have more to say about producing vowels in the next chapter.

For the moment, however, let's combine frontness and roundness to make a front rounded vowel sound. Start by making the vowel [i], as noted just above. Pay attention to what you are doing with your lips and your tongue when you make this sound. Your lips are probably spread as if you are about to smile, and your tongue is bunched toward the front of your mouth. In order to make the new sound [y], all you need to do is protrude your lips when you say the vowel, as you would if you were making an [u] sound, as in *boot*. However, do not change the position of your tongue; just move your lips from a spread to a protruding (or rounded) position. Congratulations: you have just made the front rounded vowel [y], as in the French word *su* [sy] 'knew'!

Let's try another one. You may have heard of sounds called "clicks" that occur in African languages like Zulu. The term "click" is used to describe a group of sounds that are made with a noise that sounds like clicking (hence the name). You should be able to make some click sounds quite easily since you already know how to make the various

Sounds, Not Letters!

Remember that we are talking about **sounds,** not the letters of the alphabet. Languages can use many different letters and symbols to characterize what is essentially the same sound. Even in a single language there can be more than one way to write a single sound. For example, in English, the letters and letter combinations 'f,' 'ph,' and 'gh' are all used to represent the same sound, as in *food, photo,* and *enough.* To simplify matters, we will use only one symbol to refer to a specific sound, regardless of what language it occurs in. For example, [f] refers to the sound at the beginning of the English words *food* and *photo* and at the end of *enough.* A chart of these IPA symbols is available for your reference at the back of the book.

movements, or **gestures,** involved. Although there are many types of click sounds (just as there are many kinds of vowels, for example), we will experiment with what is called an "alveolar click," characterized by the IPA symbol [!]. Begin by making the English sound [k] as in the word *back.* As you say *back,* hold your tongue in place when you make the [k] sound. Feel how your tongue is bunched up toward the upper back of your mouth. In fact, the top back portion of your tongue will be touching the roof of your mouth.

Now make the English sound [t], like in the words *table, two.* Feel where the front part of your tongue is. It will probably be touching the hard ridge located a short distance behind your teeth. To make the alveolar click, you need to put your tongue in both of these locations at the same time; that is, place the back of your tongue at the upper back part of your mouth (as in [k]), and put the front of your tongue up against the front top of your mouth (as in [t]). There should be a small space left between the back and front of your mouth above your tongue. Now create suction in this space and release your tongue abruptly from the roof of your mouth. If you hear a clicking sound, congratulations: you have just made an alveolar click found in the Zulu language!

The goal of these brief demonstrations is to show that learning to pronounce new sounds is doable if you start with some investigative work regarding the sounds. You can begin by getting information about what the various gestures of the new sounds are. You should be able to get this from, for example, a language instructor, language textbooks, websites, or even by having a native speaker describe how she makes the sounds.

The next step is to compare the new sound with similar sounds in English. What components of the new sound are different from sounds that you are already familiar with? Make use of the knowledge that you already have and apply it to sounds of the language that you are trying to learn. The gestures that combine to make sounds are independent from one another to a great extent and so can be combined in different ways to produce different sounds.

We believe that by understanding how you make the sounds in your own language, you will have tools to produce all kinds of new, exotic sounds. We include some exercises below to help you analyze the sounds of the language(s) that you are learning. Yet, before proceeding, we need to point out that not all information about making speech sounds is presented in the following pages. Instead, we have chosen to focus on those aspects that we feel are most relevant to the language learner. Many colleges and universities offer courses in phonetics and phonology, the fields concerned with this subject matter, and we encourage you to consider taking such courses should you be interested in expanding your knowledge about these topics.

Creating Speech Sounds

Most speech sounds are created when air is pushed out of the lungs and up through the vocal tract. The term "vocal tract" refers to the passage that air follows from the vocal folds (or cords) to the front of the mouth, as shown in Figure 3.1. It also includes the nasal cavity since air can also flow out of the nose to make sounds. If you think of the vocal tract as a long tube, it is easy to see how different qualities of sound can be created. When there is nothing to obstruct the air as it moves up through the mouth, you will make the sound [h] as in _hi_, _ha_, _ho_, or something similar to it. However, if you narrow the tube at various locations along the tube, these modifications will result in differing acoustic effects and, as a result, different sounds.

You can get a feel for how this works by shaping your hand into a tube. To do this, put your hand in a loose fist so that you are making an "O" with all fingers touching the tip of your thumb. Bring the "O" up against your mouth, with the end of the tube and your thumb touching your face. Blow air through the hole (you may need to blow pretty hard). Listen to the kind of noise that is produced. Now close your fist just a bit and blow again. Did you hear a difference in the quality of noise? Try it again, closing your fist even more. You should have noticed that by narrowing the diameter of the tube created by your fist, you were able to create different sounds.

In a similar fashion, we can make different speech sounds by varying the width of the air passage from the vocal folds to the lips. Narrowing the passage in one part of the mouth will filter the air to create a particular sound, while narrowing it in a different location will produce a different sound. In the case of clicks, as we saw above, the passage is narrowed in two locations, giving rise to a clicking sound.

Making a Consonant Sound

- What parts of the vocal tract are involved in making the sound?
- Where in the vocal tract is the air passage narrowed?
- How narrow is the air passage?
- Does air flow through the nose and/or the mouth?
- What is the position of the vocal folds?
- How long is the consonant?

In order to make a consonant, you should keep several general points in mind, as shown in the box on page 34. Each of these questions will be addressed below.

Parts of the Vocal Tract Involved in Making Sounds

Let's begin by familiarizing ourselves with the parts of the mouth that are important for making speech sounds, beginning with the **vocal tract** where sounds are produced. Starting at the front of the mouth, as shown in Figure 3.1, sounds can be made using the **lips** and the **teeth.** Just behind the upper teeth you can see a change in the angle of the roof of the mouth; this is called the **alveolar ridge** and is also an important location for consonants in English and other languages. The roof of the mouth is divided into the **hard palate** and the **soft palate,** or **velum.** You should be able to feel the difference between these two parts of the palate with your tongue—as you run your tongue from front to back along the roof of your mouth, you should feel that the surface is harder in the front than it is in the back. At the back of the throat is the **uvula,** the soft, dangling tissue that hangs down at the back of the soft palate. As noted above, above the roof of the mouth is the **nasal cavity.**

Shifting our focus to the **tongue,** as you no doubt know, the tongue is one of the most flexible complex of muscles of the human body. Different sounds are made by

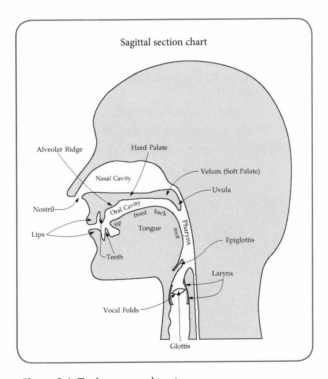

Sagittal section chart

Alveolar Ridge · Hard Palate · Velum (Soft Palate) · Uvula · Nasal Cavity · Nostril · Oral Cavity · front · back · tip · Tongue · Pharynx · root · Epiglottis · Lips · Teeth · Larynx · Vocal Folds · Glottis

Figure 3.1 The human vocal tract.

using the tongue to filter the air as it moves through the vocal tract. Some of the tongue positions that we will discover to be particularly important for making speech sounds are listed below in (1). Can you figure out which consonants are made at each of these locations?

(1) **Tongue positions**
- raised toward the top of the mouth
- pulled back toward the back of the throat
- tongue tip curled back so it touches the roof of the mouth
- tongue front pushed up against the upper set of teeth
- tongue tip pushed between the upper and lower sets of teeth

For our purposes, it is helpful to divide the tongue into four parts; moving from front to back, we have the **tip,** the **front,** the **back,** and the **root.** As we show below, each of these parts plays a key role in making consonants. Below the root of the tongue, you will see the **epiglottis,** a fold of tissue that helps cover the larynx (Adam's apple) during swallowing to help make sure that food goes into the stomach and not the lungs. The **larynx** houses the **vocal folds** (or vocal cords), and the space between the folds is known as the **glottis.**

Places Where the Air Passage Is Narrowed for Consonants

In this section, we go over where in the vocal tract the air passage is narrowed and identify some of the consonants that correspond to these locations. In the IPA charts of consonants at the back of this book, this aspect of a consonant is referred to as its **place of articulation.**

We begin with the lips. Sounds that make crucial use of the lips in their production are called **labial** sounds. If both lips are used, the sounds are called **bilabials.** English has the bilabials [p, b, m, w] which occur in words such as [p] *peat,* [b] *beat,* [m] *meat,* [w] *wheat.*

(2) **English bilabials**
[p]   peat, cap
[b]   beat, cab
[m]   meat, camera
[w]   wheat, tower

The sounds [f] (*fan*) and [v] (*van*) are also made with the lips; in this case, the bottom lip rests on the upper teeth. These sounds are called **labiodentals.** In addition to raising the lip to the teeth as in making labiodentals, you can also put your tongue between your teeth. Sounds made with this gesture are called **interdentals** and correspond to the sounds [θ, ð] in the English words *bath* and *bathe,* respectively.

(3)   **English labiodentals and interdentals**

    [f]   <u>f</u>an, lea<u>f</u>

    [v]   <u>v</u>an, lea<u>v</u>e

    [θ]   <u>th</u>in, ba<u>th</u>

    [ð]   <u>th</u>e, ba<u>th</u>e

You can also push the tip of your tongue against the back of your teeth to make a consonant. Sounds made in this manner are called **dentals** and occur in many languages, including French, Spanish, and Italian. The Italian word for 'table,' for example, begins with the dental consonant [t̪] *t̪avola*.

The Italian sound differs from the 't' in English partly because the English 't' is made further back in the mouth, against the alveolar ridge. Sounds made in this area are called **alveolars.** English has the alveolar consonants listed in (4). A common pronunciation error made by English speakers is to pronounce dental consonants as alveolars. Although the consonants sound quite similar to English ears, they are a sure mark of a foreign accent to native speakers of a language with dentals. In Chapter 6 we discuss some strategies for overcoming this pronunciation error.

(4)   **English alveolars**

    [t]   <u>t</u>wo, boa<u>t</u>, re<u>t</u>ire

    [d]   <u>d</u>o, ri<u>d</u>e, re<u>d</u>uce

    [ɾ]   le<u>tt</u>er, ma<u>dd</u>er

    [s]   <u>s</u>ue, fa<u>c</u>e, bat<u>s</u>

    [z]   <u>z</u>oo, ri<u>s</u>e, dog<u>s</u>

    [n]   <u>n</u>ew, bo<u>n</u>e, ba<u>nn</u>er

Moving further back in the mouth, the tongue can be raised so that it touches or comes near to the **hard palate,** the hard part of the roof of the mouth. Sounds made in this area are called **palatals.** They are sometimes also referred to as **palato-alveolars** or **alveopalatals,** but to keep things simple, we will just use the term **palatal.** English has the following palatal consonants:

(5)   **English palatals**

    [tʃ]   <u>ch</u>eck, ba<u>tch</u>

    [dʒ]   <u>j</u>ack, ba<u>dge</u>

    [ʃ]   <u>sh</u>ack, ba<u>sh</u>

    [ʒ]   <u>J</u>acques, gara<u>ge</u>

    [j]   <u>y</u>ak, v<u>i</u>ew

Another type of sound made with the tongue close to or in contact with the hard palate is a **retroflex** consonant. A retroflex sound is made by curling the tip of the tongue back toward the hard palate. For some speakers, the English [r] sound is made in this way.

(6) **English retroflex consonant** (for some speakers)

[ɹ]   r̠un, car̠

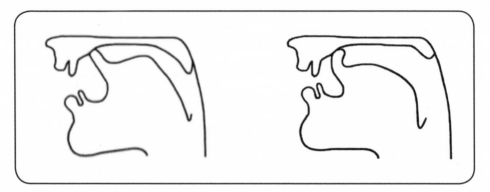

Figure 3.2 The position of the tongue for the retroflex consonant [ʈ] in Hindi (left) and Tamil (right). Based on an article published in *Journal of Phonetics* 11, Peter Ladefodged and Peri Bhaskararoa, "Non-Quantal Aspects of Consonant Production: A Study of Retroflex Consonants," 291–302. Copyright Elsevier (1983), with permission from the publisher.

Figure 3.2 shows X-ray tracings of the retroflex consonant [ʈ] produced by speakers of Hindi and Tamil. A comparison of the two tracings indicates that the way that this sound is made can vary from language to language. The different articulations of this sound, though, do share one thing in common: both involve the tongue reaching up so that it approaches the hard palate.

The tongue can also approach or make contact with the velum (soft palate) to produce what is referred to as a **velar** consonant. You should be able to feel this for yourself when you say the first consonant in the English word *c̲old*. There are three velar consonants in English:

(7) **English velars**
   [k]   c̲old, jo c̲k
   [g]   g̲old, jog̲
   [ŋ]   so n̲g, mi n̲gle

Let's continue to move back in the mouth toward the uvula. While the English language does not make use of the uvula for any of its consonants, knowing how to make sounds using it will be helpful for people learning, for example, French, Hebrew, or Arabic languages.

Try this small exercise to get a feel for where the uvula is located. Begin by making the sound [k] as in *c̲at*. Notice that the back of your tongue is bunched up toward the upper back part of the roof of your mouth (the velum). What you need to do now is move your tongue back just a bit further. It should now be making contact with the uvula, the soft dangling tissue that hangs down at the back of your throat. In some languages, the back

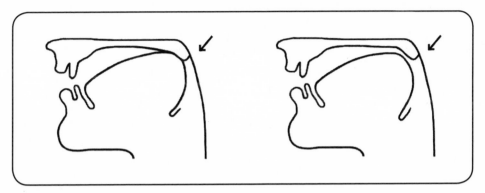

Figure 3.3 The uvular stop [q] (left) and uvular fricative [ʁ] (right) consonants, as pronounced by a speaker of Arabic. *Source:* Based on Zeroual 2000.

of the tongue is moved up toward the uvula to make sounds. These sounds are called, not surprisingly, **uvulars,** and the sound that you were just attempting to make, [q], is a common sound in Hebrew and many Arabic languages, e.g. Hebrew *qeber* 'grave'.

The leftmost image in Figure 3.3 shows a drawing of an Arabic speaker producing the uvular consonant [q]. Notice that the back of the tongue is located right up against the uvula. You can compare this with how you would say the velar consonant at the beginning of *cat*, where your tongue would be touching the soft palate and therefore would be slightly further to the front of your mouth.

Another uvular consonant, shown on the right in Figure 3.3, occurs in some Arabic languages, as well as in many varieties of French, including Parisian French, where it is spelled with the letter 'r', e.g. *rouge* 'red'. This sound, characterized by the IPA symbol [ʁ], has the same place of articulation as the [q] sound, but it is made by letting a bit of air pass between the tongue and the uvula. This creates the turbulent noise that you can often hear associated with the sound. We will return to this topic in the next section.

We will go back one more step in the mouth, to the pharynx. If you move the root of the tongue back toward the pharyngeal wall, that is, the back of your throat, you can make what is called a **pharyngeal** consonant. While English does not have consonants made at this location, many Arabic languages include pharyngeals in their inventory of sounds. The Maltese language, spoken on the island of Malta just south of Italy, has the pharyngeal sound [ħ], e.g. *ħeles* 'he set free'. The consonant sounds a bit like the English [h] in *hat*, but the tongue is pulled further back which then affects the acoustics of the sound. Figure 3.4 shows the tongue position for [ħ] as pronounced by a speaker of Arabic.

There are two additional places in the vocal tract that are used to make consonants: the epiglottis and the glottis. Since epiglottal sounds are extremely rare, we will focus only on consonants made at the glottis. You will recall that the vocal folds are located at the glottis. By manipulating the position of the vocal folds, you can produce different **glottal** sounds. One such sound is English [h] (*hi*) that we discussed above. In the case of [h], the vocal folds remain open and the air passes freely through the vocal tract. The other most common glottal sound is made by closing and then quickly opening the vocal folds. This produces a sound called the **glottal stop** [ʔ] which occurs in the English

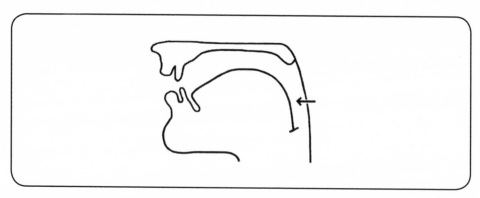

Figure 3.4 The pharyngeal consonant [h], as pronounced by a speaker of Arabic. *Source:* Based on Zeroual 2000.

expression, *uh_oh*, for example. While it is not used to differentiate words in English as the consonants [b] and [p] do (e.g. *bat* vs. *pat*), it is distinctive in other languages, including Arabic and Maltese. Notice that the only difference between the Maltese words for 'to taste' and 'this' in (8) is the quality of the last consonant; that is, whether it is [ʔ] or [n].

(8) **Maltese glottal stop: differentiating words**
daʔ   vs.   dan
'to taste'   'this'

Thus far, we have been focusing largely on consonants made where the air passage is narrowed in one location in the vocal tract. Interestingly, in some languages the air passage is narrowed in two places, creating what are called **doubly-articulated consonants** (recall that the click consonant described above has two articulations). With the possible exception of 'r' mentioned above, the closest that English comes to this type of consonant is the sound [w], e.g. *will* and *tower*. Most English speakers pronounce [w] with the lips protruded (1st location) and the back of the tongue raised toward the velum (2nd location). Hold your mouth in the position to make the [w] sound and see if you are making a sound with two places of articulation.

While not common in English, other languages can have many doubly-articulated sounds, and these can pose a challenge to the language learner. Russian's sound inventory, for example, is rich in doubly-articulated consonants. The language combines a palatal sound similar to [j] in *yellow* with what would otherwise be a basic labial, dental, or velar articulation to create what are called **palatalized** consonants. Recall that a palatal is made with the tongue raised up toward the hard palate. A palatalized consonant is similar to sequences of consonant + [j] at the beginning of English words like *view, cue, hue, pew*.

An important difference between English and Russian is that, psychologically, a native English speaker will generally consider the consonant and palatal [j] to be a sequence of two consonants, while a Russian will hear the consonant and palatal as a single sound.

A [w]-like sound can also be added to a basic consonant sound to create what are called **labialized** consonants, e.g. [pʷ], [tʷ], [kʷ]. English does not make use of this fea-

Exercise 1: English Consonant + Palatal

Say the pairs of English words below out loud, focusing on the beginning of each word. Notice the [j]-like sound after the beginning consonant, i.e. [vj] in *view,* [kj] in *cue,* [hj] in *hue,* and [pj] in *pew.* (Try not to be distracted by the spelling of the word, which does not consistently represent the palatal.) Compare the pronunciation of each word on the left with the similar word to its right. The words in the column on the right do not have a [j] sound after the first consonant, while those on the left do.

1st Consonant Sound + [j]	1st Consonant Sound, No [j]
pew	Pooh
hue	who
cue	coupe
view	voodoo

Exercise 2: Russian Palatalization

Practice saying the following Russian words first with a plain consonant and then with a slight [j]-like pronunciation added. Notice that when the palatal articulation is added, the meaning of the word changes.

Russian Plain and Palatalized Consonants

Plain		Palatalized	
mal	'little'	m^{j}al	'crumple'
nos	'nose'	n^{j}os	'he carried'
sok	'juice'	s^{j}ok	'he lashed'
zof	'call'	z^{j}of	'yawn'

ture systematically, although, as we mentioned above, lip protrusion is found with some English consonants including [ʃ], e.g. *shoe,* and [ɹ] *run.* On the other hand, labialized consonants do occur widely in some languages of Africa (e.g. Hausa, Berber, Igbo) and in some Native American languages (e.g. Navaho, Chipewyan, Bella Coola), as well as in Ancient Greek and Siberian Eskimo, among others.

Narrowness of the Air Passage

In addition to thinking about where in the mouth a particular consonant is made, it is also important to take into account how narrow the passage is for the air to move through. This property is typically referred to as a consonant's **manner of articulation.**

For example, if you jam your tongue up against the roof of your mouth, you will produce a different sound than if you leave a small space between the tongue and the roof. Try this by saying the following pairs of sounds:

(9) [t] vs. [s] e.g. <u>t</u>wo vs. <u>s</u>ue
    [d] vs. [z] e.g. <u>d</u>o vs. <u>z</u>oo

The consonants in each pair are alveolars because the tongue front is at or near the alveolar ridge. The place of articulation is then the same. What distinguishes [t] from [s] and [d] from [z] is the narrowness of the passage between the tongue and the alveolar ridge. When you pronounce [t] or [d], you will notice that your tongue actually touches the ridge, which has the effect of blocking the passage of air momentarily. Sounds made in this way are called **stops.** Now pronounce [s] or [z]. Unlike with [t] and [d], notice that the air is not blocked at all. Instead, your tongue rests very close to the alveolar ridge without touching it. This is what gives [s] and [z] their noisy quality. Consonants that have this turbulent noise quality are called **fricatives.**

There are basically three degrees of narrowness that we need to take into account when describing how narrow the air passage is at a consonant's place of articulation. Below each category, we list the corresponding consonants from English.

DEGREE 1: COMPLETE CLOSURE

There is no space for air to pass through. Sounds produced in this way are called **stops** (or **plosives**).

(10) **Stops (or plosives)**
    [p, b]   <u>p</u>at, <u>b</u>at   bilabial stops
    [t, d]   <u>t</u>all, <u>d</u>oll   alveolar stops
    [k, g]   <u>c</u>age, <u>g</u>auge   velar stops
    [ʔ]   uh_oh   glottal stop

English has another stop-like sound, [ɾ], that occurs in words such as *le<u>tt</u>er, ma<u>tt</u>er,* and *ma<u>dd</u>er.* Like a stop, the air flow is briefly interrupted while passing through the mouth. The term **flap** is used to describe sounds made in this way. It may be difficult for you to hear the difference between [t] and [ɾ], or [d] and [ɾ] if you are a native speaker of English. This is because the presence of [ɾ] in a word is completely predictable and so we tend not to pay attention to it. Since the flap is used in languages like Spanish to distinguish the meaning of words, it will come up again in Chapter 6 when we discuss common pronunciation errors.

(11) **Alveolar flap**
    [ɾ] la<u>dd</u>er, le<u>tt</u>er

Exercise 3: Bilabial Fricatives

Unlike languages such as Spanish and Ewe, English does not have bilabial fricatives. This exercise is designed to help you practice making a bilabial fricative, using the degrees of narrowness discussed in this section.

Start with Degree 1. Close your lips and open them. You have made a **labial stop** like the ones in English <u>p</u>at and <u>b</u>at. Now open your lips slightly for Degree 2. This will allow you to make **labial fricatives,** like the ones you find in the African language Ewe (you can ignore the vowel symbols).

Ewe Labial Fricatives

eva 'he polished'	vs.	English 'epa'
εβε 'Ewe (the language)'	vs.	English 'ebe'

Now open your lips even further for Degree 3. By doing this, you make a **labial glide** as in English [w] <u>w</u>in. The position of your lips when making a bilabial fricative is just between what you would be doing to make a bilabial stop and a bilabial glide. Congratulations! You've made a bilabial fricative!

In Spanish, the letters 'b' and 'v' are pronounced as the bilabial fricative [β] in certain contexts, such as between vowels, e.g. la <u>b</u>oca 'the mouth,' i<u>b</u>a 'was,' la <u>v</u>aca 'the cow,' so la<u>v</u>o 'I wash.'

DEGREE 2: NEAR CLOSURE

There is just enough space so that noise is produced when the air passes through the mouth. These sounds are called **fricatives.**

(12) **Fricatives**

[f, v]	<u>f</u>at, <u>v</u>at	labiodental fricatives
[θ, ð]	ba<u>th</u>, ba<u>the</u>	interdental fricatives
[s, z]	<u>s</u>ip, <u>z</u>ip	alveolar fricatives
[ʃ, ʒ]	<u>sh</u>ack, Jacque<u>s</u>	palatal fricatives
[h]	<u>h</u>ello	glottal fricative

You can actually combine degrees 1 and 2 and make another type of sound. We call this Degree 2½. These sounds have a complete closure, like a stop, followed by a near closure, like a fricative. These sounds are called **affricates.**

(13) **Palatal affricates**

[tʃ, dʒ]	<u>Ch</u>o, <u>J</u>oe

DEGREE 3: RELATIVELY OPEN

The air passage is narrowed, but the air can still pass through the mouth without making a lot of noise. These sounds are called **approximants** and include all **vowels, glides, and liquids.**

(14) **Approximants**

[w]	<u>wh</u>ack, <u>w</u>in	bilabial glide
[l, ɹ]	<u>l</u>ack, <u>r</u>ack	alveolar liquids
[j]	<u>y</u>ak	palatal glide

Air Flow through the Nose and Mouth

Whether the air passage is open or closed is also important for distinguishing between sounds that are made with the air flowing through the mouth and those where it also passes through the nose. Say the following pairs of words out loud and see if you can determine whether the air is coming out of your mouth or your nose. It may help to put your hand in front of your face to try to feel the air:

(15) [b] <u>b</u>a   vs.   [m] <u>m</u>a
     [d] <u>d</u>a   vs.   [n] <u>n</u>a
     [g] ag   vs.   [ŋ] a<u>ng</u>

If you determined that the air is exiting the mouth for [b, d, g] and going through the nose (and perhaps also the mouth) for [m, n, ŋ], you are absolutely right. In distinguishing these pairs of sounds, what matters is whether the air passage going into the nasal cavity is open or closed. When it is open, the air is able to go through the nasal cavity, and a nasal sound such as [m, n, ŋ] is made; when the air passage is closed, the air can only go through the mouth, and the sound is oral, e.g. [b, d, g]. The **velum** (soft palate) is responsible for controlling the flow of air through the nasal or oral cavities. If the velum is lowered as is the case in Figure 3.1, there is an opening that allows air to flow out through the nose. If the velum is raised, the opening is blocked, and no air can flow through the nose. As stated above, sounds made with air coming out of the nose are called **nasals.** The English sound inventory includes the following three nasal consonants:

(16) **English nasal consonants**
     [n] <u>n</u>ose, ca<u>n</u>
     [m] <u>m</u>ouse, sa<u>m</u>e
     [ŋ] si<u>ng</u>, mi<u>ng</u>le

Most, if not all, languages have at least one nasal consonant. The Dravidian language

Exercise 4: Nasals

Practice trying to move your velum to contrast nasal and oral sounds. Start by saying the vowel [ɑ], as in f_a_ther, several times; the velum is raised in this case. Now say [ɑŋ] as in so_ng_, several times. In this case, the velum is lowered to let the air pass through the nose as well as the mouth. Now alternate: [ɑ], [ɑŋ], [ɑ], [ɑŋ], [ɑ], [ɑŋ], [ɑ], [ɑŋ]. Focus on your velum and try to sense it moving up and down. With enough practice, you should be able to feel the movement of the velum as it lowers and rises to create nasal and oral sounds. If you are able to do this, you should be able to pronounce unfamiliar nasals by turning a familiar oral sound into its corresponding nasal sound.

Malayalam is particularly impressive in this regard because it has five nasals: labial, dental, alveolar, retroflex, and velar, as shown in (17) (the symbol [ʌ] characterizes the vowel sound in the English word b_u_tter).

(17) **Malayalam nasals**
    Labial: kʌmmi 'shortage'
    Dental: pʌnni 'pig'
    Alveolar: kʌnni 'virgin'
    Retroflex: kʌnni 'link in chain'
    Velar: kuŋŋɪ 'crushed'

Position of the Vocal Folds

The narrowness of the air passage through the vocal folds can also affect the quality of sound that is being produced. The vocal folds are tissue that stretches across the airway to the lungs; they can vibrate against each other, providing much of the sound that we hear when someone is talking. Just like the tongue, the vocal folds are used to filter air as it comes out of the lungs. Depending on their position, the quality of the air differs, and, as a result, so does the sound produced. Let's consider a number of different vocal fold positions that are used in languages to make consonants.

The vocal folds can be closed tightly and then released. This produces a sound called the **glottal stop** [ʔ] which, you will recall, is used marginally as in the English expression uh_oh. The vocal folds can also be held very close together though not closed, which allows them to vibrate. Sounds made in this way are called **voiced** sounds. Vowels are voiced, as are some consonants, including [z] (vs. [s]), _z_oo vs. _s_ue and [d] (vs. [t]), _d_o vs. _t_wo. Nasal consonants, e.g. [m, n, ŋ], are also voiced. Sounds that are made without vibration of the vocal folds are called **voiceless** sounds.

(18) **English voiceless sounds**

[p]	ca<u>p</u>	voiceless bilabial stop
[f]	cal<u>f</u>	voiceless labiodental fricative
[θ]	pa<u>th</u>	voiceless interdental fricative
[t]	ca<u>t</u>	voiceless alveolar stop
[s]	Ca<u>ss</u>	voiceless alveolar fricative
[ʃ]	ca<u>sh</u>	voiceless palatal fricative
[tʃ]	ca<u>tch</u>	voiceless palatal affricate
[k]	pa<u>ck</u>	voiceless velar stop
[h]	<u>h</u>i	voiceless glottal fricative
[ʔ]	uh_oh	voiceless glottal stop

(19) **English voiced sounds: all vowels, nasals, liquids, and glides, plus the following:**

[b]	sla<u>b</u>	voiced bilabial stop
[v]	slee<u>v</u>e	voiced labiodental fricative
[ð]	see<u>the</u>	voiced interdental fricative
[d]	see<u>d</u>	voiced alveolar stop
[z]	sei<u>z</u>e	voiced alveolar fricative
[ʒ]	sei<u>z</u>ure	voiced palatal fricative
[dʒ]	sie<u>g</u>e	voiced palatal affricate
[g]	slu<u>g</u>	voiced velar stop

Many languages differentiate words solely on the basis of the voiced and voiceless distinction in consonants. This means that the only difference in the pronunciation of two words will be that the vocal folds are vibrating for some sound in one of the words, while they are not vibrating in the other. This is the case with English words like *ca<u>b</u>* (voiced) and *ca<u>p</u>* (voiceless), ignoring possible differences in the length of the vowel.

The vocal folds can also be kept wide apart. When there is a considerable amount of air passing through them in this state, a small puff of air will be released at the end of a consonant made in this way. Say the pairs of words below with your hand in front of your mouth. Notice the difference between the underlined sounds of each pair.

(20) <u>p</u>ot s<u>p</u>ot
<u>t</u>op s<u>t</u>op
<u>c</u>ore s<u>c</u>ore

You should be able to feel a small puff of air after [p, t, k] at the beginning of the words in the left column. These sounds are called **aspirated** sounds. The corresponding stops in the right hand column are **unaspirated,** since no puff of air accompanies the consonant.

While English has both aspirated and unaspirated consonants, the presence or absence of aspiration is never the only property distinguishing two words. As a result, there are no two words that both begin with a voiceless stop and that are identical in all respects but where one is aspirated while the other is unaspirated; English has only voiceless *aspirated* stops in this position, e.g. *<u>p</u>am*. Nor are there two words beginning with

---

Exercise 5: Voiced and Voiceless Consonants

Try to get a feel for what the difference is between a voiced and a voiceless consonant. To do this, touch your palm to your throat by your larynx. Now say the following pairs of words, paying special attention to the underlined sounds:

z̲oo   s̲ue
v̲at   f̲at
d̲o   t̲o

Can you feel your vocal folds vibrating when you say the first consonant of the words on the left? For the words on the right, there will be vibration associated with the vowel, but you should still be able to notice that there is no vocal fold vibration associated with the first consonant.

---

[s] followed by two identical voiceless stops except that one is aspirated and the other is unaspirated: only *unaspirated* voiceless stops occur in this position, e.g. *spam*.

In Hindi, on the other hand, pronouncing an aspirated consonant without aspiration, or an unaspirated consonant with aspiration, can change the meaning of a word. Compare the pairs of words given in (21). The only difference between the members of each pair is aspiration: the word on the left is aspirated, while the one on the right is unaspirated.[1]

(21) **Hindi aspirated and unaspirated voiceless stops**
      [pʰal] 'knife-edge'   [pal] 'take care of'
      [t̪ʰan] 'roll of cloth'   [t̪an] 'mode of singing'
      [kʰal] 'skin'   [kal] 'era'
      [t̪ʰal] 'place for buying'   [t̪al] 'postpone'

Because aspiration is not distinctive in English, it is easy for an English speaker to mispronounce aspirated and unaspirated words in languages that have different rules from those of English. In Chapter 6, we review some of these errors and ways to avoid them.

Length of the Consonant

An interesting property used to distinguish words in some languages concerns consonant length, that is, how long the articulation of the consonant is held. Saying a sound in an English word for a longer or shorter amount of time does not change the meaning of the word. Take the word *sun*, for example. If you hold the 's' twice as long as you normally would, the word may sound rather strange, but it does not make it a new word.

---

1. We thank Ila Nagar for supplying us with these Hindi examples.

Yet, this is exactly what happens in many languages. In Italian, for instance, the words for 'fate' and 'made' are distinguished solely by the length of the consonant 't.' In 'made' the consonant is about twice as long as its counterpart in 'fate,' a quality indicated in the Italian spelling system by doubling the letter.

(22) **Italian consonant length**
  fato 'fate' vs. fatto 'made'

While English words can also be spelled with double letters, e.g. *matte, assure, babble*, this doubling is not telling the reader that the consonant is to be made twice as long as a word with only a single letter, e.g. *matte* vs. *mate*. As noted above, consonant length is not used to distinguish word meaning in English. Double letters in English can nonetheless give us clues about how words are pronounced. In *matte* (vs. *mate*), for instance, the double letters provide information about the quality of the preceding vowel.

Summary

To summarize what we have covered in this chapter, we have identified the following points concerning the production of consonants:

1. The parts of the vocal tract that are involved:
   - lips, teeth, alveolar ridge, hard palate, velum, uvula, pharynx, vocal folds
   - tongue tip, tongue front, tongue back, tongue root

2. Places where the air passage is narrowed for consonants:
   - lips, teeth, alveolar ridge, hard palate, velum, uvula, pharynx, vocal folds

3. The narrowness of the air passage:
   - Degree 1: closure (no sound; air flow is interrupted)
   - Degree 2: near closure (turbulent noise is produced)
   - Degree 2½: a combination of 1 and 2 (no sound followed by turbulent noise)
   - Degree 3: relatively open (no turbulent noise)

4. Does air flow through the nose and/or the mouth?
   - through the mouth: oral consonants (and vowels)
   - through the nose (and mouth): nasal consonants (and vowels)

(continued on next page)

Summary (continued from previous page)

5. What is the position of the vocal folds?
   - tightly closed and released: glottal stop
   - close together to produce vibration: vowels, voiced consonants
   - opened without vibration: unaspirated
   - opened with increased volume of air: aspirated

6. How long is the consonant?
   - longer
   - shorter

   Keeping these points in mind, you should be able to tackle the pronunciation of new sounds. To do so, start by understanding how a new sound is made. This may involve asking your language teacher to say the sound slowly so that you can repeat it. Some language books actually describe the particular sounds using labels similar to the ones used above. Once you understand the components of the new sound, go slowly, putting the components together. Finally, PRACTICE, PRACTICE, PRACTICE! And practice slowly. Remember: you have had years to practice making the sounds of your native language!

Additional Exercise: Comparing Consonants

Here is an exercise to help you better understand how the consonants in a language that you are learning differ from those in English.

1. On the inside back cover of this book you will find consonant charts from the International Phonetic Association giving the symbols needed to describe the speech sounds in all the languages of the world (many more than you will ever need!). On the page opposite to the IPA chart, you will see a simplified chart containing the consonants of English.

   - Make a copy of the IPA consonant chart (or draw your own).
   - Circle all the consonants from English.
   - Then, taking information that you have gathered from your language book, your instructor, the web, or other sources, draw a triangle around the consonants of the language you are learning. You could also sit down with a native speaker of the language and have her say each sound individually. You can ask her to describe how she is making the sound, or you can imitate the sound, asking her to let you know how native-like you sound. You can then determine for yourself how the consonant is made and put a triangle around the appropriate symbol in the chart.

- The next step is to compare the sounds in the circles and triangles you have drawn. Are there triangles without corresponding circles? If so, look for English consonants that share some of the same properties, for example, place of articulation, voicing quality, and so on, and use your knowledge of producing these familiar sounds to create new ones, as we did at the beginning of this chapter with clicks and front rounded vowels.

References

Ladefoged, Peter, and Bhaskararao, Peri. (1983). Non-quantal aspects of consonant production: A study of retroflex consonants. *Journal of Phonetics* 11: 291–302.

Zeroual, Chakir. (2000). *Propos controverses sur la phonétique et la phonologie de l'arabe marocain.* PhD dissertation. Université Paris. 8.

How to
Make a Vowel

Introduction

When you are learning how to pronounce vowels of a new language, it is useful to keep a number of points in mind. As with consonants, you will obviously want to be aware of the parts of the vocal tract that are involved in making a particular vowel. In addition, the narrowness of the passage through which the air exits the mouth is important. We saw that by varying the degree of narrowness of the air passage between, for example, the tongue and the hard palate, we can create different consonants. The same is true for vowels.

It is also important to consider where the narrowing occurs for vowels, as well as whether the air exits just the mouth or exits the nose as well. Also, just as consonants can be long or short, we also want to be aware of how long a vowel is and whether the quality of the vowel changes during its production. Finally, the shape of the lips—that is, whether the lips are protruded to form a small 'o' or are spread apart—is also relevant, perhaps more so than for consonants. In this chapter we will look at all these aspects of making a vowel.

In order to make a vowel, you should keep several general points in mind, as shown in the box at the top of page 52. Each of these questions will be addressed below.

Parts of the Vocal Tract
Involved in Making Vowels

Since all speech sounds are made by filtering the air as it passes through the mouth or

Making a Vowel Sound

- What parts of the vocal tract are involved in making the vowel?
- Where in the vocal tract is the air passage narrowed?
- How narrow is the air passage?
- What is the shape of the lips?
- Does the quality of the vowel change from start to finish?
- Does air flow through the nose as well as through the mouth?
- How long is the vowel?

nasal cavity, you should not be surprised to learn that similar parts of the vocal tract are used to create consonants and vowels. Yet, vowels differ from consonants in a number of ways. For example, we generally do not use the tip of the tongue to make a vowel. For vowels, it is movements involving the middle and back of the tongue that are especially important; together these two areas are often referred to as the **tongue body.** In addition, air flow is never completely obstructed in the vocal tract as it is for some consonants (stops). Despite this, vowels can be differentiated by more degrees of narrowness than consonants are. Because of these differences, it is worthwhile to have a closer look at the production of vowels in English and other languages.

Places Where the Air Passage Is Narrowed for Vowels

In this section we discuss an important function of the tongue: its back-and-forth movement in the mouth.

There are three basic positions used by speakers of most languages to make vowels. The first involves bunching the tongue toward the front of your mouth, as in [i] (b<u>ee</u>t).

Exercise 1: Horizontal Tongue Movement

To get a feel for your tongue moving back and forth, say the vowel in [æ] as in c<u>a</u>t; then say the vowel in [ɑ] as in c<u>o</u>t. Repeat a number of times, concentrating on where in your mouth the tongue body is. It may help to look in a mirror while you are doing this.

You can also use your index finger to sense the movement: touch the tip of your index finger to the front of your tongue when you say the vowel in c<u>a</u>t; now, make the vowel in c<u>o</u>t without moving your finger. Your tongue should be moving away from your finger, toward the back of your mouth, when you say the vowel in c<u>o</u>t.

This may be more noticeable when you contrast it with the pronunciation of [u] (b<u>oo</u>t), although you should ignore any differences in the shape of your lips. Vowels that are made with the tongue bunched forward are called **front** vowels.

(1) **Front vowels in American English**

     [i]   b<u>ee</u>t

     [ɪ]   b<u>i</u>t

     [eɪ]   b<u>ai</u>t

     [ɛ]   b<u>e</u>t

     [æ]   b<u>a</u>t

In the second position, the tongue is pulled toward the back of the mouth; vowels made in this way are called **back** vowels. Comparing again the front vowel [i] (b<u>ee</u>t) with the back vowel [u] (b<u>oo</u>t), notice that when you say [u], the back of your tongue is pulled back so that it almost touches the back of your throat. The front-back distinction is very important and is used in virtually all languages.

(2) **Back vowels in American English**

     [u]   c<u>oo</u>l

     [ʊ]   c<u>ou</u>ld

     [oʊ]   c<u>oa</u>t

     [ɔ]   c<u>au</u>ght[1]

     [ɑ]   c<u>o</u>t

In the third position, the tongue is neither bunched up at the front of the mouth nor pulled all the way back, but rather it is positioned in between the two. This is the case in English for the sound that occurs in the word b<u>u</u>t; vowels with this third tongue position are called **central** vowels.

Exercise 2: Front, Central, and Back Vowels

Compare the pronunciation of **front, central,** and **back** vowels in English. To do this, say just the vowels in the following words slowly one after the other: b<u>ai</u>t [eɪ], b<u>u</u>t [ʌ], b<u>oa</u>t [oʊ]. Try to feel where your tongue is for the front vowel [eɪ], the central vowel [ʌ] and the back vowel [oʊ]. Practice this until you are able to feel your tongue moving back as you pronounce the three vowels. (Note that the vowel in *but* is sometimes written as [ə], a vowel referred to by linguists as 'schwa.')

---

1. Not all speakers of American English make a distinction between the vowels in *caught* and *cot*. For those that do not, the vowel [ɑ] is generally used. See the discussion in the next section.

(3) **Central vowels in American English**
   [ʌ] or [ə]   c<u>u</u>t

Taking what you know about tongue placement in English, consider the front-central-back distinction among some vowels in the Korean language, as shown by the three forms in (4). English has [i] (b<u>ee</u>t) and [u] (b<u>oo</u>t), but not the central vowel [ɨ].

(4) **Korean**

Front	*Central*	*Back*
[i] [kil] 'road'	[ɨ] [kɨl] 'letters'	[u] [kul] 'oyster'

In both languages, the vowel [u] is pronounced with the lips protruded. Similarly, in both English and Korean, the vowel [i] is made with the lips spread, not protruded. Korean obviously differs from English in that it also has a central vowel [ɨ] where the tongue body is positioned between where it would be for [u] and [i]. You can come fairly close to making a Korean [ɨ] by drawing on your knowledge of English vowels. Start by making [i] (b<u>ee</u>t). Now, without protruding your lips, draw your tongue back toward its position for [u] (b<u>oo</u>t), though not completely. By doing this, you are approximating the pronunciation of the central vowel [ɨ] which occurs not only in Korean but in Chinese, Turkish, and many other languages.

Narrowness of the Air Passage

We turn now to the narrowness of the air passage. The different degrees of narrowness that are used to distinguish vowels are generally referred to as **vowel height** distinctions. To be more precise, it is the height of the **highest part of the tongue** with respect to the roof of the mouth that is relevant. The higher the tongue, the narrower the air passage.

   To get a feel for what we mean by the height of the tongue, say the vowel in the word b<u>ee</u>t and then the vowel in b<u>a</u>t. Repeat several times, focusing on the position of the middle of your tongue in relation to the roof of your mouth. Notice that for the vowel in b<u>ee</u>t, your tongue is very high in your mouth, almost touching the hard palate. If it were any higher, you would be making a fricative or stop consonant. For the vowel in b<u>a</u>t, on the other hand, the space between your palate and tongue is much greater. Your jaw will be much lower in this case as well. This is why doctors ask us to say "aaah" and not "eeeh"!

   The image in Figure 4.1 shows X-ray tracings of the tongue position of an English speaker saying the vowels [i] (b<u>ee</u>t), [u] (b<u>oo</u>t), [æ] (b<u>a</u>t), and [ɑ] (b<u>o</u>ttle; b<u>ou</u>ght). Look for the narrowest passage between the tongue and the roof of the mouth in each case; it is closer to the middle of the mouth for [i] and closer to the back of the mouth for the other three vowels. Compare the very different tongue heights for the vowels you were just saying: [i] (b<u>ee</u>t) and [æ] (b<u>a</u>t). Of all of the vowels illustrated, [i] and [u] have the highest tongue positions and so are referred to as **high** vowels. The vowels [æ] and [ɑ] are called **low** vowels because the tongue is low in the mouth.

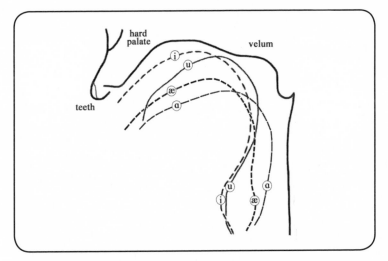

Figure 4.1 Side view of tongue positions in the production of four English vowels: [i], [u], [æ], [ɑ]. *Source*: Based on Joseph Perkell, *Physiology of Speech Production*, 1969, with permission from MIT Press.

There are five different degrees of narrowness (or vowel height) used in American English, illustrated by the front vowel sounds in (5). They can be described on a scale from high to mid to low, with the height of the two intermediate vowels labeled "higher mid" and "lower mid."

(5)   **Vowel height in American English front vowels**

High	[i]	b<u>ee</u>t
Higher mid	[ɪ]	b<u>i</u>t
Mid	[eɪ]	b<u>ai</u>t
Lower mid	[ɛ]	b<u>e</u>t
Low	[æ]	b<u>a</u>t

Practice feeling the height differences among the vowels in (5). Begin by pronouncing the vowel in *b<u>ee</u>t* by itself, without the two consonants. Notice that the tongue is very high in your mouth, close to the hard palate. Add a small bit of space between the tongue and the palate while keeping everything else in the same position. By doing this, you will be making the vowel in *b<u>i</u>t*. Lower the tongue a bit more and you will have the vowel in *b<u>ai</u>t*. Lower it one more step and you will be making the vowel in *b<u>e</u>t*. Now lower the tongue even further, drop the jaw, and you will have the vowel in *b<u>a</u>t*. Try this a few times to familiarize yourself with the feeling of your tongue moving closer to and further away from the roof of your mouth.

American English also uses different vowel heights to distinguish back vowels, as shown in (6).

(6)   **Vowel height in American English back vowels**

High	[u]	c<u>oo</u>l

Higher mid	[ʊ]	c<u>ou</u>ld
Mid	[oʊ]	c<u>oa</u>t
Lower mid	[ɔ]	c<u>au</u>ght
Low	[ɑ]	c<u>o</u>t

As noted earlier, not all speakers of American English make use of five height distinctions for back vowels. For many speakers, the vowels [ɔ] and [ɑ] are not differentiated. Instead, words like *cot* and *caught* are both pronounced as [kɑt]. Determine for yourself whether or not you distinguish between these two vowels.

English is rather uncommon in having five vowel heights, given that most languages have three or four. This is good news for people who already know English and are learning another language. The odds are that you will already be familiar with the heights of the vowels in the new language. This means that producing the vowels and hearing differences among them will probably not be as difficult as it would be if you were going from, for example, a three-height to a five-height system.

Many languages have three vowel heights, including languages such as Arabic, Bulgarian, Greek, Hawaiian, Hebrew, Hungarian, Japanese, Korean, Latin, Farsi, Serbo-Croatian, Spanish, Swahili, Turkish, and Yiddish. In Spanish, Hawaiian, and Swahili, for example, the three back vowels are [u], [o], and [ɔ].

A number of other languages have four vowel heights, including Dutch, French, German, Italian, Polish, Russian, and Swedish. Dutch, for example, has the back vowels [u], [o], [ɔ], and [ɑ].

The Shape of the Lips

We saw in the last chapter that some consonants are made with the lips protruded, as in [w] <u>w</u>in. Lip protrusion is often referred to as lip rounding because the lips form a small circle when protruded. Rounded vowels are quite common in languages. English, for example, has a number of rounded vowels, including [u] <u>boot</u>, [oʊ] <u>boat</u>, and, in some dialects, [ɔ] <u>bought</u>. While all the rounded vowels in English are also back, in other languages front vowels can be rounded as well, for example, French, German, Hungarian, Korean, Swedish, and Turkish, to name a few.

French, for example, has an especially rich inventory of front rounded vowels, as shown in (7).

(7) **French front rounded vowels**

High front rounded	[y]	*pu*	[py] 'could'	*lu*	[ly] 'read'
Mid front rounded	[ø]	*peu*	[pø] 'little'	*le*	[lø] 'the'
Lower mid front rounded	[œ]	*peur*	[pœr] 'fear'	*leur*	[lœr] 'their'

Making front rounded vowels is not difficult if you start with vowels that you are familiar with. Picking up from our discussion above, begin by making the vowel [i] as in *beet*. Now protrude your lips as you would if you were producing [u] (*boot*), remembering to keep your tongue near the front of your mouth. You have just made the high front rounded vowel [y]! Now practice it a number of times to give your muscles a chance to remember how they are positioned when you make this vowel.

Let's try another. To make the front mid rounded vowel [ø], start by making the English vowel [eɪ], as in *bait*. Now protrude your lips, again without moving your tongue. This is the vowel in French words like [pø] *peu* 'little' and [lø] *le* 'the.'

To produce the remaining French front rounded vowel, that is, the lower mid front rounded vowel [œ], begin with the lower mid front vowel [ɛ], as in English *bet*. Once more, protrude your lips. You have now made the vowel that occurs in words like [pœr] *peur* 'fear' and [lœr] *leur* 'their.' Congratulations!

Now practice pronouncing all three vowels one after another: [y], [ø], [œ].

Once again we have illustrated how you can make unfamiliar sounds from another language by drawing on the knowledge that you already have from your own language.

Changing Vowel Quality from Start to Finish: Diphthongs

Most of the vowels that we have discussed so far are similar in that the quality of the vowel stays the same from beginning to end. For instance, the vowel [i] in *bee* is consistently pronounced as [i] from when it starts after the consonant [b] to when it ends. Vowels of this type are called **monophthongs.** Not all vowels have this property, however. The vowel [ɔɪ] in the word *boy* for example, begins as a mid back rounded vowel [o] but ends up as a higher mid front unrounded vowel [ɪ]. A vowel of this type is called a **diphthong:** a vowel that starts out with one quality and ends up with another quality.

The full set of diphthongs in English is shown below in (8), including two that we have already seen: [eɪ] (*bait*) and [oʊ] (*boat*). Note that the change in quality is most detectable when the diphthong occurs at the end of a word, since in this position it is fairly long, allowing the end of the vowel to be more fully produced: compare *bait* vs. *bay*.

(8) **English diphthongs**
    [aʊ]   c<u>ow</u>, tr<u>ou</u>nce
    [oʊ]   g<u>o</u>, s<u>ew</u>, t<u>oa</u>d
    [aɪ]   b<u>uy</u>, b<u>i</u>de
    [ɔɪ]   s<u>oy</u>, b<u>oy</u>
    [eɪ]   r<u>ay</u>, s<u>ay</u>

Many languages do not have diphthongs, only monophthongs, including Arabic, Bulgarian, Ewe, Parisian French, Greek, German, Hawaiian, Hebrew, Hungarian, Italian, Japanese, Navaho, Spanish, Swahili, Zulu, and many others. In fact, all languages have monophthongs, while only some, like English, have diphthongs.

Pronunciation Errors with Diphthongs and Monophthongs

Substituting a diphthong for a monophthong is a common pronunciation error made by English speakers when learning a language without diphthongs. This substitution is especially easy when the monophthong of the foreign language is similar to a diphthong of English. For example, the English diphthongs [eɪ] and [oʊ] are very similar to the vowels [e] and [o] which occur in most of the languages noted just above. If you are a native speaker of English and you want to sound more like a speaker of a foreign language with [e] and [o], see Chapter 6 for some suggestions on how to accomplish this.

Air Flow through the Mouth and Nose

In addition to the topics above, another point to keep in mind when producing vowels is whether the vowel is nasal or oral. Just as we saw for consonants, whether the air exits the nose or the mouth can be meaningful. If the air exits only the mouth, we have an oral vowel. If it also exits the nose, the vowel is nasal.

The vowels of English are all basically oral. That is, we do not use the distinction between nasality and orality in vowels to change the meaning of words, as we do with vowel height, e.g. ([i] b*eet* vs. [ɪ] b*it*). This means that there are no two words in English that differ solely on the basis of whether the vowel is nasal or oral. Yet many languages do use this distinction.

Recall that to make a nasal consonant, the velum is lowered so that air can exit the nose. This is the case with consonants like [m] *some,* [n] *sun,* and [ŋ] *sung.* Not surprisingly, nasal vowels are also made by lowering the velum.

Try to make a nasalized [ɑ] (the oral [ɑ] occurs in words like *father*). Start by pronouncing the sound [ɑ], followed by [ŋ], as in so*ng*. Notice that the back of your tongue is touching the roof of your mouth in order to make the consonant. To remove the consonantal articulation but keep the nasality, lower the back of your tongue slightly so that it is no longer touching the top of your mouth. You should still be making a nasal sound, and if you are, then your velum is in a lowered position. You might even be able to feel air coming out of your nose. Now try to make just the vowel [ɑ] with the velum lowered, that is, the nasal vowel [ɑ̃]. (A tilde ˜ over a vowel indicates that the vowel is nasal.) Practice this several times to get a sense of what a nasal vowel feels and sounds like.

As we mentioned above, in some languages the only difference between two words can be whether the vowel is nasal or oral, and so the meaning of a word depends on this quality of the vowel. In Polish, for example, there are two mid nasal vowels, spelled 'ę' [ɛ̃] and 'ą' [ɔ̃]. The latter differentiates words that mean 'I' (which contains an oral vowel) and 'she' (which contains a nasal vowel), as shown in (9). The consonant [j], the height of the vowel, and the position of the tongue body and lips are the same.

(9) **Polish oral and nasal lower mid back rounded vowels**
    [jɔ] 'I, me'
    [jɔ̃] 'she, her'

In Polish, nasality on a vowel is "spelled" with a diacritic under the vowel, i.e. 'ę' and 'ą'. Another common way to denote nasality in spelling is to write a nasal consonant after the vowel, as is done in French and Portuguese. In French, for example, the word for *good* is spelled *bon* yet pronounced as [bɔ̃]; the 'n' in the spelling is not pronounced as a consonant, but instead indicates that the preceding vowel is nasal. As discussed in Chapter 6, a common mistake made by English speakers is to pronounce the 'n' as the consonant [n], rather than as nasalization on the vowel. Understanding the spelling conventions of the language that you are learning will help you to avoid this kind of error.

Length of the Vowel

An additional property of vowels that may be important is vowel length. In some languages, the amount of time that you hold the pronunciation of a vowel can be used to distinguish the meaning of words. Examples from the Turkish language, shown in (10), illustrate that in some words it is only the length of the vowel that differentiates words (a colon : after a vowel indicates that the vowel is longer than the same vowel without the colon). For example, the words for 'beware' and 'quiet' are identical, except that the first word [sakin] has a short [a] while the second word [saːkin] has a long vowel [aː].

(10) **Turkish short and long vowels**

Shorter Duration	*Longer Duration*
[sakin] 'beware'	[saːkin] 'quiet'
[meme] 'breast'	[meːmur] 'official'
[iman] 'faith'	[iːman] 'imam'
[surat] 'face'	[suːret] 'manner'

English vowels can also differ in duration, but these differences do not change the meaning of a word as they do in Turkish. Rather, the duration of the vowel is completely predictable from its context. A vowel is pronounced with a shorter duration if it comes before a **voiceless** consonant, such as [t, p, k, s, . . .], as in the word *beat*. A vowel is longer when it comes before a **voiced** consonant, such as [d, b, g, z, . . .], as in *bead*. Compare the vowel [i] in *beat* to the one in *bead*. Can you tell that the second one is longer? Now compare these two to the vowel [i] in *bee*. It should sound even longer, because in English the duration of a vowel is longest when it comes at the end of a word. A vowel in English, then, is short before a voiceless consonant, longer before a voiced consonant, and longest at the end of a word. Since we can predict the relative length of a vowel by knowing what, if anything, follows it in a word, vowel length in English is not distinctive. On the other hand, it is distinctive in Turkish, as we saw in (10).

Summary

In this section we discussed six areas involved in the production of vowels that may be important to you as you learn new vowels.

(11)   **Dimensions of difference for vowels**
   * the height of the vowel: high, higher mid, mid, lower mid, low
   * the horizontal position of the tongue body: front, central, back
   * the position of the lips: rounded, unrounded
   * whether the vowel is a monophthong or a diphthong
   * whether the vowel is oral or nasal
   * whether the vowel is long or short

These are the most common properties associated with vowels, and if you are aware of these, they will take you a long way in learning how to produce the sounds of another language.

Being familiar with these aspects of vowels, as well as with the additional components that we discussed in the previous chapter for consonants, should enable you to produce, with practice, almost any speech sound, even those very unusual sounds that may occur in only a few languages. Remember that when you are learning to make a new sound, it can be helpful to start from a sound that you already know. Recall that this was our strategy for producing the front rounded vowel [y]; we started from the English vowel [i] _beet_ and added lip rounding, similar to English [u] _boot_. If you are unsure about how the new sound is produced and you are studying in a formal language learning setting, ask your instructor to describe where in the mouth and how the sound is made. Alternatively, you could ask a native speaker. Watch as the person pronounces the sound, and listen carefully. Then imitate the best you can, asking him for feedback on your pronunciation. Once you have it, there is only one thing left to do: PRACTICE, PRACTICE, PRACTICE! There is no substitute in language learning for practice.

Additional Exercise: Comparing Vowels

This exercise is similar to the one for consonants at the end of the previous chapter. The goal is to help you better understand how the vowels in a language that you are learning differ from those in English.

1. On the inside back cover of this book and the page opposite it, you will find charts with symbols for vowels in English and other languages.

    *   Make a copy of the English vowel charts (or draw your own). Note that there is one for monophthongs and one for diphthongs.
    *   Taking information that you have gathered from your language book, your instructor, the web, or other sources, draw a triangle around any English vowel that also occurs in the language you are learning. Take care to determine whether the vowels of your new language are monophthongal or diphthongal. Add any vowels from your new language that do not occur in English.
    *   Now compare the vowels in the two languages:
        »   What differences in the two systems do you notice? If there are vowels in your new language that do not occur in English, in what ways are they similar to or different from English vowels?
        »   What aspect of pronouncing the new vowels do you find particularly challenging? How can you draw on your knowledge of English vowels to help overcome the challenges?

Reference

Perkell, Joseph. (1969). *Physiology of speech production.* (Research Monograph, No. 53.) Cambridge, MA: MIT Press.

5

Putting Sounds Together

Introduction

Our focus in the preceding two chapters has been on learning how to pronounce consonants and vowels. Obviously, learning to do this is crucial if you want to sound like a native speaker of some other language. But sounds rarely occur by themselves. Instead, sounds combine to form words, and learning to speak another language also involves learning to pronounce new words. In many cases this requires learning how to combine sounds in unfamiliar ways.

As with any new activity that involves the coordination and sequencing of complex movements, learning to pronounce new words requires lots of practice. In this chapter we look at how the sequences of sounds in English differ from those in other languages. Perhaps not surprisingly, we will see that some languages have more complex systems than English, while others have simpler ones. Of course, knowing which sequences of sounds can and cannot occur in English is not going to make you a master of some other language. We believe, however, that it will help you to think analytically about the sound system of English, a system that you already have a lot of experience with. Equipped with this knowledge, you can then use it as a basis for comparison with any new language that you choose to learn. Being familiar with the sound sequences of English will also give you a glimpse into potential areas of difficulty that you might expect to encounter when learning a new language.

So how can you learn to combine unfamiliar sounds in unfamiliar ways to create new words? It may be helpful to break a difficult word down into smaller, more manageable sequences and practice pronouncing these shorter sequences <u>very slowly</u>. Practice the sequence over and over to give your vocal organs a chance to learn the new combination.

Slowly combine the smaller chunks together, practicing larger and larger chunks. The important point through all of this is to practice, practice, practice—slowly.

But what constitutes an unfamiliar sequence of sounds? To answer this question, we will start by describing which strings of sounds occur in English. Notice again that we say <u>sounds</u>, not spelling! Depending on the particular dialect, English has approximately 24 distinctive consonants—that is, the sounds that are used to distinguish the meanings of words, e.g. [n, m], <u>run</u> vs. <u>rum</u>. A list of the consonants that occur in most dialects of American English is given in Table 5.1. Stops, fricatives, and affricates are grouped together under the cover term **obstruents,** while nasals, liquids, and glides form the group of **sonorant** consonants.

What combinations of consonants can begin a word in English? We know that [bɹ], [st], and [pl] are possible combinations because of words like <u>brown</u>, <u>stop</u>, and <u>please</u>. But are all combinations of two consonants possible at the beginning of a word? If they were, with about 24 consonants in the language we would expect 24!/(24 − 2)! possible

● **TABLE 5.1**
   Consonants that occur in most English dialects.

OBSTRUENTS		SONORANTS	
Stops:		*Nasals:*	
[p]	<u>p</u>ill	[m]	ru<u>m</u>
[b]	<u>b</u>ill	[n]	ru<u>n</u>
[t]	<u>t</u>ill	[ŋ]	ru<u>ng</u>
[d]	<u>d</u>ill		
[k]	<u>k</u>ill		
[g]	<u>g</u>ill		
Fricatives:		*Liquids:*	
[f]	<u>f</u>an	[l]	<u>l</u>ock
[v]	<u>v</u>an	[ɹ]	<u>r</u>ock
[θ]	<u>th</u>in		
[ð]	<u>th</u>is		
[s]	<u>s</u>ue		
[z]	<u>z</u>oo		
[ʃ]	<u>sh</u>ack		
[ʒ]	<u>J</u>acques		
[h]	<u>h</u>i		
Affricates:		*Glides:*	
[tʃ]	<u>ch</u>unk	[w]	<u>w</u>ar
[dʒ]	<u>j</u>unk	[j]	<u>y</u>our

combinations, that is, 552. In reality, there are fewer than 50 in the language. As a native speaker of English you already know this, even though you may not be consciously aware of the fact that you do. Yet, for a non-native speaker of English, these combinations have to be memorized. In the next section, we will look in more detail at what the possible sequences of English are. With this as a basis, we will then consider sequences in other languages and the challenges that an English speaker might encounter when learning them.

Sound Sequences in English and Other Languages

Knowing the sequences that occur at the beginning and at the end of a word will generally tell us the kinds of sequences that can occur within the word. Word-internal sequences are typically a combination of possible word-final sequences and word-initial sequences. For example, we know that [ɹt] is a possible word-final sequence in English because it occurs after a vowel in words like _cart, Burt, sort_. We also know that [m] is a possible word-initial consonant in English because it occurs before a vowel in words like _men, map, melon_. Given this, it is not surprising to find the sequence [-ɹtm-] occurring between vowels in an English word like _apartment_. So although we do not talk specifically about word-internal sequences in what follows, conclusions can be drawn from the other information provided.

ENGLISH SOUND SEQUENCES: WORD-INITIAL

Before looking at what occurs in other languages, let's begin by thinking about possible sequences of sounds in English. The term **phonotactics** is used to refer to which sequences occur and do not occur in a language. We start by considering English phonotactics at the beginning of a word.

In English, words can begin with either a consonant or a vowel sound, e.g. _big, supper, in, airplane_. The number of consonants that can come before a vowel at the beginning of a word ranges from one to three. Any consonant can start a word, with two exceptions. First, there are no words in English that begin with the sound [ŋ] (the sound that occurs at the end of words like _song_ [sɔŋ]). Second, the sound [ʒ] is very uncommon at the beginning of an English word, and those that do occur generally have a foreign flavor to them, e.g. _Jacques, Zsa Zsa (Gabor)_.

As we increase the number of consonants at the beginning of a word, the number of restrictions also increases. In most English words that begin with **two consonants,** the first consonant is a stop or a fricative, and the second is a liquid ([ɹ, l]) or a glide ([j, w]). The only exception to this rule is that there are sequences of two consonants in which the first is the fricative [s] and the second is either a nasal consonant, e.g. _snore, smoke_, or an oral plosive, e.g. _spot, stop, sky_. Some examples of two-consonant sequences are given in (1). (An asterisk before a sequence indicates that the sequence does not actually occur.)

(1)   **Two-consonant sequences**

p + consonant:

[pl] please

[pɹ] price

[pj] pure

*[pw] (except in foreign words like *pueblo*)

b + consonant:

[bl] black

[bɹ] brother

[bj] beautiful

*[bw]

t + consonant:

[tɹ] trim

[tw] twin

*[tl], *[tj] (though [tj] is possible in some dialects as in *tune*)

d + consonant:

[dɹ] drug

[dw] dwell

*[dl], *[dj] (though [dj] is possible in some dialects as in *dude*)

k + consonant:

[kɹ] crutch

[kl] clean

[kw] quick

[kj] cute

g + consonant:

[gɹ] grow

[gl] glad

[gw] Gwen

*[gj]

θ + consonant:

[θɹ] three

[θw] thwart

*[θl], *[θj]

f + consonant:

[fɹ] fresh

[fl] flat

[fj] few, funeral

*[fw]

v + consonant:

[vj] view

*v + consonant (except in foreign words, e.g. *Vladimir*)

s + consonant:

[sp] spot

[st] stop
[sk] score
[sm] smile
[sn] snore
[sl] slimy
[sj] Sierra (for some speakers)
[sw] swim
*[sɹ]
ʃ + *consonant*:
[ʃɹ] shriek
*[ʃl], *[ʃj], *[ʃw] (except in foreign words, e.g. *schlep, Schwinn*)
*z + *consonant,* *ʒ + *consonant,* *ð + *consonant*

You will notice that the voiced fricatives generally do not occur before a consonant at the beginning of a word, so you do not get words like *znew* or *vlop*. An exception is found with the Russian name *Vladimir*, which when used in English provides a nice illustration of how the introduction of words from other languages can expand the inventory of sound sequences in one's own language. Also missing are sequences made up of the consonants [t, d, θ] + [l], [θ] + [j], and [p, b, f] + [w]. None of these sequences occur at the beginning of words in English.

Word-initial sequences of **three consonants** are even more restricted. In fact, in English the first consonant in this kind of sequence has to be [s], the second consonant has to be a voiceless stop, [p, t, k], and the third consonant has to be an approximant, [ɹ, l, w, j], e.g. *sprain* [spɹejn], *spleen* [splin], *spew* [spju], *strew* [stɹu], *scream* [skɹim], *sclerosis* [skləɹosis], *squall* [skwɑl], *skew* [skju].[1] You will see in (2) that even within this restricted set, not all possible combinations are found (✓ means that the sequence occurs, x means that it does not).

(2) **Possible word-initial, three-consonant sequences in English**

	j	w	l	ɹ
sp	✓	x	✓	✓
st	x	x	x	✓
sk	✓	✓	✓	✓

WORD-INITIAL SEQUENCES IN OTHER LANGUAGES

Languages can differ from English in terms of word-initial sound sequences in a number of ways. A language may allow fewer consonants to occur at the beginning of a

---

1. Note that in some dialects of American English, [ʃ] can occur in these three-consonant sequences, particularly before [tɹ], e.g. *street* [ʃtɹit].

word, or it may allow more consonants. Or a language may permit a similar number of consonants as English but have different restrictions on which consonants can combine with each other. A language can also differ in the types of sounds that words can begin with.

Arabic is an example of this last point; it is more restrictive than English concerning the types of sounds that a word can start with. Recall that in English, words can begin with either a consonant or a vowel. In Arabic, however, all words must begin with a consonant. This means that, unlike English, there are no words like *apple, inside,* and *eat* that begin with a vowel.[2] Interestingly, there are no languages where all words must begin with a vowel.

Other languages are more restrictive than English in terms of the number of consonants that can occur at the beginning of a word. Fijian (Boumaa), for example, allows only a single consonant to occur at the beginning of a word, though any consonant in the language can occur in this position (Dixon 1988). In Zulu, Swahili, Mandarin Chinese, and Korean, to name a few, no more than two consonants can begin a word, and the second consonant can only be a glide, e.g. [w, j].[3] Some examples of Korean words beginning with two consonants are [kwicok] 'nobleman,' [tjulip] 'tulip,' [pʰjemul] 'jewelry.' One consequence of this restriction was noted in Chapter 2, where we noted that when Korean speakers pronounce English words that begin with a sequence of consonants, they may insert a vowel between the consonants; for example, the word *strike* may be pronounced with a short vowel between each of three initial consonants.

Languages that allow fewer consonants at the beginning of the word, such as those just mentioned, often pose less of a challenge to an English speaker learning these languages than those that allow more consonants or a greater variety of consonant sequences. Polish, for example, exemplifies a language that allows more consonants in sequence at the beginning of a word, as discussed below, and thus may pose particular problems to the language learner. At the same time, problems may be encountered when the specific consonant sequences that are allowed in a given language are *different* from those of the native language, even if they are not more numerous. Greek provides a good example of a language with a similar number of permitted consonants as English but different phonotactics.

Greek is similar to English in that up to three consonants can occur at the beginning of a word (Joseph and Philippaki-Warburton 1987). A number of the clusters with three consonants will be familiar to English speakers, such as [spl], [splína] 'spleen'; [spr], [spróxno] 'push'; [str], [stratós] 'army'; and [skr], [skrápas] 'idiot.' Two other possible sequences are not found in English: [skn], [sknípa] 'kind of mosquito'; and [sfr], [sfrajíða] 'stamp.' Sequences of two consonants also present some patterns not encountered in English. These include sequences of fricative + fricative ([sθ, sx]), fricative + stop ([ft, xt]), and stop + fricative ([ps, ts, ks]). Notice that a word of Greek origin like

---

2. Although some words in Arabic may appear to have a vowel at the beginning of a word, these are preceded by a glottal stop or another type of consonant when they are pronounced.

3. Some scholars have claimed that the glide actually forms a diphthong with the following vowel. If this is the case, Korean is even more restrictive since we would need to say that words can begin with no more than one consonant.

psychology with the non-English [ps] is pronounced in English with a single [s]. (See Chapter 6 for discussion.)

In Polish, between one and four consonants can begin a word. Words beginning with two consonants are most frequent, making up approximately 88% of words beginning with consonant clusters. Those with three consonants make up about 9%, and those with four consonants approximately 2%. It is impressive to note that there are over 230 different types of two-consonant sequences and close to 200 different three-consonant clusters (Bethin 1992).

Despite the large number of different consonant clusters in Polish, there are several generalizations about how strings of sounds combine that the language learner can use to learn the sequences, rather than memorizing each string of sounds individually. For example, not unlike English, most consonant clusters that come before a vowel are made up of an obstruent (stop, fricative, affricate) followed by a sonorant (nasal, liquid, glide), e.g. [sn, sm, s̩r], or a fricative followed by a stop, e.g. [sk, zb, st]. Unlike English, however, a sonorant consonant can also precede an obstruent at the beginning of a word, giving sequences such as [rv, rt, rd]. Another difference is that for some consonants, both orders are possible, e.g. [bz] *bzu* 'lilac', [zb] *zbir* 'thug.'

ENGLISH SOUND SEQUENCES: WORD-FINAL

Now let's consider possible sequences at the ends of words. Words in English can end with up to four consonant sounds, e.g. *sick* [sɪk] (one), *six* [sɪks] (two), *sixth* [sɪksθ] (three), *sixths* [sɪksθs] (four). Of course, words can also end in only a vowel, e.g. *see* [si]. The only consonant that is systematically excluded from occurring at the end of an English word is [h]. As we noted above, [h] occurs only before a vowel. (Remember, we are talking about sounds—the *letter* 'h' can come at the end of a word in English, but the *sound* [h] cannot.)

In some dialects of English, [ɹ] has a similar distribution to [h] in that it does not occur after a vowel, only before one. This is the case, for example, in the variety of English spoken by the Queen of England (referred to as Received Pronunciation or RP English), as well as in the American variety of English spoken in the Boston area. Speakers of both dialects share similar pronunciations of words like *car* [kɑ] and *park* [pɑk] (though the quality of the vowels can differ).

When a vowel is followed by two consonants, the first may be a fricative, a stop, or a sonorant (nasal or liquid). If the first is a fricative or a stop, the second will also be a fricative or a stop, as in the words *act* [ækt], *desk* [dɛsk], *rest* [ɹɛst], *wisp* [wɪsp], and *fifth* [fɪfθ]. If the first consonant is a sonorant, then the second will be a stop, a fricative, or an affricate, as in the words *send* [sɛnd], *camp* [kæmp], *sink* [sɪŋk], *cinch* [sɪntʃ], *art* [ɑɹt], *help* [hɛlp], *twelve* [twɛlv], *Welsh* [wɛlʃ], and *welch* [wɛltʃ].

There are, however, some further restrictions on word-final sequences. For one, when a nasal is followed by an oral stop consonant [p, b, t, d, k, g], both consonants must have the same place of articulation, e.g. *rant* [rænt], *sink* [sɪŋk], *pump* [pʌmp]. There are no words like *ranp or *pimt. This restriction is relaxed if the final consonant is the past-tense marker [t, d]; these consonants can follow any verb ending in a consonant whether they have the same place of articulation or not, e.g. *banged* [bæŋd], *rammed* [ɹæmd].

An additional restriction holds between a vowel and the consonants that follow. If a nasal + stop consonant sequence follows a diphthong, the nasal can only be [n] and the stop can only be [t, d]. Note that for this restriction, [i] and [u] behave like diphthongs and are written [ij] and [uw]. Examples are given in (3). There no words in English with these diphthongs followed by a velar or labial nasal and stop.

(3)   **English diphthong + [nt] or [nd]**

    [ɑɪ]   pint, find, mind

    [ɑʊ]   count, mount, mound, ground

    [ɔɪ]   point, anoint

    [ij]   fiend

    [eɪ]   paint, faint

    [uw]   wound

    [oʊ]   won't

But when the vowel is a monophthong, there is no such restriction: you can get a velar or a labial nasal and stop, as illustrated by the examples in (4).

(4)   **English monophthongs + nasal and stop sequences**

    [æ]   land, lamp, bank

    [ɪ]   lint, limp, ink

    [ɛ]   tent, hemp

    [ʌ]   hunt, hump, hunk

In sequences of three consonants at the end of a word, the first two consonants can be any of the permissible two-consonant sequences noted above. However, the consonant coming after these consonants can only be alveolar ([t, d, s, z]), e.g. *acts* [ækts], *wounds* [wuwndz], *lamps* [læmps], *inked* [ɪŋkt], *calmed* [kɑmd].

WORD-FINAL SEQUENCES IN OTHER LANGUAGES

As with word-initial sequences, languages can differ from English in a number of ways when it comes to possible sequences at the ends of words. Some languages, like Fijian, have no words at all that end in a consonant. Others, such as Japanese, permit only a limited number of consonants. Although there are approximately 20 consonants in the language, only one, [ŋ], can occur at the end of a Japanese word.

Greek is also interesting from the perspective of the consonants that occur at the end of a word. There are only two consonants that can appear at the end of a word of Greek origin: [s] and, less frequently, [n] (Joseph and Philippaki-Warburton 1987). Words of foreign origin can end in other types of consonants, e.g. [kláb] 'club' and [rúz] 'rouge.' Final consonant clusters are also uncommon except in words of foreign origin, e.g. [fjórd] 'fjord.'

Polish would appear to be at the other end of the spectrum since there can be up to five consonants at the end of a word. It should be noted, though, that four- and five-consonant sequences are not very common. The vast majority of final consonant sequences contain two consonants. Like English, many have a sonorant followed by another consonant, e.g. [rm, ln, mp, rtʃ, rf, lk]. Polish also has words with final obstruent-obstruent sequences such as [ʒb, ʃtʃ, kʃ, ps, ptʃ]. The language differs most from English in allowing some words to end in an obstruent followed by a sonorant, e.g. [ʒm, kl, zn, dr, tr]. In English, a sonorant can precede an obstruent only at the end of a word, e.g. *ramp, fault, art.*

Summary

As we have seen, English seems to be situated in the middle of the continuum when it comes to phonotactics. There are many languages that have fewer possible sound sequences, but there are also many others that allow for more possibilities. As noted above, those with a subset of the combinations that English allows should pose less of a problem for the learner, assuming that the sounds are the same as well. For those with unfamiliar sounds or sequences, a useful strategy in learning them is to begin by breaking the word or sequence of sounds down into smaller parts. If possible, begin with what you know and build on that, as we did with individual sounds. Practice pronouncing the smaller parts slowly, and then slowly combine the sounds, getting feedback on your pronunciation from a native speaker if possible.

Exercises

1. **Investigating word-initial consonant sequences**

   Do some investigative work into the consonant sequences that occur at the beginning of words in a language that you are learning. Here is one method of doing this:

   - Start with a list of all the consonant **sounds** that occur in the language.

     (a) *Sequences of two consonants:* .

       » Make a chart with a **row** for each consonant in the language. Put the IPA symbol for each consonant in the leftmost column of a single row. Each row should then be assigned to a particular consonant. It can be useful for seeing patterns later to list the consonants in order of manner and place of articulation, e.g. p, b, t, d, k, g, s, z, m, n, l, r, y, w.

» Add a **column** for each consonant in the language, and label the top of the column with the IPA symbol for the sound in the same order as above.

» Beginning with the consonant in the first row, go across each column, checking each cell where the consonant can occur at the beginning of a word. Proceed with the consonants in each of the other rows until your chart is complete.

» What **generalizations** can you make about the place and/or manner of articulation of consonants that can begin a word? What generalizations can you make about consonants that can come second? How do these patterns compare to the sequences that can occur in English? Given the differences between English and your new language, where do you anticipate having difficulty? How might you deal with these challenges?

(b) *Sequences of three consonants:*

» If your language allows three consonants at the beginning of a word, create a chart similar to the one above with the following modification:
  - Since three-consonant sequences will be composed of possible two-consonant sequences, label each row with one of the two-consonant sequences that you have identified above.

» Columns are identical to the ones in (a).

» Follow the same procedure as in (a), putting a check in each cell that corresponds to a possible three-consonant sequence.

(c) *Sequences of more than three consonants:*

» Follow the same procedure as above, delimiting the rows of the new chart to only those sequences that were possible in the preceding chart.

2. **Investigating word-final consonant sequences**

To discover what consonant sequences can occur at the end of a word, follow the same procedure as in Exercise 1 above for word-initial sequences, with the following modifications:

• The consonant that appears in each **row** will correspond to the consonant that comes immediately after a vowel.

• The consonant at the top of a **column** will be the consonant that potentially follows the consonant occurring in a row.

• Follow the same procedures as for word-initial sequences, putting a check in each cell that corresponds to a possible consonant sequence.

• Repeat with additional charts if more than two consonants can occur at the end of a word. Each sequence identified in the previous chart will appear in its own row in the new chart.

References

Bethin, C. Y. (1992). *Polish syllables: The role of prosody in phonology and morphology.* Columbus, OH: Slavica Publishers.

Dixon, Robert M. W. (1988). *A grammar of Boumaa Fijian.* Chicago: University of Chicago Press.

Joseph, Brian D., and Philippaki-Warburton, I. (1987) *Modern Greek.* London: Croom Helm.

Common Pronunciation Errors

*I*n the previous chapters we have seen a number of ways in which English differs from other languages in terms of how words and sentences are pronounced. Because of these differences, an English speaker is bound to make mistakes when learning to speak another language, and that, of course, is what makes the speaker's accent sound foreign. The discussion in the preceding chapters should make it easier for you to pinpoint the areas where you are most likely to have trouble and give you some tools to help deal with them.

In this chapter we bring together some of the typical pronunciation errors made by English speakers when learning another language. Perhaps these are some of the same errors that you make. If so, the following discussion will remind you of the differences between English and other languages and will also offer some guidance about how to avoid common errors.

Interpreting Unfamiliar Symbols

As we saw in earlier chapters, each language has its own conventions for representing in writing how a sound is pronounced. These conventions are arbitrary rules decided upon at some stage in the language's development. Because they are arbitrary, the same sound could potentially be represented by as many different letters combinations as there are languages! It is not quite as bad as that, but conventions do differ, as we have seen.

Nasalized vowels are a good example of a type of sound that is represented in different ways. Recall from Chapter 4 that in Polish, the two nasal vowels are represented with a cedilla under the vowel: 'ę' and 'ą.' In French and Portuguese, on the other hand, nasalized vowels are written with the letter for the vowel followed by the letter for a nasal consonant, as shown in (1) for French.

(1) **French nasal vowels**

Pronunciation	Spelling	Example
[ɔ̃]	on	*bon* 'good'
[ɑ̃]	an	*banc* 'bench'
[ɛ̃]	ain, aim, in	*bain* 'bath,' *faim* 'hungry,' *fin* 'end'

As you know, when 'n' or 'm' follows a vowel in English, we typically pronounce the consonant, as in the words 'sun' and 'some.' Because of this, a native English speaker may be inclined to pronounce French and Portuguese words that have similar letter sequences the same way as in English, and thus incorrectly. That is, the speaker will tend to pronounce the vowel followed by a nasal consonant rather than just a nasalized vowel. Native speakers of French and Portuguese will be quick to identify this speech as foreign. You can avoid this pitfall. If you, the learner, are familiar with the spelling conventions for nasal vowels in these languages, you will know that the same sequence of letters in English and in French or Portuguese are pronounced differently.

Where can you find this kind of information? The front matter of a bilingual dictionary is a very good place to start. A good dictionary, whether it be in electronic or hard copy format, will contain a key to how the spelling symbols of the language are pronounced. Alternatively, you could check with your language instructor or consult an introductory language textbook, which should also contain important information about pronunciation.

Aspiration

Another common error made by native speakers of English involves the property of aspiration. You will recall from Chapter 3 that an aspirated consonant is made with a small puff of air expelled (typically) after the consonant. We find this with the English stops [p, t, k] when they occur before a stressed vowel and are not preceded by [s]. If you place your hand a couple of inches in front of your mouth when you say the pairs of words listed in (2), you should feel a puff of air after the consonants at the beginning of the words on the left, but not after the corresponding unaspirated consonants in the words on the right. As a native speaker of English, you learned at a very early age that in some contexts stop consonants are pronounced with aspiration and in other contexts they are not.

(2) **English aspirated and unaspirated stops**

Aspirated Stops	Unaspirated Stops
p̲ot [pʰɑt]	s̲p̲ot [spɑt]
t̲o [tʰu]	s̲t̲ew [stu]

k̲ey [kʰi]   s̲k̲i [ski]

The unaspirated stops that occur after [s] actually sound very much like [b, d, g]. To discover this for yourself, try saying *spot, stew,* and *ski* first as you would normally and then as follows: replace the [p] in *spot* with [b], the [t] in *stew* with [d], and the [k] in *ski* with [g]. Can you tell the difference between *spot* and *sbot?* If not, you are like most English speakers in not being able to distinguish a voiceless stop from a voiced stop when it comes after [s]. This is because voicing differences between stop consonants in this position are not used to distinguish the meaning of words in English. That is, there are no words in English like *ski* and *sgi* which differ only in whether or not the stop after [s] is produced with vocal cord vibration. If, on the other hand, there were pairs of words such as this in the language you learned as a child, part of your language acquisition would have involved learning to listen for the subtle acoustic details when these or comparable words were spoken that would have then enabled you to tell them apart.

Turning to errors that English speakers make, two of the most common mistakes involve aspiration. In the first case, English speakers produce aspirated stops where they do not occur in the language being learned, and in the second, English speakers fail to produce aspiration where it does occur in the new language. In the first case, English

Exercise 1: Aspirated and Unaspirated Consonants

Try this simple exercise to get practice pronouncing unaspirated stops in unfamiliar contexts (that is, contexts that you are not used to when you speak English).

* Begin by pronouncing a word with an unaspirated stop, such as *Stan,* from column A. Notice that there is no puff of air after the 't' as there is in the word *tan,* for example.
* Now try pronouncing the same word from column A again, but this time, suppress the 's' at the beginning (for example, by saying the 's' silently before saying the rest of the word out loud). If you are doing it correctly, you will be pronouncing the stop consonant as unaspirated. In fact, pronouncing the word *tan* with an unaspirated stop will, to an English speaker's ears, make the word sound very much like 'dan,' which begins with an unaspirated (voiced) stop.
* Try this a few times for each of the words in column A or at least until you can comfortably produce an unaspirated voiceless stop at the beginning of an "English" word.

Column A	Column B	Column C
Stan	Stan	dan
span	span	ban
scan	scan	gan

speakers transfer the aspiration rules of English to the pronunciation of words in lan-guages that do not have aspirated stops, such as French, Italian, Spanish, and Greek. As a result, English speakers pronounce voiceless stops before a stressed syllable with aspiration. The problem is that aspiration is simply not a feature of these languages. In Italian, as with the other languages mentioned, voiceless stops like [p, t, k] are *unaspi-rated* regardless of where they occur.

Pronouncing stops with aspiration is a common characteristic of English-accented speech and one that can be avoided with practice. But first it is important to be able to hear and feel the difference between an aspirated and an unaspirated stop. Recall that you should feel a small puff of air come out of your mouth when pronouncing an aspirated consonant, as in 'to,' but not with an unaspirated consonant, as in 'stew.' The unaspirated 't' in this latter context is similar to how 't' is pronounced in Spanish, French, and Italian (and many other languages with unaspirated stops). The tricky part for an English speaker is to be able to produce the unaspirated stop in contexts where, in English, one would normally find an aspirated stop, for example, at the beginning of a word such as 'to.' In other words, you will need to learn to **undo** the rule of aspiration that you acquired as a child. (See boxed Exercise 1 on page 75.)

In English, there is no difference in spelling between the aspirated and unaspirated consonants, probably because they are not distinctive and so do not serve to distinguish the meaning of words as place of articulation does, e.g. [t] 'tea' vs. [k] 'key.'

As we saw in Chapter 3, aspiration can be distinctive in languages. In Hindi, for example, pronouncing an aspirated consonant without aspiration, or an unaspirated consonant with aspiration, can change the meaning of a word. Because aspiration is not distinctive in English, it is easy for an English speaker to mispronounce Hindi words. The speaker may incorrectly pronounce a voiceless unaspirated stop at the beginning of a word with aspiration or pronounce a voiced aspirated stop without aspiration. Each pronunciation will give the speaker English-accented Hindi and perhaps even change the meaning of the Hindi word.

Before leaving Hindi, it is interesting to note that aspiration does not appear only on voiceless consonants, as it does in English. As the examples in (3) show, voiced conso-nants also contrast for aspiration.

(3) **Hindi aspirated and unaspirated voiced stops**

[b^{h}al] 'forehead'	[bal] 'hair'
[ḍ^{h}an] 'paddy'	[ḍan] 'charity'
[ḍ^{h}al] 'shield'	[ḍ^{h}al] 'branch'
[g^{h}al] 'confusion'	[gal] 'cheek'

This fact makes Hindi particularly fascinating since it results in a four-way distinc-tion for consonants in terms of voicing and aspiration:

(4)

[k^{h}al] 'skin'	[kal] 'era'
[g^{h}al] 'confusion'	[gal] 'cheek'

Being aware of the differences between English and languages with distinctive aspiration like Hindi is a good start in learning how to pronounce the words correctly. With this knowledge you can focus on hearing and producing aspirated and unaspirated consonants in unfamiliar contexts.

Alveolar vs. Dental Consonants

Not only are sounds similar to English 't' and 'd' common in the world's languages, but they are also the most frequent consonants in English. This means that we have had lots and lots of practice pronouncing and listening to them.

The challenge for learners of other languages is that these sounds are not always pronounced exactly like the sounds of English, even though they may be spelled with the same letters *t* and *d*. We have already seen that they can be aspirated, unaspirated, or both in a given language. They can also be made at a different place of articulation than the sounds of English.

Recall from Chapter 3 that the consonants [t] and [d] in English are **alveolar** stops:

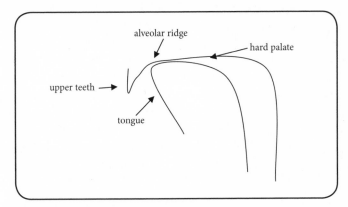

Figure 6.1 Alveolar place of articulation of English [t, d].

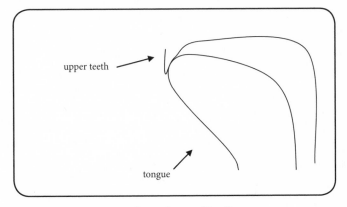

Figure 6.2 Dental place of articulation of [t̪, d̪].

they are made by raising the front part of the tongue against the alveolar ridge as approximated in Figure 6.1.

In some languages, such as Italian, Spanish, and French, the sounds spelled by the letters 't' and 'd' are classified as **dental,** as opposed to alveolar. This means that the front of the tongue (including the tip) is positioned behind the upper teeth, as illustrated in Figure 6.2.

While positioning the tongue against the teeth as opposed to the alveolar ridge may seem like a small difference, it is enough to alter the acoustics of the sound. This means that if an English speaker pronounced the first sound in the Italian word *tavola* 'table'

Exercise 2: Dentals and Alveolars

This exercise is most effective if you do it in front of a mirror.

Practicing an alveolar:

- Begin by slowly repeating the English syllables [da, da, da]. While you are saying these sequences, look at your mouth closely in the mirror, and focus on the position of your tongue while making the alveolar consonant.
- Continue to repeat the syllables [da, da, da, . . .], slowly focusing now on feeling where your tongue is touching the top of your mouth. The front part of your tongue behind the tip will be positioned slightly behind your teeth, touching the alveolar ridge.

Practicing a dental:

- Now move the front and tip of your tongue forward so that it rests behind your top teeth. When you look in the mirror, you will likely be able to see your tongue protruding slightly below your top teeth. It shouldn't protrude as much as when you make a 'th' sound, as in *the.*
- With your tongue in the dental position, slowly repeat the sequences [d̪a, d̪a, d̪a] (to make the IPA symbol for a dental sound, add [̪] below the symbol used for the alveolar). Feel and see the position of your tongue when you make the dental consonant. When you feel confident that you can make a dental sound, try the following exercise.

Practicing both together:

- Compare the pronunciation of the two types of sounds by slowly repeating the following sequences:

  [da, da, d̪a, d̪a, da, da, d̪a, d̪a, . . .]
  [da, d̪a, da, d̪a, da, d̪a, . . .]

  Feel the difference between the pairs of sounds. Look in the mirror and pay attention to where your tongue is. Listen closely and see if you can hear the difference between the alveolar and dental consonants.

with an alveolar stop instead of a dental stop, an Italian speaker would be able to identify the accent as foreign. Similarly, if an Italian speaker said the English word *table* with an initial dental stop, we would likely consider the pronunciation non-native.

Making a dental sound is not difficult; it just takes practice in remembering to shift the position of your tongue slightly forward when you are speaking a language that has them. Try Exercise 2 in the box on page 78 to familiarize yourself with the difference between dental and alveolar consonants.

Exercise 2 focuses on dental and alveolar voiced stops ([d̪, d]), though it is important to note that the distinction between dentals and alveolars is not limited to voiced stops. The voiceless counterpart of 'd' can also be dental ([t̪]) or alveolar ([t]), as can nasal consonants ([n̪], [n]). Similarly, there are both dental ([s̪], [z̪]) and alveolar ([s], [z]) fricatives.

As a rule of thumb, in a given language, all sounds in these categories will typically be either dental or alveolar. In English, for example, the voiced and voiceless stops [t, d], the fricatives [s, z], and the nasal stop [n] are all alveolar. In French, on the other hand, the stops ([t̪, d̪]), the fricatives ([s̪], [z̪]), and the nasal ([n̪]) are all dental. This does not

Exercise 3: Voiceless Alveolar and Dental Stops [t, t̪]

Repeat Exercise 2, but replace the voiced stop with the voiceless alveolar stop [t] and the voiceless dental stop [t̪].

Note: It is typical for dental stops to be **unaspirated,** as is the case in French, Italian, and Spanish.

Exercise 4: Dental and Alveolar Nasals and Fricatives

Nasals:

Repeat Exercise 2, but replace the voiced stop with the alveolar nasal [n] and the dental nasal [n̪].

Fricatives:

Similarly, repeat Exercise 2, but replace the voiced stop first with the voiced alveolar fricative [z] and the dental fricative [z̪], and second with the voiceless alveolar fricative [s] and the voiceless dental fricative [s̪]. When you make the fricatives, your tongue will be close to but not touching the alveolar ridge and top teeth.

mean that a language cannot have both dental and alveolar consonants, though it is uncommon. Malayalam, seen in Chapter 3, is a language with both: [pʌṉṉi] 'pig' and [kʌnni] 'virgin.'

To further hone your skills at producing alveolar and dental consonants, do boxed Exercises 3 and 4 (on page 79) involving voiceless stops, nasals, and fricatives.

Flapping

Say the English words *atomic* and *atom,* paying attention to how you pronounce the *t* in each word. If you are a native speaker of North American English, you probably pronounce the *t* in *atomic* as a voiceless aspirated alveolar stop. In *atom,* on the other hand, the letter *t* is most likely voiced and unaspirated, sounding similar to a quick *d* sound. This latter sound is called a **flap,** characterized by the phonetic symbol [ɾ], and is the typical pronunciation of English *t* and *d* when, simplifying somewhat, they occur between vowel sounds, if the first vowel is stressed. Compare *atomic* and *atom* once again, paying attention this time not only to how the *t* is pronounced but also to which syllable is stressed in each word. In *aTOmic,* the second syllable is prominent, while in *Atom,* the first syllable has the most stress. The *t* in *atom* therefore occurs between vowels the first of which is stressed, the context where flapping occurs. Other examples of words with a *t* or *d* pronounced as a flap include *wriᴛing, ruᴅᴅer, faᴛᴛer,* and *ouᴛ of here.*

Here are some facts about the flap in North American English. First, it is an alternate pronunciation of *t* and *d.* This means that pronouncing the *t* in the word *writer* as the flap [ɾ] as opposed to [t] does not change the meaning of the word; that is, [t] and flap are not distinctive in English; nor are [d] and flap. Second, the flap occurs in only one context in English: between vowel sounds if the first is stressed. Thus, <u>where</u> the flap is pronounced is completely predictable. The predictable, non-distinctive nature of English flap tends to make speakers less conscious of its presence; in fact, if we had not specifically drawn your attention to the fact that the *t* in *writer* is pronounced differently than, say, the *t* in *top, stop,* or *pot,* you may not have been aware of any differences. But now that you are aware, you are in a better position to correct any mispronunciations you may have involving this sound when speaking another language!

In other languages, the flap may not be a predictable pronunciation of another sound. Rather, it may be a distinctive sound in and of itself. This is the case with the flap in Spanish, written as a single letter *r,* e.g. *pero* 'but,' *para* 'for,' *tocar* 'to play.' We know that the flap is distinctive in Spanish because replacing it with a similar sound can affect word meaning. Compare the two words *pero* [peɾo] 'but' and *perro* [pero] 'dog' (*rr* is pronounced as a trill). The fact that the flap in Spanish is written with *r* instead of *t* or *d* as in English may lead a learner of Spanish to conclude that the letters represent different sounds. This is incorrect. Regardless of spelling, American English speakers already know how to produce the flap sound. This should then make it relatively easy to pronounce words such as Spanish *pero* where the flap occurs in the same context as in English.

Pronouncing a flap at the end of a word as in *tocar* [tokɐɾ] 'to play' may be more challenging since it is not a context where flaps are produced in English. A simple exercise to practice doing this is given in (5), using the Spanish words *cara* 'face' and *tocar* 'to play':

(5) a. cara, cara, cara
     b. cara carɐ, cara carɐ, cara carɐ
     c. cara carɐ tocar, cara carɐ tocar, cara carɐ tocar
     d. tocar, tocar, tocar

Begin by repeating the word *cara* several times (5a), taking notice of how you are making the flap; *cara* [kɑɾɐ] will sound similar to English *gotta* [gɑɾə], though beginning with an unaspirated [k] instead of a [g]. Now try the sequences in (5b). In this case, the final vowel in the second word of each pair is suppressed. While you should not hear a full vowel after the flap in *carɐ,* releasing the front of your tongue from the roof of your mouth when making the flap may create a very small vowel sound. Now try row (5c) in which *tocar,* with a word-final flap, has been added. Notice that the final syllable in *tocar* will essentially be pronounced the same way as *carɐ.* Finally, repeat *tocar* several times alone, paying attention to your pronunciation of the flap at the end of the word.

Spanish provides a good example of a language that has a flap like English, though it uses the flap distinctively and in different contexts. Not surprisingly, many other languages do not use the flap sound at all. In these languages, native speakers of American English commonly mispronounce *t* and *d* as a flap if it occurs in the English flapping context. As subtle as it may seem to American English ears, pronouncing a word like *data* as [dɑɾɑ] instead of [dɑtɑ] will sound very foreign to a native speaker of a flapless language. Obviously, the way to avoid this type of error is to suppress the flap pronunciation. This is much more challenging than it sounds because pronouncing a flap for a *t* or *d* is automatic for an American English speaker. However, awareness of the English flapping rule and the tendency to pronounce *t* and *d* as [ɾ] is half the battle. Practicing how to say [t] between vowels in words like [dɑtɑ] is the other half!

Released and Unreleased Stop Consonants

Another characteristic of English pronunciation involves the pronunciation of the stops *p, b, t, d, k, g,* particularly at the end of a word. To illustrate, say each of the sentences in (6) out loud several times at a normal speaking rate. Listen to how you say the consonant at the end of each of the underlined words.

(6) The cat stood on the <u>sack</u>.
     I called a <u>cab</u>.
     The rug she bought was <u>neat</u>.

Was there a small burst of aspiration at the end of any of the final consonants (called a consonant *release*)? Or did you hold the closed part of the consonant a bit longer so that the air was not released after the consonant? Experiment a bit, pronouncing each of the consonants at the end of the underlined words. Practice producing the consonants with a release and then without a release.

This short exercise is intended to illustrate that whether or not a stop consonant is released at the end of a word in English is optional. Both are acceptable pronunciations of the same word.

This is not the case in all languages. As potentially subtle as this property may seem, the presence or absence of a consonantal release can contribute to creating a foreign accent.

In some languages, such as Korean, stop consonants are never released at the end of a word. In other languages, stops are always released in this position. German is an example of this latter type. Note that adding a release to a Korean consonant or pronouncing a stop in German without a release will not change the meaning of the word. It will, however, characterize the pronunciation as non-native.

Avoiding a foreign accent in this case does not require learning how to make a new sound or gesture since English speakers already know how to pronounce a consonant with a release as well as without. Rather, it begins by being aware that whether or not a consonant is released in English is optional, and that there may be differences between English and the language being learned.

Full and Reduced Vowels

Let's look at another property of the English language that can give away your identity as a non-native speaker in no time at all! This involves pronouncing full vowels as reduced vowels. It is probably easiest to explain the difference between full and reduced vowels with an illustration.

In the section on flapping above, it was pointed out that the words *atom* and *atomic* differ in terms of which syllable is stressed, that is, which syllable is the most prominent. In *atom,* the first syllable is stressed, while in *atomic* it is the second. Recall that the pronunciation of 't' as a flap [ɾ] or an aspirated stop [tʰ] depends in part on the stress of adjacent syllables, as indicated in the phonetic transcriptions of the two words: [ǽɾəm], [ətʰámɪk]. Notice that there is also a change in the quality of the vowels across the two words. Compare, as shown in the diagram below, the first vowel of each word. In *atom,* the 'a' is pronounced as [æ], while in *atomic* it is a schwa, [ə]. Schwa also occurs as the second vowel of *atom,* even though the second vowel in *atomic* is [ɑ]. Can you predict when schwa occurs?

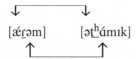

If you said that schwa occurs when the syllable is not stressed, you are absolutely right. As a native speaker of English, you will typically pronounce any vowel in a non-prominent syllable as [ə] or [ɪ], sometimes called reduced vowels. This means that all the vowels in the following words that do not have an accent mark indicating stress are pronounced as a reduced vowel: *message* [mɛ́sɪdʒ], *campus* [kǽmpəs] (or [kǽmpɪs]), *computer* [kəmpjútɚ], *porcupine* [pɔ́ɹkjəpàjn].[1] Vowels that occur in a stressed syllable in English are referred to as full vowels. This observation about English may seem confusing since the spelling of a word does not generally distinguish between full and reduced vowels. However, by paying careful attention to how a word is pronounced, you should be able to identify the syllable(s) in a word with the most prominence, those with the least prominence, and hence those with full and reduced vowels.

The challenge for speakers of English is that not all languages distinguish between full and reduced vowels. In Czech, Greek, Spanish, and many other languages, vowels are always pronounced in their full form regardless of whether the syllable they appear in is stressed or unstressed. So the Greek word for 'bicycle' is [poθílato] with no reduced vowels at all. An English speaker not aware of the fact that he learned to pronounce vowels differently in stressed and unstressed positions (regardless of the spelling) will then probably turn the vowels in Greek [poθílato] into the incorrect form *[pəθílətò], and be immediately recognized as a non-native speaker!

To avoid this, determine whether unstressed vowels are reduced in the language you are learning. Listen to and ask your instructor; listen to and ask native speakers. Are some syllables more prominent than others? Is an 'o' in the spelling pronounced the same in all positions in a word and in all types of syllables, stressed or unstressed? What about 'u' or 'a' or 'i', or whatever the vowels in the language are? If so, you will need to pay special attention to how you pronounce vowels, especially in syllables without stress. In short, you will need to unlearn the pattern that you so successfully learned and have practiced for so many years.

Monophthongs vs. Diphthongs

As we saw in Chapter 4, the English vowel system is quite complex because it contains monophthongs like [i] *beat,* [ɪ] *bit,* [ɛ] *bet,* [æ] *bat,* and [ʌ] *but,* as well the diphthongs in (7).

(7) **English diphthongs**

[aʊ]	c<u>ow</u>, tr<u>ou</u>nce
[oʊ]	g<u>o</u>, s<u>ew</u>, t<u>oa</u>d
[aɪ]	b<u>uy</u>, b<u>i</u>de

---

1. The two different accents (´acute, ` grave) on the word *porcupine* represent the two types of stressed syllables in English: primary stress and secondary stress. As the terms suggest, primary stress is stronger. Secondary stress is not as prominent as primary stress, but it is more prominent than a syllable with no stress at all.

| [ɔɪ] | s<u>oy</u>, b<u>oy</u> |
| [eɪ] | r<u>ay</u>, s<u>ay</u> |

A great many languages have only monophthongs and no diphthongs. In Chapter 4, we identified the following list of languages, though many more could be added: Arabic, Bulgarian, Ewe, French, German, Greek, Hawaiian, Hebrew, Hungarian, Italian, Japanese, Navaho, Spanish, Swahili, and Zulu. It should be clear what the challenge is for a speaker of English when pronouncing vowels in these languages: to try to avoid saying a monophthong as a diphthong.

Substituting a diphthong for a monophthong is a common mistake made by English speakers when learning a language without diphthongs. This is especially easy when the monophthong of the foreign language is similar to a diphthong of English. The English diphthongs [eɪ] and [oʊ], for example, are very similar to the vowels [e] and [o] which occur in most of the languages noted just above. If you are a native speaker of English and you want to sound more like a native speaker of a foreign language that has [e] and [o], you will need to practice saying the vowels [e] and [o] without adding an [ɪ] or [ʊ] pronunciation to the end. Boxed Exercise 5 is designed to help you accomplish this.

Exercise 5: Diphthongs to Monophthongs

- Say the vowel in *s<u>ay</u>* slowly. Concentrate on not moving your tongue or jaw upwards toward the end. This will have the effect of making the vowel seem much shorter and end more abruptly. Note that the tongue and jaw movement may be very subtle.
- Repeat with the vowel in *s<u>o</u>*.
- Once you feel that you are able to pronounce the vowels as monophthongs, try saying a short word in the language that you are learning that contains these vowels. If you are learning French, for example, you might choose the words *fée* [fe] 'fairy' and *faux* [fo] 'false.' You could compare your pronunciation of the French words with the monophthongs to the English words *Faye* and *foe;* the English words end in a diphthong while the French ones do not.
- Repeat with other monophthongal vowels from your new language.

Unrounded Back Vowels

The final common pronunciation error discussed in this chapter involves back unrounded vowels, particularly the high vowel [ɨ], in languages such as Japanese, Korean, and Turkish. Remember from Chapter 4 that this vowel is made a bit like the [u] in *suit* but without rounded lips. Try saying *suit* as you would normally. Now, say it with your lips somewhat spread as if you were smiling. Your pronunciation should be similar to [sɨt].

It is really not that hard for a native English speaker to make this sound. In fact, some people already use the vowel in English words such as *roses* [roziz] (others may say [roziz] or [rozəz]).

Yet, it is not uncommon for English speakers to pronounce a back unrounded vowel as rounded, that is, to pronounce [ɨ] as [u]. One of the reasons for this is that in some languages, the vowel [ɨ] is spelled or transcribed with the letter 'u'. This can be confusing unless you are aware that the spelling does not match up with how you would pronounce 'u' in English.

Another reason for the mispronunciation can be that an English speaker may actually perceive the foreign vowel [ɨ] as [u] since both sounds share some similar acoustic properties. From this perspective, when a person says the misperceived [ɨ] as [u], she is simply repeating what she heard.

While there are certainly other reasons why an English speaker may mispronounce a back unrounded vowel, we note one more to conclude this chapter: the person has simply not had sufficient practice making a back vowel without rounding the lips since all non-low back vowels in English are rounded.

Knowing that vowels and indeed all sounds are composed of independent gestures that can be combined in different ways, you should be in a better position to understand how to control your lips independently of where the back of your tongue is positioned. In short, in order to sound more like a native speaker of the language that you are studying, you can learn to undo some of what you have spent so many years practicing.

Summary

In this chapter we have focused on a few of the more common errors of pronunciation that North American English speakers make when learning a new language. Naturally, the types of errors you might make will depend on how the languages that you speak well and the language that you are learning differ. We believe that the information covered in this chapter and the preceding chapters will provide you with tools to analyze these differences and be more aware of how you pronounce the sounds and words of the language you are learning.

II: Thinking like a Native Speaker

7

The Work That Language Does

*I*n this chapter we look at the factors that determine how a sentence of a language is understood. The basic idea is that the **form** of a sentence, that is, how the words are ordered with respect to one another in time (or on the printed page), and the precise shape of the words, that is, how the words are pronounced, determine the kind of sentence that is being uttered. This form determines the basic **function** of the sentence (for example, whether it is a statement, a question, or a command). The form of the sentence, together with the context in which the sentence is uttered, defines the **meaning** of the sentence, the idea that the speaker is intending to convey.

Accent: A Feeling for Form

Part of a native speaker's knowledge of language involves the proper form of words, that is, how they are to be pronounced. In Chapter 6, we discussed the fact that non-native speakers of a language typically have a **foreign accent** because they are unable to precisely match the form of the words that they are trying to pronounce. To a considerable extent, a foreign accent arises from the fact that the sounds of a speaker's native language are produced differently from the sounds of his non-native language.

In the same way, non-native speakers may typically show a "foreign accent" in the way that they construct the form of sentences. They may put things in the wrong order, leave things out, or put things in that don't belong.

Now let's look at some examples that will help us distinguish form, function, and meaning. Here are some typical things that non-native speakers of Standard English say:

(1) a. Sun is hot.
    b. She lawyer.
    c. He lives in the Peru.
    d. The Professor Smith is very dynamic.
    e. Store on corner is closed.
    f. They still discussing the problem.
    g. I study here for a year.
    h. She avoids to go.
    i. Good grades receives every student in the class.
    j. The enrolled in community college student (is my friend).
    k. I want that you stay.
    l. Is raining.
    m. My father he lives in Columbus.
    n. Here is the student which you met her last week.
    o. I gave the forms to she.
    p. My sister dropped his purse.
    q. Four new lamp . . .
    r. The book is on the table is mine.
    s. I have helpfuls friends.
    t. They don't know nothing.

What we want to focus on at this point is that these sentences don't sound like "correct" English, regardless of how the words are pronounced. Native speakers of English understand the sentences but recognize that they deviate in certain ways from what is understood to be "correct." To take just one example for now, (1a), *Sun is hot,* is less than perfect English because in English we have to say <u>The</u> *sun is hot.* Other languages, however, may not have a word for *the*. Speakers of such a language might leave out *the,* either because they don't know how English works or because they are unable to always remember to put in *the* where it belongs.

As we work through our survey of what speakers of English know about their language and what speakers of other languages know about theirs, we use errors of this type to highlight precisely what it means to speak "without an accent." In an important way, recognizing what causes an accent helps us to recognize what it means to speak without one.

We turn next to an example of how the form of a sentence is related to aspects of its meaning and how it is used to communicate in discourse. The point to keep in mind is that in order for us to understand how languages work, we must recognize the differences in how the form, the meaning, and the function are different from one another in different languages.

An Example: Communicating an Idea

Suppose that you are in a restaurant, and you want a cup of coffee and you want the waiter to give you one. You could say:

(2)   Give me a cup of coffee.

(3)   Can you give me a cup of coffee?

Of course, you could say many other things that you could reasonably expect would have the effect of the waiter giving you a cup of coffee, a topic which we will get to shortly.

What do these two sentences have in common? They are about the event of the waiter giving you a cup of coffee. Examples (2) and (3) in part express the same **literal meaning,** or what we refer to as **content,** which is this idea of the waiter giving you a cup of coffee.

Moreover, they both communicate the same, more complex idea: your desire for a cup of coffee and your intention that the waiter will give you a cup of coffee because of this desire. We call this more complex idea the **force** of the sentence.

Notice that neither sentence literally says that you want a cup of coffee. You could say this, though:

(4)   I want a cup of coffee.

And this sentence, like (2) and (3), has the same force. But it has a different content, since it doesn't actually express the event of the waiter giving you a cup of coffee.

Thus, each of these three sentences has a different form, and each literally expresses a different (but related) meaning.

- Sentence (2) is in the **imperative** form, marked by the fact that it lacks an explicit subject. What this sentence does is express a command (or make a request, particularly with the addition of the politeness marker *please*). It literally and directly expresses your request that the waiter give you a cup of coffee.
- Sentence (3) is in the **interrogative** form, marked by the fact that *can* precedes *you.* This sentence asks a question. It is literally a question about whether the waiter has the **ability** to give you a cup of coffee. It expresses neither your desire nor your intention. But you can ask for a cup of coffee this way because you can reasonably expect the waiter to draw the intended conclusion, again by recognizing that this is the sort of thing that people say in restaurants when they are ordering a cup of coffee.
- Sentence (4) is in the **declarative** form. It makes a statement. It expresses your desire for a cup of coffee, but it does not express your intention that the waiter should do anything. The literal meaning is that you want a cup of coffee. The waiter must draw the conclusion that he should give you a cup of coffee because you expressed your desire for a cup of coffee, and because of the context (after all, you are in a restaurant).

The differences between these sentences highlight the difference between (i) the form of the sentence, what we call its structure or its grammar or grammatical form; (ii) the literal meaning that depends on this form; (iii) the function of the sentence, that is, whether it makes a request, asks a question, or makes a statement; and (iv) the force of the sentence, that is, the more complex idea that it communicates.

Example (4) also shows that it is possible for a sentence to express literal content and at the same time to communicate a more complex idea indirectly, because of the ability of speakers to draw conclusions about what other speakers have in mind when they say certain things. The direct idea is that the speaker wants a cup of coffee; the indirect idea is that the waiter should give it to him.

In fact, you could express your desire for a cup of coffee by simply saying:

(5)   A cup of coffee, please.

This is not even a sentence, yet it has the same force as the other ways of asking for a cup of coffee—again, because of the context.

Just as the same idea can be expressed in a number of different ways, so can the same form express a number of different ideas. Take a look again at sentence (3), *Can you give me a cup of coffee?* This sentence has the form of a question, but it is used to express a request. The following sentences are all questions but can convey different types of ideas.

(6)   Is it time to leave yet?

(7)   What kind of dog is that?

(8)   Do I look like a maid to you?

(9)   What kind of idiot do you take me for?

Sentence (6) appears to ask a very straightforward question—it is asking whether it is time to leave yet, and the expected answer is either yes or no. Sentence (7) is a different kind of question as far as its form is concerned, but it also seems to be very straightforward—it is asking the hearer to identify the type of dog that is being observed.

Sentence (8) has the same form as sentence (6), but it does not seem to invite a yes-or-no answer—a normal interpretation is that the speaker is objecting that he or she is definitely not a maid (and should not be treated like one, perhaps). Similarly, sentence (9) suggests that some idea that has been expressed in the conversation is stupid. Both of these last two sentences have the indirect force of a statement, not a question, even though they have the form of a question.

Finally, consider sentences (10)–(12):

(10) The waiter gave me a cup of coffee.

(11) I got a cup of coffee from the waiter.

(12) This is the cup of coffee that the waiter gave me.

These sentences express a relation between the speaker, the waiter, and a cup of coffee. It is the same relation expressed literally by sentences (2) and (3), namely, the relation "the waiter gives me a cup of coffee." Notice that this relation is a constant whether the sentence makes a request, makes a statement, or asks a question. This relation forms part of the content of the sentence. The total content of a sentence consists of the relation or relations that the sentence expresses between the people and things referred to in the sentence, as well as less concrete things like times, places, reasons, and events.

Form, Content, Function, and Force

Summarizing, these examples show that we need to distinguish four aspects of sentences. First, there is the form of the sentence. The major forms of English sentences are illustrated by sentences (2)–(9). Second, there is the content of the sentence, which expresses the relationships between the people and things referred to. Third, there is the function of the sentence, for example, to make a request, to make a statement, or to ask a question about that content. Fourth, there is the intended force of the sentence, the meaning that the speaker intends the hearer to understand.

Let's look again at sentence (3)—*Can you give me a cup of coffee?*—to distinguish these four aspects. The sentence has the form of a question: the verb *can* precedes the word *you*. In contrast, in a statement, the order would be the other way around: *You can give me a cup of coffee.* The content, as we have seen, is the relation "give" between the hearer (in this case the waiter), the speaker, and a cup of coffee. The function of the question is to ask whether the hearer is able to give the speaker a cup of coffee. And the intended force is that the waiter should give the speaker a cup of coffee.

Let's look at another example, sentence (6), *Is it time to leave yet?* Again, the sentence has the form of a question: *is* precedes *it.* The content concerns the time of an event, that of leaving. The function is to ask whether it is time to leave yet. And the intended force is that the hearer should answer the question yes or no.

Exercise 1: Form, Function, and Force

To be sure that you understand the distinctions being made here, write down what the form, function, and force are of sentences (7) and (9). The answers are on page 95. (The content is the same in all cases.)

Language Meaning

- All human languages provide their speakers with the resources to express and communicate exactly the same basic contents, functions, and forces.

Language Form

- Every human language has its own particular ways of signaling the content and function of sentences.

When we talk about "the work that language does," we are referring both to the capacity of language to express functions and forces like those that we have just examined, and to precisely how the form of a language is used to do this. There are two basic facts about language that we focus on in the next few chapters—we highlight them in the box at the top of this page.

What we have summarized here is the fact that the speaker of a language has to know how to arrange words to form a sentence in that language, and the hearer has to know how to interpret this arrangement of words. EVERY SPEAKER OF EVERY LANGUAGE knows precisely how to do this for his language. EVERY LANGUAGE has a complex set of rules for how to do this; there are no "primitive languages" that lack rules.

As we discuss later in this book, there are often very closely related languages or "dialects" that share many rules but differ slightly in a few rules. In such cases, speakers of each dialect may feel that the speakers of the other language do not obey the rules of the language. But this is not true—they are all obeying rules; it's just that there are different rules for different dialects. Because there are different dialects, the "languages" that they are speaking are different in very subtle but noticeable ways. Speakers of a language are extremely sensitive to language differences and can always tell when someone does not speak exactly like they do. Speakers of different dialects and languages follow the rules of their own dialects and languages. It is important to understand this phenomenon because there are often social and cultural factors associated with different languages.

When languages are more distantly related, applying the rules of one language to another often produces very noticeable errors. For example, many languages do not have different forms of verbs to express temporal relations, while English does have such forms. Speakers of such languages may simply fail to produce the correct English forms, giving rise to errors such as *He have a good time yesterday* and *The singer have big band.* Or they may misuse certain forms: *I am wanting to leave now* and *She enjoys to play tennis.* Understanding the differences in rules between languages allows the learner to anticipate and deal with likely errors.[1]

---

1. A good sample of these "transfer errors" can be found in Ann Raimes, *Keys for Writers,* 2000.

Grammar: The Role of Form in Language

We have said that the form signals the content, function, and force of a sentence. Exactly what do we mean by form? Consider again the English sentence (2), *Give me a cup of coffee*. We called this an **imperative** sentence, referring to its particular form. This sentence lacks an explicit phrase that refers to the hearer, and thus it has a special form that distinguishes it from other English sentences. Its function as an imperative is thus defined by this aspect of its form. In another language, the same function might be signaled in other ways. For example, in Italian, the imperative sentence may have a special form of the verb. The imperative form of the verb meaning 'give' in Italian is *da*, while the declarative form is *dà*, as illustrated in (13) and (14). (Notice also that the word for 'me' goes in a different position in the imperative and in the declarative—it follows the verb in the imperative and precedes it in the declarative.)

(13) Dammi una tazza di caffè.
      give-me a   cup of coffee
      'Give me a cup of coffee.'

(14) mi dà   una tazza di caffè
      me (s)he-gives a   cup of coffee
      '(S)he gives me a cup of coffee.'

We look more closely at the types of functions that sentences have and the use of form to mark these functions in the next chapter.

The form of a sentence also plays a role in determining its literal content. In English, where a phrase goes in a sentence determines whether it is the actor in an event or the object that is undergoing the action. An example is provided in (15).

(15) The dog bit Sandy.
      Sandy bit the dog.

Answer to Exercise 1: Form, Function, and Force

Sentence (7) has the form of a question, in particular, what is called a "wh-question" (because these questions begin with words beginning with 'wh-', like *what*). It has the function of asking what kind of dog that is. The force is that the hearer should provide the answer to the question. Sentence (9) is also a wh-question. It has the function of asking the hearer what kind of idiot the hearer takes the speaker for. But it has the force of saying that the speaker thinks that the hearer is an idiot.

The same individuals are involved in this event of biting, but the relation is different in the two cases. We look more closely at how form determines literal content in the remaining chapters in this section.

The relationship between form, content, and function, particularly the form part, is familiar to many readers as "grammar." And for many of those readers, "grammar" is something that they were made to learn about in high school, might have disliked intensely, and may well have largely forgotten.

The reason grammar is hard for many people is that it does not appear to have any immediately useful purpose. After all, by the time we learn grammar, we are already fluent speakers of our own language—what does knowledge of grammar give us that we don't already have?

There are two reasons that some knowledge of grammar is useful. The first is that there are important differences between spoken language and written language, and these differences can be most effectively described in terms of grammatical concepts and categories. Knowing about grammar helps us write better, because we are more aware and in control of what is required in the two styles of language, spoken and written. Moreover, in thinking about the written language, we can talk explicitly about the differences in form between two or more ways of expressing the same content and can evaluate which works better to convey our ideas, and why.

The second reason, which is most central to the focus of this book, is that the grammar of a language is a summation of the knowledge that a speaker has about how that language works. We have already seen that an understanding of how form works is essential to understanding how languages express content and function, that is, how they allow us to communicate. We already know intuitively how our own language works; the challenge is to acquire knowledge about how another language works. And we want that knowledge to be usable.

To put it another way, the grammar of a language is the set of "rules" (or "instructions," if you like) that specify how units are arranged to form phrases and sentences and how the parts of a sentence correspond to its meaning. For anyone who wants to learn how to communicate thoughts in another language, some insight into the grammar of that language can be very useful, and in some cases it may even be essential.

For these reasons, we introduce in this section of the book the most important grammatical terms and concepts. Wherever possible, we illustrate them first using English, and then we look at examples from other languages to provide a broader perspective. Because the rules involve both form and meaning, we compare languages in two basic respects.

First, we look at how languages differ in their form. In learning a second language, it is very important to be aware of the grammatical differences. Knowing how a language arranges its units allows us to focus on the areas where we have to devote special attention to expressing things in the right way.

Second, we look at the various aspects of meaning that languages can express. Different languages use different grammatical devices to express the same components of meaning. Some languages explicitly express certain of these components that are implicit in another language; as speakers, we have to know what has to be said explicitly and what needs to be implied. Such differences pose particular difficulties for the language learner and warrant special attention and practice.

What Is Structure?

A little while back we introduced the term **structure** of a sentence or a phrase and said it was another way of referring to the form. The word "structure" refers specifically to the way in which a sentence or phrase is organized into parts, how the parts are grouped together, and how they are ordered with respect to one another. Consider yet again sentence (2):

(2) Give me a cup of coffee.

There are several things that our intuitions as speakers of English tell us about the structure of this sentence. First, we recognize that the words are of different categories or types: *give* is a verb, *me* is a pronoun, and so on. Second, we recognize that the order of words is special; scrambling them up would not produce a sentence of English.

Third, we recognize that *a cup of coffee* is a phrase that is used to refer to a particular thing. *Me a* is not a phrase, nor is *Give me a.*

We explore aspects of structure in the remaining chapters of Section II. We introduce some minimal terminology that will allow us to refer clearly to the parts of sentences and phrases. To illustrate the structure of sentences, we use the simple device of bracketing words together to show how the parts of a sentence are arranged and what they consist of. For example, the structure of *Give me a cup of coffee* can be shown as follows:

(16) [Give me [a cup of coffee]]

Putting brackets around *a cup of coffee* represents the fact that it is a phrase. And grouping *give* and *me* with [*a cup of coffee*] represents the fact that *give me a cup of coffee* is also a phrase (a **verb phrase,** to be precise).

The arrangement of the words into phrases and the sequencing of these phrases are what constitute the structure of a sentence. Those familiar with "sentence diagramming"

Exercise 2: Scrambling

How many ways can you scramble the words of *Give me a cup of coffee*? Are any of them possible sentences of English?

know how to sketch out the structure of a simple sentence and how to assign a function to each part of the structure. This type of exercise may not be especially challenging for simple examples like *Give me a cup of coffee*. However, it becomes quite challenging when sentences get complicated, even in one's own language. Having the ability to see clearly the structure of one's own language, and understanding the ways in which its structure corresponds to that of another language, can substantially facilitate the task of learning the other language.

Categories

Let's consider in more detail how languages have rules about structure that are known to the speakers of those languages and how these rules can vary from language to language. Think of the words *the, dog,* and *barked*. How many different ways can we arrange these three words? The following list shows that there are in fact six ways to arrange three words:

(17) a. the dog barked   d. dog the barked
     b. the barked dog   e. dog barked the
     c. barked the dog   f. barked dog the

Are all of these sentences of English? No, only (17a) is. Someone who knows English has to know what *the, dog,* and *barked* mean and has to recognize that these words can be combined to express the thought 'the dog barked.' But the person also needs to know that the words have to go in a particular order.

When we have more than one participant in an action, each of whom plays a particular role in the action, the English sentence uses the order of words to indicate who is doing what to whom. Consider these two sentences:

(18) The dog chased the cat.
     The cat chased the dog.

The words used in the two sentences are exactly the same, but the meanings are vastly different.

This example illustrates a very important point about the meaning of a sentence that we will get into in more detail later in this chapter: The structure of a sentence specifies the roles played by the participants in a relationship expressed by a sentence; the rules of the language say how the parts of the structure match up with these roles.

If you are aware of such facts about English, will that help you when you try to learn another language? Not directly, it turns out, because some other languages work differently from English. Of course, it does help to know that another language could use a different order of words, but we have to know precisely what that order is. In other words, we know what questions we should ask about how another language forms questions, but we do not necessarily know what the answers are going to be.

How would we say *John read that letter* and *Did John read that letter?* in Japanese, for example? We could say these sentences in this way:

(19) John ga sono tegami o yon-da.
John   that letter   read-PAST
'John read that letter.

John ga sono tegami o yon-da-ka.
John   that letter   read-PAST-QUESTION
'Did John read that letter?'

Notice that the verb comes at the end in these Japanese examples. In fact, it must come at the end of the sentence that it belongs to; this is a rule of Japanese. And in the second sentence, the particle *ka* is added to the verb at the end of the question sentence to indicate that it is a question. Japanese also has the particles *ga* and *o* that have the function of indicating which phrase is the subject and which is the object.

What about Bulgarian? Here we have other possibilities:

(20) Kuche-to lae-she
dog-the   barked
'The dog barked.'

Lae-she kuche-to.
barked dog-the
'The dog barked.'

Both orders of subject and verb are possible, appropriate to different contexts. Notice also that the Bulgarian word for *the* follows the word for *dog,* in contrast to what happens in English.

What about Spanish? In Spanish we could say the following:

(21) El perro raspó.
the dog barked
'The dog barked.'

Or we could say this:

(22) Raspó el perro.
barked the dog
'The dog barked.'

What we would say depends on the context. *El perro raspó* answers the question 'What did the dog do?', while *Raspó el perro* answers the questions 'What happened?' or 'Who barked?'

Spanish is like English in that it has a word for *the* that appears before the word for *dog*, but there seem to be other differences in terms of what order the words appear in.

We can see that observations about the order of words in English are not special things about the particular words *the, dog,* and *barked,* and the same is true for other languages. If we think about similar English examples with *a, this, that,* and *cat, pig, rooster,* and *hissed, grunted, crowed,* and so on, we find that the pattern holds true for the entire language. So in English, only the pattern exemplified by *the dog barked* is used.

Let's look at Table 7.1. Using the "Chinese Menu Approach," suppose that we take one word from column A, one from column B, and one from column C. Doing so will give us reasonable sentences, if we go straight across a row as in (23).

● TABLE 7.1
Menu for simple English sentences.

A	B	C
the	dog	barked
a	cat	hissed
this	pig	grunted
that	rooster	crowed

(23) The dog barked.
       A cat hissed.
       This pig grunted.
       That rooster crowed.

But we can also skip around, still going from left to right, column by column, but moving up and down between the rows and combining the words in funny ways, e.g. *This cat crowed* or *That rooster hissed.* These may not be natural sounds for a cat or a rooster to make, but these are definitely sentences of English and we understand what they mean.

This last point is important enough to restate: A string of words that has all the words in the right place and is completely interpretable but has a strange meaning is a grammatical sentence. But if a string of words has the words in the wrong order, it is ungrammatical, even if we can figure out some kind of intended or approximate meaning. So *This dog hissed* may be strange, but it is grammatical, while *Pig the grunted* is **not** a grammatical sentence, even if you and every other native speaker can reliably decipher the meaning.

Notice that we must take just **one** word from column A, **one** from column B, and **one** from column C. And we must order the words according to this order of the columns. If we do not, then in general we get a string of words that is not a sentence of English—e.g. *The barked, *Cat hissed, *Grunted crowed, *Dog a cat, *This that pig,* and so on. (We use the symbol * to indicate that a string of words is not a possible expression of the language under discussion, in this case, English.) And we cannot take more than one word from each column in some haphazard way; doing so also produces ungrammaticality: *the a dog barked, *the dog cat rooster crowed barked; *the dog barked a.*

Not surprisingly, it is possible to construct a Chinese menu for simple sentences of any language. Consider the following sentences of Mandarin Chinese:[2]

这　　是　　书·
Zhèi　shì　shū.
This is a book.

我　　是　　学生·
Wǒ　shì　xuéshěng.
I am a student.

先生　　　是 中国　　　人·
Xiānshěng　shì　Zhōngguó　rén.
The teacher is Chinese (LIT.: China person).

Table 7.2 will produce these sentences if we take one word from each column in left-to-right order. Notice that there is only one item in column B, so we have to take that one for any sequence of words from this menu.

● TABLE 7.2
Menu for simple Chinese sentences.

A	B	C
这 Zhèi this	是 shì is	书· shū. book
我 Wǒ I		学生· xuéshěng. student
先生 Xiānshěng teacher		中国　人· Zhōngguó rén. Chinese

2. Adapted from *Modern Chinese: A Basic Course,* 1971.

Because of the sorts of patterns that we have just seen, we say that the words in a language are members of **categories.** A category consists of all those words that can go in the same column. The words in the columns in Tables 7.1 and 7.2 are just a small sampling of the total set of words in each of the categories. And sometimes a word can be a member of more than one category, for example, the word *can* in English, which is both a noun and an auxiliary verb.

Categories

The words of a language are grouped together into **categories,** sometimes called "parts of speech."

For convenience, we give the categories names like **noun, verb,** and so on. The nouns of a language form one category, and the verbs another. In the next three chapters, we look more closely at what determines the membership of the most important categories.

Sentences of a language are formed by arranging words of particular categories in specific orders. Statements about the particular categories and the particular orders in which they can be arranged are often called **grammatical rules.** Words in the same category participate in the formation of phrases in the same way. The rules of grammar that native speakers know are not about individual words but about categories of words.

A grammatical rule of a language says how to form a sentence, by taking a word from one category, followed by a word from another category, and so on. For example, Table 7.2 illustrates a rule of Chinese that we can state as follows: "Make a sentence by taking a noun (that is, a word from column A), followed by 'is,' followed by another noun (that is, a word from column C).

Summary

So, what do we have to know in order to speak and understand a language using sentences from the language?

- We have to know the words and what they mean and how they are pronounced.
- We have to know what category (or categories) each word is a member of.
- We have to know the grammatical rules.

And we also have to know how the meaning of a sentence is determined by the meanings of the words, their precise shapes, and the structure of the sentence. In the next few chapters, we look more closely at the ways in which languages use form to express meaning.

Additional Exercises

1. Look again at the sentences in (1). If you are a competent speaker of English, you should be able to correct each error fairly easily. But it is more challenging to say what the error is and why the correction works. In the text we suggested what you might say about sentence (1a). Do the same for the remaining sentences in (1).

2. We noted that it is possible to ask for a cup of coffee in a restaurant by saying "A cup of coffee, please." Think about what the conditions are for such a request to be successful. Does it matter who this phrase is addressed to? Why? What would happen if the same thing was said in a different environment, say, the post office or the ticket counter at an arena? Why? How do things work at the post office and the ticket office? What sorts of phrases would produce the desired result in a restaurant, and what sorts would not (e.g. "a chair, please"; "a dog, please"; "ten dollars, please")? Why? Does it matter if you don't say "please"?

3. An English noun phrase typically contains a noun, like *dog,* and may contain a number of descriptive words that specify a property of the thing that the noun refers to. Some of these words are called **adjectives:** e.g. *furry, happy, smart, pink.* Construct a menu that shows how these adjectives can combine with the nouns *dog, cat, pig,* and *rooster* and the words *the, this, a.* Are all combinations predicted by the menu grammatical noun phrases in English? Are there any combinations that are fully grammatical but strange because of their meaning? What does this tell you about the relationship between grammatical form and meaning?

4. Construct four English verb phrases with structures that are different from the one in (16) and different from each other. Each of these should be a verb phrase that lacks something that the one in (16) has, or has something that (16) lacks, or both. To do this, start by observing that *give me [a cup of coffee]* contains a verb and two noun phrases.

5. Construct two verb phrases in a language other than English that you know is different from the structure of the sentence in (16). Describe the difference between these verb phrases and the one in (16) in terms of the phrases that they contain and the order in which they appear.

6. For a language that you know, other than English, state as clearly as you can how that language forms (a) imperatives and (b) interrogatives. Compare with how English forms imperatives and interrogatives, focusing on where English is the same and where it is different.

References

Peking University. (1971). *Modern Chinese: A basic course.* Mineola, NY: Dover Publications.

Raimes, Ann. (2000). *Keys for writers.* Boston: Houghton-Mifflin.

8

Talking about Things

Introduction

*O*ne of the basic functions of language is to talk about things: we need to refer to and describe things in the world. This chapter is about how languages perform these functions.

The words that refer to things are typically called "nouns." We explore these questions about nouns:

- What kinds of meaning do nouns have?
- Where do nouns go in the order of words in a phrase and in a sentence in various languages?
- How do nouns contribute to the meaning of a sentence?
- What special forms do nouns have in different languages?

In the simplest cases, a single word can be used to refer to something, for example, *Susan* or *computers*. But in more complex cases, where we want to express some properties of what we are referring to, it is necessary to construct a phrase, for example, *this computer*, or *every red chair*, or *the person that you said you were talking to*. Although all languages can perform the function of expressing such properties, they vary dramatically in how they do this in terms of linguistic form. For example, in some languages, the words for 'every' and 'red' would follow the noun, not precede it as in English. Other languages lack words meaning 'the' and express the meaning conveyed by 'the' by locating the phrase containing the noun in a particular location in the sentence.

Nouns

To gain some perspective, we begin with some errors that non-native speakers make in English:

(1) a. Sun is hot.
            Store on corner is closed.
       b. He lives in the Peru.
            The Professor Goldmund is very dynamic.
       c. Student in this class very friendly.
       d. I bought a book. He was very expensive.

Let's compare these sentences with their correct counterparts. In (2), an underlined word is one that we have added to correct the sentence, and a word marked with a strike-out has to be removed to correct the sentence.

(2) a. <u>The</u> sun is hot.
            <u>The</u> store on <u>the</u> corner is closed.
       b. He lives in ~~the~~ Peru.
            ~~The~~ Professor Goldmund is very dynamic.
       c. <u>The</u> student<u>s</u> in this class <u>are</u> very friendly.
       d. I bought a book. ~~He~~ <u>It</u> was very expensive.

The examples in (2a) were discussed in the previous chapter; in English, words like *sun* (when referring to our sun) must be preceded by *the* (which is called the **definite article**). The examples in (2b) show that phrases in English that refer to particular people or places typically do not have an article. Example (2c) shows that English makes a distinction in the form of the noun between singular and plural. And Example (2d) shows that English uses the neuter pronoun *it* to refer to inanimate objects, rather than the pronouns *he* and *she,* which distinguish masculine and feminine gender.

We will see later on that some other languages in fact omit the definite article and use other ways to express the notion of definiteness. Other languages distinguish categories of words as "masculine" and "feminine," a distinction that may get translated literally (but incorrectly) into English as *he* and *she* instead of *it.* And some languages do not distinguish singular and plural by marking the word, as English does. Speakers of such languages are likely to make errors of the sort seen in (1), and speakers of English are likely to have comparable difficulties in learning such languages.

A word that refers to a thing, like *dog,* is a type of noun. Words of this type can appear in English after *the, a,* etc. Let's look more closely at the English examples that went into the construction of Table 8.1, which we used in the previous chapter. The words in column B are similar to one another in two ways. First, their meanings have something in common (they all refer to physical objects, in particular, to animals). Second, they

> ● **TABLE 8.1**
> **Menu for simple English sentences.**
>
> | A | B | C |
> |---|---|---|
> | the | dog | barked |
> | a | cat | hissed |
> | this | pig | grunted |
> | that | rooster | crowed |

appear in similar sequences of words to form sentences—they can follow *the, a, this,* and *that,* and they precede words like *barked, hissed,* and so on.

The fact that these similarities go together is not accidental. In general, words that share some essential part of their meaning in a particular language tend to behave the same in terms of their distribution in phrases and sentences. For this reason, we group them together into the same **category.** But the converse does not hold—not all the words in a category share some part of their meaning. Within the category containing *dog* and *cat,* for example, there are words that refer to substances, such as *water;* to imaginary entities, such as *unicorn;* to emotions, such as *anger;* and so on. But it is correct to say that the category noun contains groups of words that do share many properties, as do the words that refer to animals.

Recognizing the general tendency of category and meaning to go together makes language learning much easier than if we had to learn the specific properties of every word. For example, if we know that *dog* refers to a type of animal, and if we know that it is possible to say *The dog is sleeping* (that is, we know that this is a good sentence of English), then if we learn that *cat* refers to another kind of animal, we can pretty well guess that *The cat is sleeping* will be a good sentence of English, too, with a very similar meaning. Even if we make up a new word for an animal that doesn't exist, say, *benoxicobe,* we can say *The benoxicobe is sleeping.* The only thing that is odd about this sentence is the fact that it contains a word that doesn't exist. But that word is in the "right" place as far as English grammar is concerned.

A rough but fairly accurate test of whether something is a noun is that it can appear with *the,* as in *the dog* and the other words in Table 8.1. Using this test, we find that a

Exercise 1

Make up a nonsense word referring to a type of animal. Make up a half-dozen sentences with the word *dog* used in different ways, and then replace the word *dog* with this new word. Are all of these new sentences grammatical?

noun may be a word that refers to:

- a physical thing, like *dog, cat, apple, foot, moon, President*;
- a physical substance, like *milk, air, dirt, wind*;
- a non-physical thing, like *idea, sentence, thirty-three, infinity*;
- organizations and other social entities, like *government, presidency, family*;
- non-physical qualities that we are able to perceive in ourselves or in others, like *imagination, sincerity, anger, aggressiveness, friendship*;
- times, like *day, hour, month*; and
- places, like *inside, city, backyard*.

This list is not exhaustive.

Do Other Languages Have Nouns?

Anyone who has studied another language knows that other languages have nouns. But even if we haven't studied another language, we would guess that they do. Why? Because speakers of other languages must be able to refer to the kinds of things that speakers of

Basic Types of Nouns

There are several basic types of nouns:

- Countable things, either physical or non-physical. These can appear with *the* and with words like *every*, as in *every dog, every cat, every apple, every foot*. These are **count** nouns.

  » A count noun can be used with a **singular** or a **plural** form in English, for example, *dog/dogs, woman/women*. However, if a word refers to a substance, it cannot be counted, so we cannot use *every*: **every milk, *every air, *every dirt, *every imagination, *every sincerity, *every anger*.

- But a substance can be measured, so we can use *a lot of* before it: *a lot of milk, a lot of air, a lot of dirt, a lot of wind*. This type of noun is called a **mass** noun.

- The type of noun that is the name of something unique, like *Paris, Albert Einstein*, or *Christmas*, is called a **proper** noun.

Here is a summary of nouns:

Type	Use	Example
Count	Refers to things that can be counted	*every dog, three books*
Mass	Refers to substances	*water, air*
Proper	Refers to unique things, places, etc.	*Albert Einstein, Paris, Frodo Baggins*

English refer to. Moreover, people need to be able to indicate whether the thing they are referring to is familiar or definite (expressed by *the* in English), unfamiliar or indefinite (expressed by *a* in English), singular or plural, and so on. Words that perform this function are what we call "nouns."

So all languages have nouns. However, the structures of phrases that contain nouns vary among languages. And languages differ in how they express such things as definiteness and number. As we have seen, English uses *the* for definiteness. *The* is called a **determiner** and, more precisely, an **article.** In many languages there are no words corresponding to *the*. Look at the following sentences from Chinese:

(3) Lai   ren   le.
     come person COMPLETED
     'Some person/people has/have come.'

     Ren   lai   le.
     person come COMPLETED
     'The person/people has/have come.'

These examples show that when the noun *ren* 'person/people' is at the beginning of a sentence, it is interpreted as definite; that is, it refers to someone believed to be familiar to the participants in the conversation. But when the verb comes first, the noun is interpreted as indefinite; that is, it introduces someone or something new into the conversation.

Most significantly, there are no Chinese words that correspond to English *the* and *some*. A literal translation of *Ren lai le* is 'Person come,' which is just like one type of error that we saw earlier: *Store on corner is closed.*

Another type of error in English has to do with marking singular and plural, as we saw in the example *Student in this class very friendly.* Notice that in the Chinese example in (3), the singular and plural have the same form. *Ren* can mean either 'person' or 'people.' This illustrates the fact that not all languages have singular and plural forms for nouns. It is natural for speakers of languages that do not have such forms to make errors when they speak a language that does have such forms. A speaker of a language that systematically distinguishes singular and plural needs to become accustomed to the fact that the number distinction has to be indicated by using a numerical expression (such as 'one' or 'many') or has to be discernible from context.

In some languages that have articles, whether the phrase is singular or plural is marked not by the noun but by the form of the article. Here are some examples from Maori and spoken French:

(4) | **Maori** | **French** | **English** |
     |-----------|-----------|-------------|
     | te ngeru | le chat | the cat |
     | nga ngeru | les chats | the cats |

The final -*t* and -*ts* are silent in the French words *chat* and *chats,* so the actual forms are [lə ʃa] and [le ʃa].

Let's look more closely at the functions of determiners and how languages express these functions.

Determiners

WHAT IS A DETERMINER?

Determiners are the words and expressions that in English (but not all languages) precede the noun and that are used to express distinctions of quantity, uniqueness, and definiteness. Here are some common determiners in English:

- one, two, every, each, some, many, much, the, a

Some determiners are used to pick out objects from a group of objects of the same type:

- this, that, these, those

We have already mentioned one rule of English, which is that the determiner must precede the noun. This rule is what tells us that any word from column A can precede any word from column B in Table 8.1.

Table 8.2 focuses just on determiners and nouns; it shows that there are a few other things that have to be noted in addition to the relative order of the words. We cannot simply combine a word from column A with a word from column B, even if we observe the ordering rule; we have to know something about the types of words we are dealing with. As we have seen, certain determiners go with mass nouns, and others go with count nouns.

In addition, some determiners go only with plural nouns:

(5) these apples, those pigs, many cats, *these dog, *those imagination

Some go only with singular nouns:

● **TABLE 8.2**
Menu of determiners and nouns.

A	B
the	dog
a	cat
this	pig
that	rooster
these	apple
those	foot
one	moon
two	idea
every	sentence
each	milk
some	air
much	dirt
many	wind
	imagination
	sincerity
	anger
	aggressiveness
	Albert Einstein

(6)   this apple, that pig, every cat, *this dogs, *those rooster

And others go with mass nouns:

(7)   some wind, some anger, much dirt, much sincerity

And still others go with count nouns:

(8)   some books, many books, several people

And, finally, proper nouns do not have determiners:[1]

(9)   *every Albert Einstein, *much Albert Einstein

AGREEMENT

The idea that certain words "go with" certain words in terms of their form is what is called **agreement** in the description of languages. We see, for example, that *this* "agrees with" singular nouns, while *these* "agrees with" plural nouns. What agreement means in this case is that it is impossible to have *this* with a plural noun or *these* with a singular noun. These observations suggest what we call the Determiner Rule for English (see the box below).

The Determiner Rule describes how to create an expression in English that is based on a noun. Such an expression is called a **noun phrase.** All languages have noun phrases, but they may differ in various ways on how a noun phrase is made up. We'll look at some examples of other ways of making noun phrases very shortly.

In the cases that we have been looking at, the determiner agrees with the noun in the property of **number:** singular determiners go with singular nouns, and plural determiners go with plural nouns.

Determiner Rule for English

Determiner precedes Noun.
Restrictions:
- Count determiners go with count nouns.
- Mass determiners go with mass nouns.
- Singular determiners go with singular nouns.
- Plural determiners go with plural nouns.
- Proper nouns lack determiners.

---

1. To be precise, they do not have determiners that imply or require that there be more than one thing with the same proper name. Emphatic *THE* is quite possible with proper names, e.g. *THE Albert Einstein.*

In some languages, agreement is quite pervasive, while other languages lack it entirely. Depending on the language, agreement may involve number and other properties of words. For example, if you look up the translation of 'this' in a French dictionary, it will tell you the following:

(10) ce (m), cette (f), cet (m) (before
      vowels)

What do (m) and (f) mean? We can figure it out if we see what happens when we put the determiners into column A and the nouns into column B for French, and start combining them freely as shown in Table 8.3.

If we take one word from column A, we get some grammatical French expressions:

(11) ce livre   'this book'
      cette maison   'this house'
      cet arbre   'this tree'
      cette table   'this table'
      cette chaise   'this chair'
      cette orange   'this orange'

● **TABLE 8.3**
Forms expressing 'this' in French.

A	B
ce	livre 'book'
ce	chien 'dog'
cette	maison 'house'
cette	table 'table'
cette	chaise 'chair'
cette	orange 'orange'
cet	arbre 'tree'

These are French noun phrases. But other combinations don't work:

(12) *ce maison
      *cette livre
      *ce chaise
      *cet orange

The reason these don't work is that there are two classes of words in French, called "masculine" and "feminine," and the form of the determiner depends on which class the noun belongs to. These classes are called **gender** classes, and the words must **agree in gender.** So, *ce* is a masculine determiner that goes only with masculine nouns, and *cette* is a feminine determiner that goes only with feminine nouns. *Cet* is the form that *ce* takes when it precedes a vowel, as in *cet arbre*.

Another important observation is that determiners in these languages typically also agree in number with the nouns. So in French, for example, the form of the determiner is singular or plural, depending on whether the noun is singular or plural. Table 8.4 lists all the French words meaning 'the,' 'this,' and 'that.'

Determiners show agreement for number, and for gender in the singular forms. The same kind of pattern holds for other determiners in French and for related languages like Italian and Spanish.

● TABLE 8.4
French determiners.

Word	Gender	Number
le 'the'	masculine	singular
la 'the'	feminine	singular
les 'the'	masculine and feminine	plural
ce 'this/that' cet	masculine	singular
cette 'this/that'	feminine	singular
ces 'these/those'	masculine and feminine	plural

Exercise 2

State the Determiner Rule for French, given the information in Tables 8.3 and 8.4. Here's the first part:

- Determiner precedes Noun.

GENDER AND SEX

It is important to recognize that gender is related to biological gender, but it is not the same as biological gender, or what we usually refer to as **sex.** There are two biological sexes for most living things—including humans, animals, and plants—namely, male and female. But inanimate things, abstract things like ideas and beliefs, and substances like water and wood do not have sexes per se, since they are not animate or even biological. But, amazingly, in languages like French, all nouns have **gender.** Everything is either "masculine" or "feminine."

Gender is a classification of the nouns into groups. It is not a necessary property of the object or substance that the word refers to. It is true that in French the nouns for females are typically feminine, and the nouns for males masculine. This makes it easy to remember the gender for words like *homme* 'man' and *femme* 'woman.' But how can you figure out the gender of *livre* 'book' and *maison* 'house'? You can't, because gender is for the most part simply a classification of the nouns.

So for most nouns, you just have to learn what the gender is. The words are masculine or feminine, but the things that they refer to are neither male nor female. The properties that determine agreement are for the most part properties of the words, not of the objects. In fact, '(the) girl' in German is *(das) Mädchen,* which is neuter, not feminine, even though girls are females. And '(the) person' in German is *(die) Person,* which is feminine, even though some persons are female and some are male.

When we first encounter gender in another language, we might say to ourselves: "Hey, these people are weird—they think of tables and houses as female and books and beds as male. What made them think of that?" But this idea is a mistake: nouns have gender, but the objects that they refer to do not actually have sexes. Gender in the category of nouns is a way of classifying them. It is just as though we said, "OK, for the fun of it let's put the label RED on all apples and the label GREEN on all peppers" (with the labels in capital letters). It is true that many apples are red in color, but many are not, like Granny Smith apples. And many peppers are green, but many are not; some are red. And some apples and some peppers are neither red nor green. It is easy to get confused because the name of the classification label RED is related to the actual color red, and many objects classified as RED (that is, apples) actually have the color red. Similarly, we have gotten confused about gender in language because we have taken the classification scheme, using the labels "masculine" and "feminine," which correlate with some real biological property of some of the objects (those that are animate), and we may have confused it with the biological property itself.

Grammatical Gender

Grammatical gender is not about biology; it is about the way that a language classifies its nouns.

Making the situation a bit more complicated is the fact that in some languages, there are three or even more noun classes based on gender. These languages do help to show that grammatical gender is primarily word classification, not biology. Typically, when there are three classes, one is masculine, one is feminine, and one is neuter, as in German. This seems odd to us when we discover that certain animates are grammatically neuter even though biologically they are either male or female. And as the number of classes gets larger, the connection with biological gender becomes less and less secure.

The arbitrariness of gender can be highlighted by considering the gender of some nouns referring to the very same thing in different languages. Usually, if a noun refers to something animate that has biological gender, the noun will be in the corresponding gender class. But if the noun does not refer to something animate, and the two languages are not related, the gender is really quite unpredictable. Table 8.5 gives some examples; (m) means "masculine," (f) means "feminine," and (n) means "neuter."

There appears to be no pattern and nothing about the meanings of these words that would predict their gender, except perhaps for 'boy,' which is masculine across all of these languages.

English appears to express gender only in the words *he/him, she/her, his/her,* and *himself/herself.* But this is, in fact, not grammatical gender. We use *he/him* and *she/her* to refer to people and animals, and the word that we use corresponds to the biological sex. *He* is used to refer to one male individual, and *she* to one female individual. English nouns do not have gender. We use *it* in English to refer to an inanimate object.

But because all French nouns must have gender, the French counterparts to English *he* and *she* have to be used to refer to all things according to their gender. Compare the following sentences:

(13) J'ai   acheté un livre   et   il était cher.
     I have bought a book   and he was expensive
     'I bought a book and it was expensive.'

     J'ai   acheté   une maison et   elle était chère.
     I have bought   a house   and   she was expensive
     'I bought a house and it was expensive.'

The words *il* and *elle* are the same words that are used to refer to people, and when they are used in that way, they can be directly translated into English as *he* and *she*. So when we see the translation 'it (masculine singular),' we might be tempted to think that it is the same as *he*, and it is true that we would use the word *il* in French to refer to a single male person. But *il* does not mean 'he'; it means 'he/it' and agrees with the gender class of the noun, not just the biological sex. So, translating *il* as 'he' and *elle* as 'she' in these sentences would be a mistake; they correspond to 'it' in English.

● **TABLE 8.5**
Examples of gender in different languages.

English	French	German	Russian	Spanish
the house	la maison (f)	das Haus (n)	dom (m)	la casa (f)
the table	la table (f)	der Tisch (m)	stol (m)	la mesa (f) la tabla (f)
the boy	le garçon (m)	der Junge (m)	mal'chik (m)	el niño (m) el muchacho (m)
the idea	l'idée (f)	die Idee (f)	ideja (f)	la idea (f)
the problem	le problème (m)	das Problem (n)	problema (f)	el problema (m)
the bed	le lit (m)	das Bett (n)	post'el' (f)	la cama (f)
the tree	l'arbre (m)	der Baum (m)	derevo (n)	el árbol (m)
the water	l'eau (f)	das Wasser (n)	voda (f)	el agua (f)
the trash	le rebut (m)	der Abfall (m)	drjan' (f)	la basura (f)

NOUN CLASSES

To see that French gender is a simple example of what can be a more complex phenomenon in other languages, consider the noun classes of Swahili, a Bantu language. In Swahili there are 15 noun classes—and thus the form of a word in the singular and the plural is determined partly by what class it is in, and agreement takes into account the noun classes. For example, the form *m-* (class 6) is attached to the beginning of a noun that refers to a person:

(14) **m**-toto   '(a) child'
      m-tu   '(a) person'
      m-geni   '(a) guest'

To make the plural, the form *wa-* (class 7) is added to the noun:

● **TABLE 8.6**
  Definite articles across languages.

Language	Phrase	English translation
Chinese	pingguo apple	an apple, the apple
Kwamera	kuri u dog this	this dog
Swedish	mus-en mouse-the	the mouse
Swahili	wa-toto class 7-child	the children
Bulgarian	kuche-to dog-the	the dog
Italian	il cane the dog	the dog
French	le livre the book	the book
Russian	voda water	water, the water
German	das Wasser the water	the water

Note: Kwamera example from Tallerman, 1998.

(15) **wa**-toto   'children'
     wa-tu   'people'
     wa-geni   'guests'

However, if the word refers to a small thing, the singular has the form *ki-* attached to it, and the plural has the form *vi-*:

(16) **ki**-toto   '(an) infant'   **vi**-toto 'infants'
     ki-kapu   '(a) basket'   **vi**-kapu 'baskets'
     ki-ti   '(a) stool'   **vi**-ti 'stools'

Notice the use of the form *toto* for 'child/children' and 'infant/infants.'

WHERE DO DETERMINERS GO?

Essentially, a French noun phrase looks like an English noun phrase, at least regarding the placement of the determiner. In other languages, though, the determiner follows the noun. In yet other languages, the meanings conveyed by English determiners are not expressed by distinct words, but are understood from context and from the overall form of the sentence. Some simple noun phrases from other languages are given in Table 8.6.

In Kwamera, Swedish, and Bulgarian, the word for *the* follows the noun. And in the other languages illustrated here, it precedes the noun. Finally, as we have seen, there are languages that lack articles and use other devices, such as word order, to indicate definiteness and indefiniteness.

LEARNING TO USE DETERMINERS

Part of the challenge of learning another language is to figure out in what ways it is different from the language or languages that you already know. This requires that you understand something about how your language works and that you be able to pinpoint those areas in which the languages differ. The relationship between determiner and noun is one such area where differences can arise.

Having recognized that differences exist between noun phrases in different languages in terms of whether there is agreement and what the order of the noun and the determiner is, the next question that we have to consider is how to learn to produce and recognize the differences most effectively.

Being able to do this goes beyond knowing what the rule is. It even goes beyond knowing that the noun *maison* 'house' in French is feminine, while the noun *lit* 'bed' is masculine. We have to get to the point where we automatically put the determiner in the right place and do the agreement without thinking about the rule. The essential step in learning how to get order, gender, and agreement right is to practice the forms together. That is, we do not want to simply memorize the following:

(17) maison (f)
     lit (m)

Memorizing the nouns alone won't help us to handle the determiners *le, la, cette, ce,* and so on, without carrying out an extra step. Here are the mental steps that we would have to go through:

1. Ask your brain: what is the word for 'house'?
1a. Answer: *maison*
2. Ask: what is the gender of *maison*?
2a. Answer: feminine
3. Ask: what is the feminine form for 'the'?
3a. Answer: *la*
4. Ask: where does the determiner go?
4a. Answer: before the noun.

By the time we go through all of these steps, our audience will be lost if we are speaking, or we will be lost if we are trying to figure out what someone is saying. Here's another way to handle the determiners:

1. Ask your brain: how do you say 'the house'?
1a. Answer: *la maison*

1. Ask: how do you say 'this bed'?
1a. Answer: *ce lit*

In other words, we need to learn not just the gender and the rule for gender agreement, but also the actual forms that are required in order for there to be proper agreement as part of the noun. Doing so will save us many costly steps.

Clearly, we must learn the rule in order to understand why some phrases are different from others. But once we know the rule, we must use the rule to construct the expressions, and then **we must learn the complete expressions so well that they become automatic.** When we want to say 'the house,' we don't want to have to waste time figuring out whether the proper form is *le* or *la;* we need to know that *la maison* means 'the house' and eliminate the extra mental steps. Learning the more complex forms reduces the amount of computational time that we have to go through, at those moments when time is precious.

DESCRIBING THINGS

Let's take another look at some examples of "foreign accent" in English.

(18) a. I gave her a rose red.

    b. I have helpfuls friends.

    c. The enrolled in community college student (is my friend).

    d. Here is the student which you met her last week.

    e. The book is on the table is mine.

What is wrong with these sentences? We can understand each of them, yet in some way, each one is wrong. Let's compare them with how they would be expressed in grammatical English. Underlines show where something should go, while strikeouts show something in the wrong place.

(19) a. I gave her a <u>red</u> rose ~~red~~.

      b. I have helpful<u>s</u> friends.

      c. The ~~enrolled in community college~~ student <u>enrolled in community college</u> (is my friend).

      d. Here is the student which you met ~~her~~ last week.

      e. The book <u>that</u> is on the table is mine.

As you can see, some of the differences are very subtle, but they have a considerable effect. Example (19a) shows that a word like *red* in English must precede the noun, not follow it. Example (19b) shows that only the noun is marked for plural; *helpful* is not. The words *red* and *helpful* are **adjectives.**

The remaining three examples illustrate properties of **relative phrases or clauses** in English. Example (19c) shows that the phrase *enrolled in community college* has to follow the noun (in contrast to *red,* which precedes it). Examples (19d) and (19e) are somewhat more complicated, and we'll come back to them later.

Adjectives and relative clauses in English have the function of describing things. All languages perform these functions. Languages differ in the form of adjectives and relative clauses and in the location of adjectives and relative clauses in noun phrases. We discuss how this works next.

Adjectives

ADJECTIVES IN ENGLISH

Adjectives are used to refer to properties of things and substances (physical and nonphysical, and real and imaginary). The following are examples of the types of properties that can be referred to with adjectives:

- overall size; e.g. *huge, big, little, small, tiny, enormous, middle-sized*
- size in a particular dimension; e.g. *tall, short, fat, slim, elongated, stubby*
- shape; e.g. *square, round, oval, squiggly, triangular, flat*
- qualities perceived by one of our senses; e.g. *loud, quiet, shrill, squeaky, wet, melodious, rhythmic, shiny, dull, dark, scratchy, rough, red, black, green, polka-dotted*

- social or personal qualities; e.g. *polite, rude, inquisitive, happy, sad, intelligent, silly, goofy*

There are many others.

As we did in the case of determiners and nouns, we can say what the rule is for adjectives in English. First consider these examples:

(20) huge dog   *dog huge
     the huge dog   *the dog huge   *huge the dog
     this huge dog   *this dog huge   *huge this dog
     every huge dog   *every dog huge   *huge every dog

We know already that the determiner has to precede the noun, so we have to look only at where the adjective goes. These examples show that the adjective also precedes the noun; moreover, the adjective has to follow the determiner. If there is more than one adjective, all the adjectives must follow the determiner and precede the noun.

(21) the huge gray dog
     the huge gray howling dog
     the huge gray happy howling dog

Adjective Rule for English

In a noun phrase, an adjective precedes the noun that it modifies and follows the determiner.

These observations allow us to formulate the English Adjective Rule (see box above).

Table 8.7 gives a small sample of the possible noun phrases of English. If we take one word from column A, one from column B, and one from column C, we get sequences that look like English noun phrases, although some of them are nonsensical and others are simply bad English. For example, if the determiner and the noun do not obey the agreement restrictions of the Determiner Rule, the sequence is bad.

● **TABLE 8.7**
Menu for simple English noun phrases.

A	B	C
the	huge	dog
a	wet	water
every	square	idea
this	intelligent	sincerity
much	happy	foot
a lot of	stubby	proposal

Let's start at the beginning. *The, huge,* and *dog* combine according to the Adjective Rule for English to form *the huge dog.* This is a proper expression of English, and we know what it means. Let's replace *dog* with the other nouns and see what we come up with.

(22) ☹the huge water
     ☺the huge idea
     ☹the huge sincerity

The first example, *the huge water,* sounds odd because it refers to a property of water that cannot be measured. Water can be heavy, or wet, or warm, but not huge. To indicate this type of oddness, we use the frowny face symbol ☹.

In comparison, an idea is a non-physical object. It can be counted (e.g. *every idea*), but because it is non-physical, it does not have a physical size. But we can talk metaphorically of a non-physical object as though it is physical, so we can use *huge* metaphorically to describe an idea. The smiley face symbol ☺ on *the huge idea* is used here to indicate this metaphorical usage.

Sincerity is a non-physical substance. So it is odd to use an adjective that measures physical dimension to describe sincerity, even metaphorically. It would be equally strange to talk about ☹ *the huge air* or ☹ *the huge water.* ☹*The huge sincerity* therefore gets the frowny face symbol assigned to it.

Notice that the sorts of things that we are describing here are not specifically about the English language, but about how we understand the world as human beings. If we translated these expressions into some other language, they would be judged equally acceptable, metaphorical, or odd, to the extent that the words that we were using conveyed the same literal concepts. So ☹*la sincerité enorme* 'huge sincerity' should be as strange in French as it is in English, and in exactly the same way.

Notice also that there does not appear to be any agreement restriction between the adjective and the noun in English. While we found that we have to use *this* with singular nouns and *these* with plural nouns, the adjectives in column B can be used with either type of noun, as in the following example:

(23) this huge dog
     these huge dogs

Exercise 3

As we have seen, Table 8.7 gives rise to a number of perfectly good noun phrases and to a number of less-than-perfect noun phrases, e.g. *much happy foot, *a lot of square water, *a stubby sincerity, *much wet idea.* For each of these bad combinations, say as precisely as you can why they're bad.

Descriptive and Restrictive Modification

An adjective is a word like the English *red, helpful, happy*. We can say
- *the happy dog*
- *The dog is happy.*

With stress on *dog,* the phrase *happy dog* means simply that the dog is happy. This is the **descriptive** or **attributive** use of the adjective. With stress on *happy,* by contrast, the adjective is used to distinguish this dog from other dogs that are not happy. This is the **restrictive** or **contrastive** use of the adjective.
- As an exercise, use the expression the *happy dog* in a sentence to simply say that the dog is happy. You should be able to hear that the stress falls on *dog.* Try this with other phrases.

This means that we do not have to add any restrictions to the Adjective Rule.

ADJECTIVES IN OTHER LANGUAGES

Now, let's consider how a language might differ from English in regard to the counterpart of the Adjective Rule that says where to put adjectives in noun phrases:

- In some other language, the adjective could follow the noun.
- In some other language, the adjective might be required to agree with the noun.

Let's take a look at the examples in Table 8.8 on the following page. These examples show that the position of the adjective depends on the language. In Swahili, French, and Spanish it follows the noun, while in the other languages it precedes the noun. (Note that some adjectives in French may also precede the noun.) The determiner that means 'the' goes in different positions in different languages, as does the determiner that means 'every'. Each of these languages has a Determiner Rule and an Adjective Rule that says what the ordering requirements are and what the restrictions are, if any. We illustrate shortly.

Remember that in some languages there is agreement between determiners and nouns. Not surprisingly, in these very same languages, adjectives must also agree with the nouns. Let's look at some examples from a language that we have not talked about yet—Italian. We indicate masculine with M, feminine with F, singular with SG, and plural with PL. First we look at noun phrases without adjectives, and then we throw some adjectives in. See if you can figure out what is going on:

(24) il   libro
      the-M.SG   book-M.SG
      'the book'

● **TABLE 8.8**
Adjective noun order across languages.

Language	Phrase	English translation
French	un chien enorme a dog huge	a huge dog
German	der vernünftige Vorschlag the intelligent proposal	the intelligent proposal
Chinese	hao xuésheng good student	(a) good student
Swedish	den hungriga mus-en the hungry mouse-the	the hungry mouse
Spanish	cada hoja verde every leaf green	every green leaf
Russian	kazhdyje zelënyje list'ja every green leaf	every green leaf
Swahili	matunda mazuri fruit nice	nice fruit
Bulgarian	zeleni-te lista green-the leaves	the green leaves

i   libri
the-M.PL   book-M.PL
'the books'

la   casa
the-F.SG   house-F.SG
'the house'

le   case
the-F.PL   house-F.PL
'the house'

il   libro   piccolo
the-M.SG   book-M.SG   little-M.SG
'the little book'

i	libri	piccoli
the-M.PL	book-M.PL	little-M.PL

'the little books'

la	casa	piccola
the-F.SG	house-F.SG	little-F.SG

'the strange house'

le	case	piccole
the-F.PL	house-F.PL	little-F.PL

'the strange houses'

What do we see here? First, as in French, the adjective follows the noun. Second, the form of the adjective varies according to the gender and number of the noun, just like the form of the determiner does. In fact, we can even make a good guess about what the form is. Look at the difference between *piccolo* and *piccola*. They are the same as far as the *piccol-* part is concerned, and they differ just in whether they end in *-o* or *-a*.

The four forms together suggest the following picture:

ITALIAN ADJECTIVE AGREEMENT

	singular	plural
masculine	-o	-i
feminine	-a	-e

But notice that these same endings appear on the nouns themselves. We have highlighted the endings in **boldface** type so that you can compare them with those for adjective agreement:

ITALIAN NOUNS

	singular	plural
masculine	libr-**o**	libr-**i**
feminine	cas-**a**	cas-**e**

And we can make a nice chart for the determiners as well. This chart very closely resembles the chart for the adjectives and the nouns:

ITALIAN DETERMINERS

	singular	plural
masculine	il	i
feminine	la	le

What these charts are telling us is that there is a pretty systematic way of indicating number and gender in Italian, and, moreover, the determiner, the adjective, and the noun all have to show number and gender and agree with one another in number and gender.

So consider the following Italian vocabulary:

(25) ragazzo 'boy'
      ragazza 'girl'
      strano 'strange (M.SG.)'

How would we say 'the strange boy,' 'the strange boys,' 'the strange girl,' and 'the strange girls'? We just follow the rules:

(26) il ragazz**o** stran**o**
      i ragazz**i** stran**i**
      la ragazz**a** stran**a**
      le ragazz**e** stran**e**

And this is the general pattern that we find throughout the language. (Maybe this is one reason is why many people find it easy to learn Italian.)

Exercise 4

Work out the Adjective Rule for Italian.

Exercise 5

What would you say is the best way to learn how to productively construct grammatical noun phrases in Italian?

As we discussed earlier, there are 15 noun classes in Swahili, meaning that the form of a word in the singular and the plural is determined partly by what class it is in, and that agreement takes into account the noun classes. Consider again the examples we discussed. For example, the form *m-* (class 6) is attached to the beginning of a noun that refers to a person:

(27) **m**-toto   '(a) child'
      m-tu   '(a) person'
      m-geni   '(a) guest'

And to make the plural, the form *wa-* (class 7) is added:

(28) **wa**-toto   '(a) child'
      wa-tu   '(a) person'
      wa-geni   '(a) guest'

But if the word refers to a small thing, the singular has the form *ki-* attached to it, and the plural has the form *vi-*:

(29) **ki**-toto 'infant'   **vi**-toto 'infants'
      ki-kapu 'basket'   **vi**-kapu 'baskets'
      ki-ti 'stool'   **vi**-ti 'stools'

Here now are some examples of noun phrases containing adjectives:

(30) **ma**-tunda **ma**-zuri
      fruit   nice
      'nice fruit'

      mi-tego **mi**-wili
      traps   two
      'two traps'

      wa-tu   ha-**wa** **wa**-zuri
      people these   nice
      'these nice people'

      vi-ti   **vi**-le **vi**-kubwa
      chairs those big
      'those big chairs'

What we see is that the class marker that attaches to the noun also attaches to the adjective and the determiner. Just as in Italian and French, Swahili shows agreement throughout the noun phrase.

Exercise 6

Work out the Determiner Rule and the Adjective Rule for Swahili.

Relative Clauses

RELATIVE CLAUSES IN ENGLISH

Here are a few errors produced by Japanese learners of English:[2]

(31) a. Based on many informations of the daughter gathered, . . .
     b. But the mystery of behind the door still remained.

As we noted at the beginning of this chapter, the other way to describe or restrict something in terms of its properties is to use a relative clause. These are ungrammatical attempts to produce a relative clause—pay close attention to what is missing that should be there and what is there that should not be in these examples. In (31a), for instance, we find *many informations*. In English, *information* is not a count noun but a mass noun, so this phrase should be *much information*. But then there is *of the daughter gathered*, which should be *that the daughter gathered*, or *which the daughter gathered*, or simply *the daughter gathered*.

(32) Based on much information <u>that the daughter gathered</u>, . . .
     Based on much information <u>which the daughter gathered</u>, . . .
     Based on much information <u>the daughter gathered</u>, . . .

Japanese learners of English use *of* to introduce a relative clause, because a relative clause follows the noun in English, whereas in Japanese a relative clause precedes the noun. The learners know that *of* can be used to separate phrases within a noun phrase, e.g. *picture **of** Sandy*, so they seize on *of* as the way to deal with this particular grammatical problem. The same strategy appears in (31b), which should be simply *the mystery behind the door*.

Let's consider more closely at how a relative clause is formed.

(33) The dog <u>that is happy</u> is eating my socks.
     I chased the dog <u>that was eating my socks</u>.
     My mother made me let go of the dog <u>that I caught</u>.

The first relative clause is *that is happy,* the second is *that was eating my socks,* and the third is *that I caught.* We call *dog* the **head** of the noun phrase. Its function with respect to the meaning of the phrase is to pick out the type of thing that the relative clause describes. We sometimes say that "the head is what the relative clause modifies."

What these examples suggest is that one way to form relative clauses in English is to take a complete sentence that says something about the head. For example, take the following clause:

---

2. From Muto-Humphrey, "Frequent Errors in English Grammar," 2005.

(34) the dog is happy

Strike out the phrase that corresponds to the head and its determiner, if there is one:

(35) ~~the dog~~ is happy

Put *that* in front of the clause:

(36) that is happy

This works for the other relative clauses in the examples. So:

(37) I caught the dog   →
      I caught ~~the dog~~   →
      that I caught

Striking out the phrase to form the relative clause means that a relative clause is a sentence with a **gap** in it that corresponds in meaning to the head. It is for this reason that there is something strange about one of the "foreign accent" sentences, (18d), which was introduced earlier in this chapter:

(38) Here is the student which you met her last week.

Because the relative clause modifies *student* and expresses the relation of meeting the student, there should be a gap after *met*. But instead we find the word *her* in this position. Some languages use a variant of the construction illustrated in (38), but standard English does not; the correct form is *which you met—last week*.

There are other ways to make relative clauses in English. One involves putting *who(m)*, *which*, *where*, or *when* in front of the clause, instead of *that*.

(39) the man whom I saw
      the dog which is happy
      the place where I put the lasagna
      the time when I first saw Paris

Some of these are not entirely colloquial for many speakers of English and are associated more with a written or formal style.

It is also possible to leave out *that*, but not when the struck-out phrase is the subject of the relative clause:

(40) The dog I caught needed a bath.
      the first time I saw Paris
      *I bought a dog was happy.

(Compare: I bought a dog **that** was happy.)

Hence we have an explanation for what is wrong with another example, (18e), which was introduced earlier:

(41) *The book is on the table is mine.

The problem here is that the word *that* must appear in the relative clause, because the struck-out phrase is the subject: *the book **that** is on the table. . . .*

The other thing that we know about English relative clauses is that they follow the head of the noun phrase.

(42) *The <u>that is happy</u> dog is eating my socks.
      *I chased the <u>that was eating my socks</u> dog.
      *My mother made me let go of the <u>that I caught</u> dog.

Thus, a third example of a relative clause error from the beginning of the chapter can be explained:

(43) *The enrolled in community college student (is my friend).

Here, *enrolled in community college* is a type of "reduced" relative clause that does not follow the noun; in a language like German or Japanese, however, such a relative clause would precede the noun.

Relative clauses, like adjectives, have two functions. One is restrictive, and the other is called "non-restrictive," "appositive," or "attributive." Consider the following examples:

(44) I saw the dog that/who was happy.
      I saw the dog, who was happy.

The first example is understood as picking the happy dog out from a group of dogs. The second example is simply stating that the dog was happy. Thus the non-restrictive function is the same as the attributive function of the adjective that we discussed earlier. Typically the two are distinguished in written language, as shown in the example: a comma separates the non-restrictive relative from the noun, but there is no comma used when the relative clause is restrictive.

RELATIVE CLAUSES IN OTHER LANGUAGES

The relative clause in French is similar to that in English in that it has a gap. The forms that appear at the beginning of the relative clause are selected on the basis of the structure in which the gap appears. If the gap is an object, the relative clause begins with *que*. If it is a subject, the relative clause begins with *qui*.

(45) l'homme que j'ai   vu
the-man that I-have seen
'the man that I saw'

l'homme qui m'a   vu
the-man that me-has seen
'the man that saw me'

Notice that by making use here of the notions of subject and object, we are able to state in a very simple way how the French relative clause is formed.

In Italian the relative clause always begins with *che*:

(46) il uomo che ho   visto
the man that I-have seen
'the man that I saw'

il uomo che mi ha   visto
the man that me has seen
'the man that saw me'

The relative clause in these languages follows the head noun, which makes it relatively easy for speakers of English to deal with them. But in other languages, the relative clause precedes the head noun. Look at the following examples from Korean:[3]

(47) John-un <u>tomangka-nun</u>   **totwuk-ul**   cap-ess-ta.
J.-TOPIC run.away-REL.IMPERF **thief-ACC**   catch-PAST-DECL
(lit. 'John <u>running away</u> thief caught.')
'John caught a/the thief who was running away.'

John-un **totwuk-i** <u>tomangka-nun</u>   **kes**-ul cap-ess-ta.
J.-topic **thief**-NOM run.away-REL.IMPERF **kes**-ACC catch-PAST-DECL
(lit. 'John <u>thief running away who</u> caught.')
'John caught a/the thief, who was running away.'

The head that the relative clause modifies is in **boldface.** In the first example, the relative clause precedes the head. There is no word corresponding to English *that* or *who,* but there is a marker *-nun* on the verb (*tomangka-<u>nun</u>*) that indicates that it is in

---

3. Examples adapted from Min-Joo Kim, "Internally-Headed Relatives," 2004. REL marks the verb as being in a relative clause, IMPERF indicates that the action lacks a fixed endpoint, NOM marks the subject, ACC marks the object, and DECL indicates that the sentence is declarative.

a relative clause. But Korean also has a construction in which the relative clause follows the noun. In this case, there is a following pronoun *kes,* similar to the Italian *che,* but following the relative clause, not preceding it.

German also has two types of relative clauses, one that precedes the noun and one that follows it:[4]

(48) der <u>in seinem Büro arbeitende</u> Mann
the in his study working man
'the man working in his study'

der Mann <u>der in seinem Büro arbeitet</u>
the man that in his study works
'the man who is working in his study'

Japanese is similar to Korean. The relative clause precedes the noun.

(49) Yamada-san ga saru o kat-te i-ru.
Yamada-Mr NOM monkey ACC keep-PART be-PRES
'Mr. Yamada keeps a monkey.'

Yamada-san ga <u>kat-te i-ru</u> saru.
Yamada-Mr NOM keep-PART be-PRES monkey
'the monkey which Mr. Yamada keeps'

The relative clause also precedes the noun in Chinese:

(50) Zhāngsān mǎi de qich hèn guì.
Zangsan buy NOM car very expensive
'The car that Zhangsan bought was very expensive.'

Summary

We began this chapter with a few examples of typical errors that non-native speakers make. Here they are again:

(1) a. Sun is hot.
Store on corner is closed.
b. He lives in the Peru.
The Professor Goldmund is very dynamic.

(continued on next page)

---

4. Examples from Avery Andrews, "Relative Clauses," 2004.

Summary (continued from previous page)

c. Student in this class very friendly.
d. I bought a book. He was very expensive.

These errors show us that some languages lack articles corresponding to *the* and *a;* that some languages use articles with proper nouns, unlike English; and that some languages make grammatical gender distinctions among nouns, while English does not.

In this chapter we looked at two kinds of modifiers of nouns, adjectives, and relative clauses. In some languages, adjectives precede the noun that they modify, and in some they follow. Like adjectives, relative clauses precede the noun in some languages and follow it in others. Relative clauses show a number of variants of form as well, in terms of whether they have something introducing them (like *that* or Italian *che*) that marks them as relative clauses, or something following them (like Korean *-nun*), or nothing at all, as in Chinese.

Additional Exercise

1. Choose a language that you are familiar with other than English. How do you construct the counterparts of the following underlined relative clauses in this language?

   a. the book <u>I bought</u>
   b. the salesperson <u>that I bought the book from</u>
   c. the salesperson <u>who sold me the book</u>

   Discuss the differences between the rules for forming relative clauses in your language and in English. Also, state clearly where the relative clause appears in the sentence with respect to the noun that it modifies.

References

Andrews, Avery. (2004). Relative clauses. Online: http://arts.anu.edu.au/linguistics/People/AveryAndrews/Papers/typrc2_june.pdf.

Kim, Min-Joo. (2004). Internally-headed relatives instantiate situation subordination. In *Proceedings of the 34th Annual Meeting of the Northeast Linguistics Society,* ed. Keir Moulton and Matthew Wolf, University of Massachusetts Amherst, GLSA. 333–44.

Muto-Humphrey, Keiko. (2005). Frequent errors in English grammar: articles and possessive markers. Online: http://library.nakanishi.ac.jp/kiyou/gaidai(31)/05.pdf.

Tallerman, M. (1998). *Understanding syntax.* London: Arnold.

Expressing Meaning

*I*n the preceding chapter we looked at noun phrases, which are used to refer to things. Typically, noun phrases form parts of sentences. Generally speaking, sentences express properties of the things that noun phrases refer to or relationships between the things. The precise literal content that a sentence expresses and the communicative function that it performs are dependent on its form, by which we mean the order in which the words appear and whether and how the words are marked grammatically.

We focus in this chapter on the two main contributions of form: (a) the literal content of a sentence, that is, the relationships that the sentence expresses and the properties that are attributed to participants; and (b) the function of the sentence, that is, whether it is a statement, a question, a request, or a command.

Some Errors in English

As before, we begin with some typical errors that learners of English make because the rules of their language are different from those of English. These errors highlight the differences:[1]

> *Dutch:*
> (1)   I must at once my sister see.

---

1. These errors are taken from Michael Swan and Bernard Smith, *Learner English* (2001), a rich compendium of errors that native speakers of languages other than English make when learning English.

German:

    (2)   You speak very well German.

    (3)   On Tuesday have we a holiday.

French:

    (4)   She lives not in Paris.

    (5)   The telephone they repaired it?

    (6)   She is the woman the most beautiful that I know.

Italian:

    (7)   Can you suggest us a good restaurant?

    (8)   Say me the truth.

Spanish:

    (9)   Do you can swim?
          Maria cans swim.

   (10)   I no understand.

Russian:

   (11)   At what are you looking? [grammatical but not colloquial]
          With whom were you talking when I saw you? [grammatical but not colloquial]

   (12)   New house is building near cinema that is near us.

   (13)   I have many money.

Polish:

   (14)   Tell me where are they.
          She wants to know what do you want.

Farsi:

   (15)   The man, which I saw him, . . .
          The book, which I gave it to you, . . .

Arabic:

   (16)   I went to the store for buy some clothes.

   (17)   He was soldier.

Chinese:

   (18)   This is a very difficult to solve problem.

Korean:

   (19)   Many foreigners exist in Seoul.

   (20)   Tomorrow will hot.

These examples demonstrate that there are two basic factors that go into expressing an idea in a language: (a) the particular words that are used and (b) the order in which they appear. For example, in the Dutch example (1), the words are well chosen, but the order is wrong—the verb *see* should come before *my sister*, which should come before *at once*. This error reflects the fact that the order in the Dutch verb phrase is the reverse of the order in the English verb phrase. On the other hand, in the Italian example (8), the error consists of the fact that the verb *say* does not function like *tell: tell me the truth* is grammatical, but **say me the truth* is not. This error reflects the fact that Italian uses the same word to express both 'say' and 'tell.'

Let's look more closely at how an English sentence is constructed and at some of the ways in which other languages differ from English.

Verbs and Verb Phrases

Verbs are the key to expressing a relation or a property, so we will begin with verbs and the phrases that are built around them. With each verb are associated a number of **roles,** which distinguish the various participants in a relation. For example, in a sentence like *The dog gave its owner the ball,* there are three roles: the thing given, the giver, and the recipient.

(21) ball   THING GIVEN
       dog   GIVER
       owner   RECIPIENT

These roles are associated with the verb and form a central part of the verb's meaning. There may be several verbs in the language that express the same general type of event; in this case, for example, there are *send, sell, lend,* and so on. Each verb refers to a relation in which something is going from one individual to another. What differs from verb to verb are the fine details of how this transmission takes place and the nature of the possession involved. So, for example, *lend* is a non-permanent transfer of possession, *sell* involves money, *send* involves some medium of transmission (such as the Internet), and so on. What is fundamentally important is that every language is able to express these relations, and it does so by distinguishing the participants in terms of what we have called 'form'—the order of words and their grammatical marking. Let's look closely at verbs and consider how they are used in sentences to express specific meanings.

The verb is the heart of a sentence. It tells us something about the scene, or state of affairs, that is being discussed and something about what the various individuals in the scene are doing and their relationships to one another. For example, if we use the verb *kick,* then we are talking about some event involving a person (or perhaps animal) performing a particular type of action against some other person or object: *Sandy **kicked** the door.*

Form and Meaning

The structure of a language serves to distinguish the participants in a relation from one another and specifies which one is playing which role.

There are two basic types of verbs: **main verbs,** which are those that describe the state of affairs; and **auxiliary verbs,** which express things such as possibility (e.g. *can*), necessity (e.g. *must*), and obligation (e.g. *should*). All languages have main verbs, but not all languages have auxiliary verbs. We will talk about the functions of main verbs here, and those of auxiliary verbs in the second half of this chapter.

We begin with a few simple sentences that we have already discussed. We can create them from the now-familiar Table 9.1 as shown in (22).

(22) The dog barked.
⊗The dog hissed.
The dog grunted.
⊗The dog crowed.

As before, we use the symbol ⊗ to indicate that a sentence like *The dog crowed* has an odd meaning. The form of these sentences is not a problem—they are the same as the good sentences, like *The dog barked.* This distinction between whether or not the meaning is good and whether or not the form of the sentence is good is an important one.

• **TABLE 9.1**
A menu for making simple English sentences.

A	B	C
The	dog	barked
A	cat	hissed
This	pig	grunted
That	rooster	crowed

Table 9.1 indicates the order in which words may appear so that they constitute a grammatical English sentence. (This is what we have called 'form.') We already know something about the noun phrase *the dog;* it is an expression that refers to some dog that we are aware of or have been talking about. It satisfies the Determiner Rule, so it conforms to a rule of English. Since the words of column C appear to function in more or less the same way to help form sentences, it is reasonable to conclude that they form a category. This category is distinct from the category **noun:** you can't put a verb into the position occupied by a noun and get a good sentence: **The hissed grunted.* We call this category **verb.**

Since all of these sentences have certain things in common, it is possible to say in a more general way what a simple English sentence looks like. Consider the sentences *The dog barked* and *The dog chased the cat.* Regardless of what follows the verb in these examples, there is a noun phrase preceding the verb. This is true no matter what form the noun phrase takes; we could use *the huge dog* or *the huge howling dog* or whatever, and it wouldn't matter.

(23) <u>The huge dog</u> barked.
<u>The huge dog</u> chased the cat.
<u>The huge howling dog</u> barked.
<u>The huge howling dog</u> chased the cat.

Our intuition is that the thing that this phrase refers to is playing the same role with respect to the action described by the verb. This role, which is that of the initiator of a voluntary act, is called **agent.** We will have more to say about roles in the next section. Since we have rules that say how to make a noun phrase in English, we do not need to list all of the possible components in separate columns. We can just use one column for all of the noun phrases, as shown in Table 9.2.

What this says is that we can create any noun phrase we want, and then follow it with a verb and so on, and we will get a sentence (perhaps a sentence with a * or a ⊗, of course).

You may have also noticed that what follows the verb *chased* and *opened* looks like a noun phrase, too. In fact, it is true that because of their meanings, some verbs must or may occur with a second noun phrase; they are called **transitive** verbs. Other verbs, because of their meaning, cannot have a noun phrase following them. They are called **intransitive verbs.** In English, the second noun phrase typically follows the transitive verb.

● **TABLE 9.2**
Preliminary rules for forming an English sentence.

A	B	C	D
[noun phrase]	barked		
[noun phrase]	chased	the	cat
[noun phrase]	grunted		
[noun phrase]	hissed		
[noun phrase]	opened	the	door
[noun phrase]	crowed		

(24) The dog chased the cat.
The dog chased the rooster.
⊗ The dog chased the door.
*The dog grunted the cat.
*The dog hissed the door.

We have called the noun phrase that follows the verb the **object;** it is sometimes called the **direct object.** We say that some verbs, like *chase,* **select** direct objects while others, like *hiss,* do not.

But notice that if a verb selects an object, the object cannot precede the verb:

(25) **Object before Verb**

*The huge dog <u>the cat</u> chased.

*The huge howling dog <u>the cat</u> chased.

*The cat <u>the door</u> opened.

*My roommate <u>the beer</u> drank.

*The fire <u>the house</u> destroyed.

Object after Verb

The huge dog chased <u>the cat</u>.

The huge howling dog chased <u>the cat</u>.

The cat opened <u>the door</u>.

My roommate drank <u>the beer</u>.

The fire destroyed <u>the house</u>

Notice also that if the verb is transitive, the specific action expressed by the sentence is expressed not just by the verb but by the verb together with the object. So *chased the cat* is one action, and *chased the rooster* is a different action.

And notice that where the noun phrase goes determines what role the object that it refers to plays in the event. In *The dog chases the cat,* the agent is the dog, and the thing chased is the cat, not the other way around. This is a very simple but important illustration of how form is used in a language to convey meaning.

These observations suggest several things. First, like the noun, the verb appears in a phrase, and it is the verb phrase (that is, the verb plus the object if it selects one) that describes the action. We can use the method of columns from Table 9.3 to summarize the form of a verb phrase in English.

What this says is that verb phrases can be formed from verbs alone (like *hissed* and *grunted*) or by combining a verb with a following noun phrase (like *chased the cat*).

Second, whether a verb phrase can consist of an intransitive verb alone or a transitive verb and an object depends largely on the meaning of the verb.[2]

The rule for the verb phrase is stated in the following box.

● **TABLE 9.3**

English verb phrases.

A	B
hissed	
grunted	
chased	[noun phrase]
opened	[noun phrase]

Verb Phrase Rule for English

A verb phrase consists of a verb, possibly followed by a noun phrase (the direct object).

Restrictions:

- A verb has a direct object in the verb phrase only if the meaning of the verb allows for a direct object.
- verb cannot have a direct object if its meaning does not allow for a direct object.

2. There are some verbs, like *eat* and *drink,* that may be either transitive or intransitive, with essentially the same meaning.

Identifying the Participants in an Event or State

As we have noted, an important function of grammar concerns the roles the participants play in an action expressed by a sentence and the way these roles match up with the phrases in the sentence. Let's now look at this function in more detail.

To see how important it is to get the roles of the various individuals right, consider the automatic translation, done by software, from English to German and back to English shown in Table 9.4. The German sentences correspond word for word to the English ones: *die* 'the,' *Kinder* 'children,' *bereit* 'ready,' *zu* 'to,' *essen* 'eat, have dinner.'

The bad translation of *The potatoes are ready to eat,* and the comparison of the examples, illustrate this very central function of verbs. The difference between #1 and #2 is that in #1, the children are the ones that will be performing the action of eating (they are **agents**), and in #2, the potatoes are, by contrast, the things that will be eaten; they will have something done to them (we say that the potatoes are the **theme** of the eating event). But the automatic translation software does not pick this distinction up and treats potatoes as though they were performing an action.

● TABLE 9.4
A German-to-English-to-German translation.

English	To German	Back to English
1. The children are ready to eat.	Die Kinder sind bereit zu essen.	The children are ready to have dinner.
2. The potatoes are ready to eat.	Die Kartoffeln sind bereit zu essen.	The potatoes are ready to have dinner.

BASIC ROLES

There are many verbs that involve only one participant. In these cases, the phrase that refers to the participant always occupies the subject position in an English sentence.

(26) Robin is snoring.
        Someone called.
        Albert fell.
        The bomb exploded.
        My goldfish died.

Some events just happen, while others are caused. When a sentence describes an event that is caused by a living creature, such as a person or an animal, the cause is called the agent. *Robin* is an agent in *Robin is snoring,* and *someone* is an agent in *Someone called*. But, as these examples show, there are many sentences where the cause is not mentioned, yet something happens. Albert falls, moving from a higher position to a lower position (ouch!). The bomb explodes, changing from an intact bomb into a bunch of pieces. My goldfish goes from the state of being alive to the state of being dead. The thing that changes state in sentences like these is also called the **theme.**

In addition, actions can be caused by inanimate things. For example, we can say *The rock broke the window*. In this case the rock was the **instrument** that caused the breaking of the window, but not an agent, because it did not act on its own to break the window.

Recall these examples:

(27) The dog chased the cat.
      The cat chased the dog.

The verb *chase* expresses a direct action, where one individual affects the other. The phrase to the left of *chased* refers to the individual that causes or initiates the action—the chaser, in this case, or, more generally, the agent. The phrase to the right of *chased* refers to the individual that is affected by the action—the "chasee," in this case, or, more generally, once again the **theme.**[3]

In English, the positions to the left and the right of the verb are special. The phrase to the left is what we have called the **subject,** and the one to the right is the (direct) **object.** These are called the **grammatical functions.** We see that the subject of the sentence plays the agent role in the event of chasing, while the object plays the theme role in this event. By distinguishing subject and object, speakers of English are able to keep track of the participants in a direct action: the agent of chasing is expressed as the subject, and the theme is expressed as the object.

This **matching up** of subject with agent and object with theme holds for the vast majority of English verbs that express direct actions. But the positions in a sentence are used to keep track of other roles as well, for example, the role of verbs that do not express direct actions but states and various types of events. So in the sentence *I received*

Basic Roles

- **Agent:** The individual (animate thing) that causes or initiates an action.
- **Theme:** The entity that undergoes a change of state or is acted on by an agent.
- **Instrument:** An inanimate thing that brings about a change.

---

3. The definition of theme given in the box is an approximate definition and sidesteps a number of complex issues that would divert us from our main concerns.

a letter, the subject does not cause the action and is not an agent; it is a recipient. This sentence has the same word order and structure as *I wrote a letter,* in which the subject *I* is an agent. The role of *I* is different in the two sentences.

For this reason, we have to distinguish the positions and the grammatical relations from the roles. Being a subject has to do with the form, while being an agent or having some other role has to do with the meaning. The subject in English is simply the noun phrase that precedes the verb and agrees with it. Its role depends on the particular verb.

Similarly, if you feel the rain on your face, you are not initiating any action, but you know that the subject of *feel* refers to the individual who is experiencing the sensation.

(28) I feel the rain on my face.

So you are not an agent in this case. But the verb is transitive: it has a subject (*I*) and a direct object (*the rain*).

In the following sentence the students are agents of the action, but the room is not physically changed by this action, so it is not a theme:

(29) The students entered the room.

The noun phrase *the students* is the subject, and *the room* is a direct object, just as it would be in the following:

(30) The students painted the room.

In (30), *the room* is the theme of *paint,* because it is physically changed by the action.

In summary, it is possible to distinguish many different roles that individuals can play, and there are more roles than we have illustrated here. The roles are part of the meaning of a verb, and they are associated with particular phrases in a sentence on the basis of the structure of the sentence. The box below summarizes our discussion thus far.

Grammatical Functions

- An English sentence typically has a **subject**.
- A sentence with an **intransitive** verb has a **subject;** a sentence with a **transitive** verb has a **subject** and an **object**.
- The **roles** associated with a subject and an object depend on the **meaning** of the verb.

GOVERNING ROLES

We say that a verb **governs** the roles that depend on it. Some verbs, like *snore,* govern one role, that of agent. Some verbs, like *bite,* govern two roles, agent and theme. In a simple case such as this, one role is associated with the subject, and a second role is associated with the object. But the situation can be more complicated. In some cases, a verb governs more than two roles. And when this occurs, one of the roles is associated with a phrase that is neither the subject nor the direct object, but something else.

Here is an example in which there are three roles:

(31) Robin gave Pat the book.

In *Robin gave Pat the book, Robin* is the agent, and *the book* is the theme. But what about *Pat?* Since *Pat* is the one who ends up with the book, the role is neither agent nor theme—it is a third role, which we call **goal.** The book changes possession from *Robin* to *Pat.*

Notice that there are two noun phrases following the verb, but only one can be the direct object; in this case, it is *the book,* which is the theme, because it undergoes a change of state (in particular, possession). The noun phrase that refers to the goal is typically called the **indirect object.** Notice also that the indirect object precedes the direct object in English.

Exercise 1: Roles and Grammatical Functions

Each of the following sentences has a subject, and some have direct objects as well. Try to explain what the differences are in the **roles** associated with the subjects and objects.

a. Sandy opened the door.
b. The door opened.
c. The key opened the door.

d. The tree died.
e. The farmer killed the tree.
f. The tree killed the farmer.

g. I fear the Abominable Snowman.
h. The Abominable Snowman frightens me.
i. It frightens me, all this talk about the Abominable Snowman.

Subject and Object across Languages

The roles assigned to the participants referred to in a sentence are part of the literal content of the sentence. How each role gets assigned depends on the form of the sentence. The need to express the roles of individuals in an event or a state is not a special property of English. It is something that all languages do, because talking about events and states is what people use language for (among other things). So all languages must have a way of indicating in a sentence which participant is the agent, which is the theme, and so on. Typically, languages do this by distinguishing the noun phrases in terms of their form.

Goal

The direction toward which a change of position, possession, or state moves.

There are three main ways in which languages distinguish subject and object. As we have just noted, English does it by position (also called **word order**). Other languages do it by **case,** which is a marking on the noun phrase, and by agreement. We illustrate each of these below.

WORD ORDER

French is similar to English in the way it uses word order to distinguish subject and object. But in French, there are no indirect objects like there are in English. Consider the examples in (32). As before, the asterisk indicates that the sentence is not grammatical in the language.

(32) Je donne le livre à Marie.
I give the book to Mary.

*Je donne Marie le livre.
I give Mary the book.

So we would say that in French, the goal role is marked by the preposition *à:*

(33) Je   donne le livre à   Marie
     agent   **theme goal**

In Ojibwa, the direct object comes before the indirect object. The subject is incorporated into the verb in this example:

(34) *Ojibwa (Algonquian)*[4]
     Ngi:mina: mzinhigan Ža:bdi:s
     I-gave-it book   John

4. Examples from Y. N. Falk, "Ditransitive Constructions."

agent   theme   goal
'I gave John a book.'

And in Palauan and Kinyarwanda, the indirect object comes before the direct object, just as in English:

(35) *Palauan:*
Ak milstęrir a ręsęchęlik a hong.
I   give my friends a book
agent   goal   theme
'I give my friends a book.'

(36) *Kinyarwanda:*
Umugóre aréereka ábáana   amashusho.
woman   shows   children pictures
agent   goal   theme
'The woman is showing the children pictures.'

Notice two things about these examples. First, the roles associated with the verb are the same to the extent that the verbs mean the same things. This is because these verbs express typical relationships that exist in all human societies, such as giving and showing, and all languages have words for these relationships. But different languages use different word orders to designate which part of the sentence corresponds to which role. As we see in the next section, there are languages in which word order is not used for this function; rather, it is done by marking the noun phrases to indicate their grammatical functions.

CASE

Case is used to mark the function of phrase in a sentence, regardless of where it is located. Consider again these examples from Japanese:

(37) John **ga** sono tegami **o** yon- da
John   that letter   read-PAST
'John read that letter.'

John **ga** sono tegami **o** yon- da- ka
John   that letter   read- PAST- QUESTION
'Did John read that letter?'

Notice that we did not say earlier what the meanings of *ga* and *o* are. That is because they have no meanings. The particle *ga* indicates that *John* is the subject of *yon-da* 'read,' while the particle *o* indicates that *sono tegami* 'that letter' is the object. Therefore, *John* gets the agent role, and *sono tegami* gets the theme role.

Because of this fact, the Japanese subject and object can be in a different order with respect to one another in the sentence, and it is still possible to figure out who is causing the action and what is undergoing it.

(38) Sono tegami **o** John **ga** yon- da.
     that letter   John   read-PAST
     'John read that letter.'

     Sono tegami **o** John **ga** yon- da- ka
     that letter   John   read-PAST-QUESTION
     'Did John read that letter?'

Similarly, when there is a direct object and an indirect object, either order of objects is possible.

(39) John **ga** Mary **ni** sono hon **o**   miseta.
     John   Mary to   that book showed
     'John showed that book to Mary.'

     John **ga** sono hon **o** Mary **ni** miseta.
     John   that book Mary to showed
     'John showed that book to Mary.'

Notice here that the noun phrase that refers to the goal is marked with the case marker *ni,* which we translate as 'to.'

This flexibility of word order is found in many other languages that use case, for example, Russian and German. In such languages, case is indicated not by particles, as it is in Japanese, but by modifications in the form of words, or their "morphology." For example, here are some forms used in Russian for the subject and object:

(40) *Russian:*

	Subject (Nominative Case)	Object (Accusative Case)
'book'	kniga	knigu
'man'	ot'ets[5]	otsa
'beer'	pivo	pivo

---

5. In the standard transliteration of Russian, the symbol ' is used to indicate palatalization. So *t'e* is pronounced "tye." Similarly, *Igor'a* in Example (41) below is pronounced "Igorya."

So if you say 'the book fell' in Russian, you use the form *kniga* to refer to the book, since it is the subject, but if you say 'I read the book,' you use the form *knigu*, since it is the direct object.

In addition to nominative (NOM) and accusative (ACC) case, Russian has four other cases: dative (DAT), instrumental (INST), genitive (GEN), and prepositional (PREP). All of these have many uses. The dative case is a typical way to indicate the goal of giving, instrumental case can be used to indicate how some action was accomplished, and genitive case is used to express possession, among other things. Example (41) shows a sentence in which five of the cases are used. We give the Russian sentence using the Russian alphabet and then transliterate it into the Roman alphabet, just for fun.

(41) Анна   руками   дала   Ивану   голубую книгу   Игоря.
      Anna   rukami   dala   Ivanu   golubuju knigu   Igor'a
      Anna-NOM   hands-INSTR   gave   Ivan-DAT   blue-ACC book-ACC   Igo-GEN

'Anna gave Igor's blue book to Ivan with her hands.'

Notice that both *golubuju* 'blue' and *knigu* 'book' are marked with the accusative case. We say that they must "agree" with one another in case. This type of agreement is similar to what we saw in Chapter 8 with respect to gender and number agreement in French and Italian noun phrases.

Exercise 2: English Case

English shows a remnant of an earlier case system in the form of the pronouns, such as *I, me, she, her, he, him, his, we, us, they, them, who, whom, whose,* but it does so nowhere else in the language.

- Which of the above pronouns are nominative case forms (used for subject), which are accusative (used for object), and which are genitive (used for possession)?
- Using your answer to this question, explain why the following sentences are ungrammatical:

  a. *Me like you very much.
  b. *Please give it to I.
  c. *Whom is hungry?

AGREEMENT

Agreement between the noun phrases and the verb is yet a third way to indicate the function of a phrase.

In a language that uses this type of agreement, the form of a noun is the same regardless of whether it is subject or object, just as in English. But the verb has a form that is determined by particular properties of the subject and, in some languages, the properties of the object.

As we noted in Chapter 8, Swahili has 15 noun classes. Interestingly, in a sentence, the verb typically displays a marker that is the same as the class marker of the subject and another marker that is the same as the class marker of the object. The verb is said to **agree** with subject and object. Agreement means that the forms match according to specific rules of the language.

Here are some examples from Swahili. The class marker is indicated by a number. Once again, SG means singular and PL means 'plural':[6]

> (42) Juma <u>a</u>-li-<u>mw</u>-on-a   Mariam.
> Juma 3SG-past-3SG-see-INDIC Mariam
> 'Juma saw Mariam'
>
> <u>M</u>-toto   <u>a</u>-ni-<u>ki</u>-soma   <u>ki</u>-tabu.
> 1SG-child 1SG-PP-7SG-read 7SG-book
> 'The child is reading the book"
>
> <u>Ki</u>-tabu   <u>wa</u>-na-<u>ki</u>-soma   <u>wa</u>-toto.
> 7SG-book 2PL-PP-7SG-read 2PL-child
> 'The children are reading the book.'

While the precise shape of the class markers attached to a verb may be different from that attached to a noun, the class marker attached to the verb is specifically chosen for the class of the noun that it agrees with.

PREPOSITIONS

In English some roles may be expressed by another type of phrase, called a **prepositional phrase.** Some examples are given in (43). The words marked in boldface are members of the category **preposition.** The prepositional phrases are underlined.

---

6. In these examples, INDIC means "indicative," which means roughly that the sentence is about a concrete reality and is not a hypothetical or an imperative, and PP means "present progressive."

(43) a. Sandy sailed **to** <u>Salem</u>.
        agent   **goal**
    b. Sandy smashed the window **with** <u>a hammer</u>.
        agent   **theme**   **instrument**

Here is another example with three roles:

(44) I borrowed this book <u>from the library</u>.

In this sentence, the role of one of the participants in the scene, the library, is identified by using a preposition. The preposition *from* in this sentence identifies the **source** of the book. The source is the origin of the change. Notice that this role is associated not with either subject or object, but with a preposition.

The reason why this example is important is that it shows that verbs and prepositions can work together to identify certain roles in the sentence. The verb governs certain roles directly, through the subject and object, and the prepositions supply the others.

We have seen that the position of a noun phrase can perform this function in English—for example, the subject of *give* is the agent, and there can be two objects. But while the concept of borrowing involves three roles—an agent, a theme, and a source— *borrow* does not appear with two objects.

(45) *I borrowed the library the book.

The proposition *from* has to be used to mark the source on behalf of the verb *borrow*.

The phenomenon that we see here is very widespread. It is so important because in order to use a verb correctly, it is necessary to know how to identify all of the participants in the scene described by the verb.

The box below summarizes the roles that we have discussed.

Summary of Roles

Agent: The individual (animate thing) that causes or initiates an action.
Theme: The entity that undergoes a change of state or is acted upon by an agent.
Instrument: The inanimate thing that brings about a change.
Goal: The direction toward which a change of position, possession, or state moves.
Source: The original location of a change.
Experiencer: The individual that has a perception, thought, or feeling.

Actives and Passives

In most languages there is more than one way to identify the roles governed by a verb. Thinking about the sentences that we have discussed, we see that there is one general pattern, which we will state as a rule. First, let's consider the pattern illustrated by the following examples:

(46) a. Robin was snoring
    b. The dog bit the cat.
    c. The bomb exploded.

In the first example, the subject refers to the agent, and there is no theme. In the second example, the subject refers to the agent, and there is a theme. In the third example, there is no agent, and the subject is the theme.

These examples illustrate a general pattern: the subject is reserved for the agent if there is one; if there is no agent, the subject can identify other roles. So we do not expect to find a simple sentence of English with an agent where the agent is not the subject. We summarize our observations in the form of the Agent/Theme Rule (see box below).

The exceptions to #3 of the Agent/Theme Rule involve verbs such as *receive*, which expresses its theme as direct object and a role other than agent as subject, as illustrated in (47):

(47) I | received | some email | today (from Pat).
    goal   **theme**   **source**

These exceptions have to be learned as part of the meaning of the particular verb.

The Agent/Theme Rule seems a bit rigid, because it says that if there is an agent, it must be the subject. Fortunately, many languages, including English, have ways to get around such rigid rules and introduce some flexibility and variety in how the roles are

---

Agent/Theme Rule for English

1. If a verb governs the agent role, this role is expressed by the subject.
2. If a verb governs the theme role, and if there is an agent, this role is expressed by:
   a. the direct object or
   b. the object of a preposition, depending on the verb.
3. If there is no agent, the theme is expressed by the subject.

Restriction:
• Clause #3 has exceptions.

identified. In English this flexibility is achieved through the use of the **passive,** illustrated by the following pairs of sentences:

(48) The dog bit the cat.
      The cat was bitten by the dog.

      Pat opened the door.
      The door was opened by Pat.

In the first pair of sentences, the agent is the dog; in the second pair, the agent is Pat. But in *The cat was bitten by the dog,* the subject is not the agent but the theme. And the agent is the object of the preposition *by.* A similar observation can be made about the second pair of sentences.

Looking closely at these sentences, we see that there is a pattern. We can use Figure 9.1 to pick out the significant features that participate in this pattern. What we see is that we can put the direct object into the subject position, and the subject into the preposition phrase with *by,* if we also change the verb *chased* into *was chased.* These two ways of identifying the roles governed by a verb are called **active** and **passive.**

The form of the verb in the passive is that of the past tense in English for regular verbs, and a special form for irregular verbs. We call this form the **passive participle;** some examples are given in (49):

(49) **Present Past**   **Passive Participle**
      Irregular:
      eat   ate   (was) eaten
      see   saw   (was) seen
      write   wrote   (was) written
      know   knew   (was) known

      Regular:
      chase   chased   (was) chased

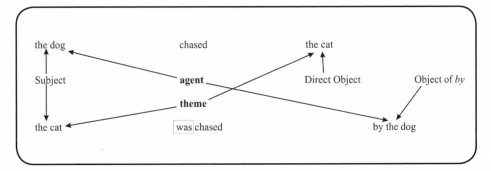

Figure 9.1 Roles of the passive construction.

deliver	delivered	(was) delivered
carry	carried	(was) carried
toss	tossed	(was) tossed

Active and passive are very general. For almost every active there is a passive, and vice versa, with some limited exceptions. The subject does not have to be an agent; it can be a **recipient,** as with *receive,* or an **experiencer,** as with *see, hear:*

(50) Robin received some email.
Some email was received by Robin.

Leslie saw the dog.
The dog was seen by Leslie.

Pat heard the music.
The music was heard by Pat.

Now, here is something very important to observe about the passive. Suppose that you wanted to express the idea that something chased the cat, but you didn't know who or what the agent was. You could say:

(51) Something chased the cat.

But you couldn't say:

(52) *Chased the cat.

as a full sentence because of the requirement that every non-imperative sentence in English has an explicit subject.

The passive gives us another way to avoid mentioning the agent in this type of case, because in the passive, the requirement that there be a subject is satisfied by the noun phrase that expresses the theme (in the case of *chase*), that is, the direct object. We can

Active/Passive Rule for English

A statement can be:
1. active, with roles expressed by subject and object or
2. passive, with:
    a. a form of *be* followed by the passive participle,
    b. the direct object role identified by the subject, and
    c. the subject role identified by the object of *by* (which does not have to be included in the sentence).

leave out the prepositional phrase and express just the idea that we want:

(53) The cat was (or was being) chased.

Because a different role is identified by the subject, the sentence has a somewhat different emphasis than the active and can be used for stylistic variety.

Notice that this trick can be used regardless of what role the direct object of the active expresses. For example, we can say the following:

(54) The door was opened.
      Some email was received.
      The dog was seen.
      The music was heard.

The role that is associated with the direct object in the active is associated with the subject in the passive. This observation gets us to our next rule, the Active/Passive Rule (see the box at the bottom of page 150).

There are two additional observations to make about the passive. First, notice that sometimes the passive can be formed when the subject corresponds to the object of a preposition:

(55) We looked at the clowns.
      The clowns were looked at.

      We talked about the proposal.
      The proposal was talked about.

      We sat on the chair.
      The chair was sat on.

What this tells us is that sometimes the preposition combines with the verb to identify the direct object. In other words, the direct object doesn't have to be a noun phrase that immediately follows the verb; it can follow a preposition that is governed by the verb.

Second, the following examples show that that subject of the passive does not have to correspond to a direct object; it can correspond to an indirect object:

(56) I gave <u>Pat</u> a passing grade.
      <u>Pat</u> was given a passing grade.

      You sold <u>me</u> a lemon.
      <u>I</u> was sold a lemon.

And when there is an indirect object, the direct object cannot become the subject of

Exercise 3: Passives

In the following groups of three sentences, there is an active, a passive, and a third type of sentence. While the roles expressed are the same, the grammatical properties of the sentences are different. Describe the grammatical differences between the first, second, and third sentence in each group of three. Which one is passive? Why?

1. The storm sank the boat.
    The boat was sunk by the storm.
    The boat sunk in the storm.

2. The wind opened the door.
    The door was opened by the wind.
    The door opened in the wind.

3. Sandy sent Leslie a letter.
    Leslie was sent a letter by Sandy.
    Leslie got a letter from Sandy.

the passive for many speakers.

> (57) (*)A passing grade was given Pat.
>   (*)A lemon was sold me.

What this means is that, strictly speaking, clause #2b of the Active/Passive Rule should refer not to the direct object but to the first object noun phrase following the verb.

Time and Truth

As we have seen thus far, a sentence expresses a relationship or a property. We have not yet discussed two other important aspects of sentences that many languages also express: the time of a relationship and the truth of a description. These are complex topics, and we will only scratch the surface here. As a language learner, you will have to come to terms with the different ways in which your native language and the language you are learning carry out these functions.

To get a feel for how this part of the language works, let's take a look at some more examples showing a "foreign accent" in English:

> (58) a. They still discuss the problem.
>   b. I study here for a year.
>   c. She avoids to go.
>   d. I want that you stay.

e. I can't to fix that!

Compare these to the correct forms:

(59) a. They <u>are</u> still discuss<u>ing</u> the problem
　　　b. I <u>have</u> <u>been</u> study<u>ing</u> here for a year.
　　　c. She avoids ~~to~~ go<u>ing</u>.
　　　d. I want ~~that~~ you <u>to</u> stay.
　　　e. I can't ~~to~~ fix that!

Example (59a) shows that in order to talk about an ongoing event, it is necessary to use a form of the verb *be* and a verb with *-ing*. For something spanning a period of time that includes the present, *have been . . . -ing* is necessary, as shown by example (59b).

The other three examples illustrate other fine details about what form of the verb appears in various contexts. The verb *avoid* occurs with a verb in the *-ing* form, as contrasted, for example, with *try*, which occurs either with *-ing* or *to*, and *manage*, which occurs only with *to*:

(60) a. She tried to go.
　　　b. She tried going.
　　　c. She managed to call.
　　　d. *She managed calling.

The verb *want* occurs with *to*, and not with a full clause that begins with *that*. In other languages, such as German, the literal translation of (58d) would be the way to say this:

(61) Ich will, dass du　bleibst.
　　　I　want that　you　stay
　　　'I want you to stay.'

And the verb *can't* appears with the 'bare' form of the verb, that is, one that lacks 'to.' In many languages, such as German, the form of the verb that appears with the counterpart to *can* is translated as the English infinitival *to*:

(62) Ich kann　nicht　das　reparieren!
　　　I　can　not　that to-repair
　　　'I can't fix that.'

Getting this aspect of the grammar right, in English and in other languages, is an important part of speaking without an "accent." Moreover, it is one of the most difficult areas of grammar for non-natives to master. Let's take a look at the kinds of meaning differences that are expressed by differences in verb form.

TENSE AND ASPECT

When a sentence is a statement, its verb can have different forms. We will use the most extreme English case to illustrate this phenomenon, that of the verb *to be:*

(63) I <u>am</u> here now.   I <u>was</u> here yesterday.
        You <u>are</u> there now.   You <u>were</u> here yesterday.
        He <u>is</u> here now.   He <u>was</u> here yesterday.
        We <u>are</u> here now.   We <u>were</u> here yesterday.
        They <u>are</u> there now.   They <u>were</u> there yesterday.

Five different forms of the verb are used in sentences like these: *am, was, is, were,* and *are.* Notice that while we say that the verb is "(to) be," the form *be* does not actually appear in this list. Moreover, some of the verb forms are used to refer to a situation in the present (*am, is, are*), while others are used to refer to a situation in the past (*was, were*).

The different forms of a word make up its **inflections.** The inflections of a verb make up its **conjugation.** The part of the conjugation (that is, the particular form) that plays a role in expressing the time is called **tense.** In these examples we have illustrated **present tense** and **past tense.** Present tense of the verb *be* is expressed by *am, is,* and *are.* Past tense is illustrated by *was* and *were.*

The reason to focus on English conjugations is, of course, not to teach you about how English works but to highlight the fact that verb form can be a critical part of what makes up a grammatical sentence in a language. Other languages have conjugations too, and they are more elaborate than those of English. The above English conjugation is translated into French in (64). The verb forms are underlined. *Vous* means 'you,' *il* means 'he,' *nous* means 'we,' and *ils* means 'they.' *Maintenant* means 'now,' and *hier* means 'yesterday.'

(64) Je <u>suis</u> ici maintenant.   J'<u>étais</u> ici hier.
        'I am here now.'   'I was here yesterday.' (etc.)
        Vous <u>êtes</u> ici maintenant.   Vous <u>étiez</u> ici hier.
        Il <u>est</u> ici maintenant.   Il <u>était</u> ici hier.
        Nous <u>sommes</u> ici maintenant.   Nous <u>étions</u> ici hier.
        Ils <u>sont</u> ici maintenant.   Ils <u>étaient</u> ici hier.

And such languages are more complex in cases where English is simple. The present tense of *sourire* 'to smile' is shown in (65). Notice that the French verb takes a number of different forms, while the English verb takes only two forms.

(65) **French**   **English**
        Je sour<u>is</u>.   I smile.

Tu sour<u>is</u>.	You (singular) smile.
Il sour<u>it</u>.	He smile<u>s</u>.
Nous sour<u>ions</u>.	We smile.
Vous sour<u>iez</u>.	You (plural) smile.
Ils sour<u>ient</u>.	They smile.

It is important to recognize that tense has to do with the form of a verb. This formal aspect of the verb must be distinguished from **time,** which has to do with **meaning.** In English we can express reference to many different times, including the future, but we do not use different forms of the verb in every case. For example, to express the future of *I see my friend* we could say the following:

(66) I <u>am</u> see<u>ing</u> my friend tomorrow.
I <u>will</u> see my friend tomorrow.
I <u>am going</u> to see my friend tomorrow.
or even
I <u>see</u> my friend tomorrow.
or
I <u>am about to</u> see my friend tomorrow.
I <u>am to</u> see my friend tomorrow.

In most of these cases, the form of the verb *see* is simply *see,* without any inflection. Moreover, the forms that are used in all of these examples are present tense: *am* and *see.* The form *will* is an auxiliary verb (see later discussion) and is also in the present tense. The use of *will* + verb, along with expressions like *am/is/are going to,* here used in the present tense form, express reference to the future, but, it is important to note, they do not do it by using future tense.

The difference between tense and time is very significant, and it is important not to confuse them. As we will see, all languages can refer to time, but not all languages use tense in order to do this. Or they may use tense in some cases (for example, present tense *see,* past tense *saw*), as in English, but may use another means in other cases (for example, future reference but present tense *will see*). **ENGLISH HAS NO FUTURE TENSE.**

Tense

Tense has to do with the <u>form</u> of a verb; reference to **time** has to do with the <u>meaning</u> of a sentence. The meaning may depend on the tense, but it may depend on other things as well, such as expressions that refer to actual times.

Exercise 4: Time and Tense

For each of these sentences, say what the time is and what the tense is:

a. We welcome your inquiries.
b. Did you hear that?
c. How long have you lived here?
d. When are you going to stop smoking?
e. [Phone rings.] That will be the cable guy.
f. So then he goes, "Yuck!"
g. Can you stop by tomorrow at around 3 P.M.?

VARIATIONS IN VERB FORM

Having come this far, we can begin to imagine other ways in which a language might be different from English. Here are some questions that we could investigate:

- How does the language indicate present time and past time? Do the verbs have inflections for tense in these cases?
- How does the language indicate future time? Do the verbs have inflections for tense in this case?
- How does the language indicate commands? Is there a special command inflection of the verb?
- What is the form of a verb phrase with a transitive verb? Does the direct object go after the verb, as in English, or before it? Or both?
- How is the subject identified? Does the subject precede or follow the verb phrase, or both? Is there perhaps some other way to express the subject?

The more we find out about how English and other languages work, the more questions we can ask, and the more possibilities we can imagine.

Every language has verbs, because every language has to be able to talk about the sorts of things that verbs express—relations between individuals with different roles, states of affairs, events, and so on. Because the verb is the heart of a sentence, it expresses the core of the idea that is expressed by the sentence. The noun phrases express the various players and assorted details about the setting, the time, the place, and so on.

We said earlier that English has only two tenses, present and past, while other languages have future as well. Here's an illustration, using Spanish next to English:

(67) The dog barked at the cat.   El perro **ladró** en el gato.
                                         the dog   barked to the cat

The dog barks at the cat.	El perro **ladra** en el gato.
	the dog barks to the cat
The dog will bark at the cat.	El perro **ladrará** en el gato.
	the dog will-bark to the cat

You can see that where English uses an extra (auxiliary) verb, Spanish simply uses another form of the verb (and thus does inflect for and have future tense). This is one of the main differences between English and other languages. Let's see how things work in Russian:

(68) 'The dog barked at the cat.'   Sobaka <u>lajala</u>   v kote.
       dog   barked at cat

     'The dog barks at the cat.'   Sobaka <u>laet</u>   v kote.
       dog   barks   at cat

     'The dog will bark at the cat.'   Sobaka <u>budet lajat'</u>   v kote.
       dog   is   to-bark at cat

Russian uses a present tense form of the verb *be* plus the verb to refer to the future in this case, and it is thus similar to English in not having a future tense and in using other means to refer to future time. For another class of verbs (the perfectives), Russian expresses the future by using the present tense of the verb itself:

(69) 'The dog will bark at the cat.'   Sobaka zalajet v kote.
       dog   barks   at cat

There are other languages that do not have tense at all. We would translate reference to different times in Chinese as shown in (70). The form *le* is a particle that denotes completion of the event or what is called "perfective aspect."

(70) Wo zuotian   qu kan   dian ying le.
     I   yesterday   go watch movie   PERF
     'I went to the movies yesterday.'

     Wo xianzai qu kan   dian ying.
     I   today go watch movie
     'I am going to the movies now.'

     Wo mingtian yao qu kan   dian ying.
     I   tomorrow   go watch movie
     'I will go to the movies tomorrow.'

These examples show that there is no inflection for tense in Chinese—the same form of the verb is used regardless of the time referred to, and the time is expressed directly by an adverb.

What these examples also show is that languages can refer to the present, the past, and the future, whether or not they have verb forms (that is, tenses) that specifically pick out a certain time. The commonly held notion that some languages cannot express the future, and that speakers therefore are unable to think about the future, is mistaken. All people can think about and refer to the future, but different languages provide different grammatical means of doing this. Some use inflectional forms, and some do not.

ASPECT

Verb forms are used to refer not only to the time of an event but also to properties of the event. The most common properties are whether or not the event has been completed and whether the event occurred at a particular point in time or over an extended period of time. These properties are called **aspect.** A completed event is said to have **perfect** aspect, and an ongoing event is **progressive.**

We saw some aspect errors earlier, in (58). Here are some more, with the correct forms in brackets:[7]

(71) a. I <u>have seen</u> him yesterday.   [saw]
     b. All my nineteenth-century ancestors <u>have lived</u> here.   [lived]
     c. I <u>know</u> him for five years.   [have known]
     d. I <u>live</u> in Amsterdam since I was a child.   [have lived]
     e. I <u>have</u> a lot of trouble with John at the moment.   [am having]
     f. This house <u>is belonging</u> to my father.   [belongs]

This area of grammar is a very difficult one in every language for the language learner. Either the other language marks the distinctions differently from the way the learner's language does, or it doesn't mark them at all. Boiling the problem down to its essentials, it is the "problem of aspect" described in the box below.

The Problem of Aspect

In English,
- when do we use the simple present: I wash
- when do we use the progressive: I am washing
- when do we use the simple past: I washed
- when do we use the perfect: I have washed
  and
- how do we express these differences in languages that do not have exactly the same distinctions?

---

7. Examples from Swan and Smith, 2006.

Consider an event that uses the verb *wash,* for example, washing a window. If you say what is happening at the moment that it occurs, you might say *I am washing the window.* This conveys the idea that the action is ongoing—it started in the past, is occurring now, and will continue for a while. If, however, you are speaking now of what happened in the past, you might say *I washed the window.* If there is a question of whether it is still an ongoing event, you might say *I have washed the window (already).* If you shift your perspective into the past and describe your ongoing action from your current position, you might say *I was washing the window.* But if you say *I wash the window,* this must mean that you do it habitually.

Given all of this, what must *I have been washing* mean? Why?

Aspect in English is expressed by combining *be* and the verb with *-ing* added to it (this is called the **progressive** form of the verb because it expresses progressive aspect), or by combining *have* and the verb with *-ed* or *-en* added to it (this is called **perfect** form because it expresses perfect aspect). All of the forms of *wash* in the present and past tense are summarized in Table 9.5.

● **TABLE 9.5**
The aspects of *wash*.

Form	Use
I wash	habitual
I am washing	ongoing now
I have washed	completed in the past, relevant to the present
I washed	completed in the past
I was washing	ongoing in the past
I have been washing	ongoing in the past extending into the present
I had been washing	ongoing in the past extending into a later time in the past

Other languages mark tense and aspect using form, but not all of them do it in the same way that English does. For example, Arabic does not mark tense and aspect by adding forms to the beginning or the end of the basic verb. Rather, it changes the pattern of vowels while holding the consonants constant:

(72) k**a**t**a**b 'write'   **a**kt**u**b 'write (completed)'

The basic form of the verb is *k-t-b,* and the various tenses and aspects (and other forms as well) are made by putting particular vowels in the slots before, after, or between consonants.

Exercise 5

The verb *go* is used in colloquial English to refer to speaking: "So she goes, 'what did you do with my notebook?'" Can all forms of *go* be used in this way, or are there restrictions? If so, what are they? Give examples.

Russian also marks aspect differently than English does. Verbs in Russian come in two varieties, called "imperfective" and "perfective."[8] The same meaning may be expressed by two verbs, an imperfective verb and a perfective verb, and the two verbs would be translated the same into English. For example, there are *pisat'/na-pisat'*, both meaning 'to write.' Typically, an imperfective verb in Russian is used in the present tense to express a habitual or ongoing action in the present, while the perfective is typically used to refer to future time when it is in the present tense. Used in the past tense, the imperfective indicates a habitual or ongoing action in the past, while the perfective is used in the past tense to indicate a completed action.[9] Here are the present and past tense forms of the Russian verb meaning 'to write':

(73) pisat   '(s/he) writes, is writing'
    napisat   '(s/he) will write'

(74) pisal   'wrote, was writing'
    napisal   'wrote (once)'

A few more pairs of verbs are listed in (75). You can see from these examples not only that the perfective is related to the imperfective in form, but also that the relationship is not a regular and predictable one.

(75) **Imperfective**	**Perfective**	
delat'	s-delat'	'to do'
prosit'	po-prosit'	'to ask'

Exercise 6

Why does the present tense form of the Russian perfective refer to future time?

---

8. The term "perfective" as used with respect to Russian verbs is not the same as the term "perfect" used above for English.

9. Boris Unbegaun, *Russian Grammar*, 1957, pp. 229–32.

davat'	dat'	'to give'
	Ja delaju	'I do, I am doing'
	Ja sdelaju	'I will do'

English Auxiliary Verbs

We said that English has two tenses, past and present. But we also said that all languages have ways to refer to all types of time, regardless of the forms that they use. Past tense is used to refer to events in the past, and present tense is used to refer to events in the present. But there are other times that we need to refer to, such as the future. We noted that English can use a variety of expressions for referring to the future, none of which are future **tense.** Here are some examples:

(76) I am seeing my friend tomorrow.
      I will see my friend tomorrow.
      I am going to see my friend tomorrow.
      I see my friend tomorrow.
      I am about to see my friend tomorrow.
      I am to see my friend tomorrow.

Let's focus on the first two examples, which are special.

The first example involves the progressive form. One key meaning expressed by the progressive is that of an event under way or in progress (which is why it's called the progressive). We can see that if meeting my friend tomorrow is in some sense already under way now, perhaps because it has already been arranged, then we can use a statement about the present to refer to an event in the future.

The progressive is complex in form; it is a **verbal cluster** made by adding -*ing* to the bare form of the verb and placing this verb after a form of the verb *be*. The -*ing* form is called the present (or progressive) participle. In this particular example, the verb *be* is inflected for present tense, so we get

(77) am going, is going, are going

The progressive can also be used with past tense to refer to an action that was under way in the past:

(78) was going, were going

A verbal cluster in English typically involves two verbs, although there can be more than two. As mentioned in the previous chapter, the last verb in the sequence is called the **main verb;** the other verb or verbs are **auxiliary verbs.** The main verb expresses the

Exercise 7: English Auxiliary Verbs

Suppose that you are teaching English to a group of non-native speakers. How would you explain the order in which the following words may appear in two-word sequences in a grammatical English sentence: *must, can, has, have, is, be, been, speak, speaks, speaking, spoke, spoken.* For example, *must* and *can* cannot appear together (*must can, *can must), but *must speak* is possible (and *speak must is* not). Rather than list all of the possible sequences, try to find the simplest way to explain what makes a two-word sequence grammatical.

---

basic scenario and, in particular, expresses the roles of the participants. The auxiliary verb expresses some aspect of this scenario that does not have to do specifically with the type of event or state of affairs involved.

Notice that there is a rule of English that says where the auxiliary verb goes in the sentence in relation to the main verb. We will come back to this in the next section.

English has a number of auxiliary verbs that express necessity, obligation, possibility, and time: *must, should, can, could, will, would.* These verbs are called modal verbs, or modals. They appear before the verb in a typical statement. In English, the position of the auxiliary verb is an indicator of the function of a sentence (that is, whether it is a statement, a question, or an imperative); other languages use other formal devices for expressing the function, as we see in the next section.

Expressing Sentence Function

THE MAJOR FUNCTIONS

The major functions of sentences are making statements, asking questions, and making requests or issuing orders, as shown in Table 9.6. The form of the sentence typically indicates what its function is.

There are particular rules that govern the form that a sentence must have in order to be understood as having a particular function. Here are some typical errors that German learners of English make that highlight how important these rules are:

(79) a. When begins the class?
      b. Bought you the textbook?
      c. Where goes this train?
      d. Speaks Ted English?
      e. Why said you that?

> ● **TABLE 9.6**
> **The major function of sentences.**
>
> | Form | Function |
> |---|---|
> | *Declarative*
Example: You are sitting down. | Makes a statement |
> | *Interrogative*
Example: Are you sitting down? | Asks a question. |
> | *Imperative*
Example: Sit down. | Makes a request or issues an order |

What is happening here? Compare these questions with the correct English forms:

(80) a.   When does the class begin?
      b.   Did you buy the textbook?
      c.   Where does this train go?
      d.   Does Ted speak English?
      e.   Why did you say that?

In each of the German sentences, the main verb, that is, the verb that expresses the relation or action, precedes the subject of the sentence:

(81) when   begins   the class
      1   2   3

But in the correct English sentence, the main verb follows the subject, and an auxiliary verb precedes the subject:

(82) when   does   the class   begin
      1   2   3   4

Notice also that *does/did* appears only if there is no other auxiliary verb:

(83) when   will   the class   begin
      1   2   3   4

We cannot say *When does the class will begin? or *When does will the class begin?

Rules such as these are challenges for learners of English. Correspondingly, English speakers learning a language such as German have to recognize that there is no *do* in German questions. The word orders in (79) reflect the normal order of German, as illustrated in (84).

(84) a. Wenn   beginnt   die Klasse?
        when   begins   the class
        'When does the class begin?'

      b. Kauftest   du   das Lehrbuch?
        bought   you   the textbook
        'Did you buy the textbook?'

QUESTIONS

There are two types of questions: yes-no or YN-questions, e.g. *Are you hungry?*, and wh-questions. The competent speaker of English knows implicitly how these functions are expressed in English. Before going on, try Exercise 8 at the bottom of the page to see if you can state explicitly what the basic differences in form are between these three types of sentences (we have already discussed some of these differences).

As we have seen, a statement in English has the following basic form: First, there is a phrase that (usually) refers to something, which is typically called the subject of the sentence. It is followed by one or more verbs, like *can, am, is, drinks, drank*, and *drinking*. One of these verbs expresses some kind of relationship or property involving the subject (like *drinks*) and perhaps other things, like time or necessity. The verb that expresses this relationship may be followed by other things, depending on the verb and the meaning to be expressed. Hence we may have the following:

(85) I can drink that cup of coffee.
      I am drinking.

Exercise 8: English Auxiliary Verbs

Suppose you are trying to explain to someone who is learning English how to make statements, questions, and imperatives. Fill in the blank for each of the following:
1. In order to form a statement, _____.
2. In order to form a yes-no question, _____.
3. In order to form an imperative, _____.
Hint: Start with the statement, and describe the question and imperative in terms of it. (Your explanation will probably take up more space than the blanks do here.)

She is drinking quickly.
A fish drinks water in the lake.
We drank it all.

In order to keep track of our observations about what we know about English sentences, we introduce the following chart. What appears between parentheses indicates material that is possible but not necessary in a sentence of this type.

Form of an English statement:

FUNCTION	ENGLISH FORM
Statement	Subject—(Auxiliary Verb)—Main Verb—(Other Stuff)

Now we see that an English question has a form that distinguishes it from the corresponding statement. While the auxiliary verb follows the subject in the statement, it precedes the subject in the question, as we saw in our discussion of errors in questions. So we have the questions in (86) which correspond to the statements in (85). Notice again that if the statement does not have an auxiliary verb, the corresponding question has the auxiliary verb *do/does/did*.

(86) Can I drink that cup of coffee?
      Am I drinking?
      Is she drinking quickly?
      Does a fish drink water in the lake?
      Did we drink it all?

So let's add questions to the chart:.

Forms of English statements and questions:

FUNCTION	ENGLISH FORM
Statement	Subject—(Auxiliary Verb)—Main Verb—(Other Stuff)
YN-Question	Auxiliary Verb—Subject—Main Verb—(Other Stuff)

Now, as we have said, other languages must express the same functions, but they may use different forms. We have already looked at German. Here are some examples from Chinese:

(87) Ni   shuo Yingyu.
      you speak English
      'You speak English.'

Ni   shuo-bu-shuo   Yingyu?
you speak-not-speak English
'Do you speak English?'

Ni hui shuo Yingyu.
you can speak English
'You can speak English.'

Ni hui-bu-hui shuo Yingyu?
you can-not-can speak English
'Can you speak English?'

For comparison, here are some YN-questions from Japanese; they are very different in form from those in English, German, and Chinese:

(88) Eigo   o   hanashi-masu.
English OBJ speak-POLITE
'You speak English.'

Eigo   o   hanashi-masu-ka?
English OBJ speak-POLITE-QUESTION
'Do you speak English?'

Eigo   o   hanas-e-masu.
English OBJ speak-can-POLITE
'You can speak English.'

Eigo   o   hanas-e-masu-ka?
English OBJ speak-can-POLITE-QUESTION
'Can you speak English?'

We notice four main characteristics of these Japanese sentences:

1. The subject is missing. In Japanese, the subject and other things that are under discussion do not have to be mentioned if they are known from the conversation or the context. Since the subject is 'you,' it is known from the context.
2. The verb always comes at the end of the sentence.
3. The auxiliary verb and the main verb are not separate verbs; they form a single complex verb.
4. The YN-question is formed by adding -*ka* to the verb.

The following chart summarizes:

Basic Japanese sentence structure:

FUNCTION	JAPANESE FORM
Statement	(Subject)—(Other Stuff)—(Complex) Verb
YN-Question	(Subject)—(Other Stuff)—(Complex) Verb—ka

WH-QUESTIONS

Finally, there are questions that ask about the identity of a participant in a relation or about such things as the manner, reason, time, or place. For example, suppose there used to be some ice cream in the freezer, and now there is an empty ice cream container on the kitchen table. We may be pretty certain that someone ate the ice cream. And "someone ate the ice cream" is the content of a sentence that we can express. But we have a particular way of phrasing a question in English to determine the identity of the person who ate the ice cream:

(89) Who ate the ice cream?

This type of question (as mentioned previously) is called a **wh-question,** because it is formed with question words that all begin with *wh-* (*how* is an exception).

Every language has a means for eliciting the specific content of a relation whose general outlines are known (or suspected). That is, every language has wh-questions. But the form of a wh-question varies from language to language. The major variable is whether the wh-word or wh-phrase is in the initial position in the sentence or whether it remains in place.

Here, for comparison, are some wh-questions from other languages with their English translations. Note where the wh-phrases appear:

(90) *Chinese:*
　　　hufei mai-le　　shenme (ne).
　　　Hufei buy-PERF　what　　PRT
　　　'What did Hufei buy?'

　　　Lisi weishenme cizhi?
　　　Lisi why　　　resign
　　　'Why did Lisi resign?'

　　　Ni　renwei Lisi weishenme cizhi?
　　　you think　Lisi why　　　resign

Exercise 9

Give an explicit statement of the rule for forming wh-questions in English.

'Why do you think Lisi resigned?'
(= 'What is the reason why Lisi resigned?')

(91) *French:*
Jean a   acheté quoi?
John has bought what
'What has John bought?'

Quel livre John a-t-il acheté?
which book John has-he bought
'Which book did John buy'?

(92) *Korean:*
Chelswu-ka   mues-ul   po-ass-ni?
Chelswu-NOM what-ACC see-PAST-Q
'What did Chelswu see?'

(93) *Japanese:*
John ga   nani o   kaimasita-ka?
John SUBJ what OBJ bought-POLITE Q
'What did John buy?'

In French, there are two ways to make wh-questions, including one similar to English in that the wh-phrase moves to the front of the sentence. In the other languages illustrated, the wh-phrase does not move to the front of the sentence.

IMPERATIVES

The last basic sentence form is the imperative, which has the function of making a request or giving an order. Before going on, try to say explicitly what the general form of the English imperative is—just keep in mind that there are no auxiliary verbs in the imperative, except *do* in the negative.

The imperative in many other languages is similar in form to that of English. Here are a few more examples of imperatives from other languages. For each one, try to identify the particular aspect of form that indicates that it is an imperative:

(94) *French:*

Vous me   donnez la   bière.
you   to-me give   the beer
'You give me the beer.'

Donnez-moi la   bière.
give-me   the beer
'Give me the beer.'

Vous lisez le   livre.
you   read the book

Lisez   le   livre.
read   the book

(95) *Polish:*

pytać   pytam   pytasz   pyta
'to ask'   'I-ask'   'you-ask'   'he-asks'
Pytaj!
'Ask!'

(96) *German:*

Sie   rauchen nicht.
you (polite)   smoke not
'You don't smoke.'

Rauchen Sie   nicht!
smoke you (polite)   not
                     'Don't smoke.'

Du   rauchst nicht.
you (familiar)   smoke not
'You don't smoke.'

Rauch   nicht!
smoke   not
'Don't smoke.'

Summary

In this chapter we looked at the content of a sentence, in particular, the relationships that the sentence expresses and the properties that are attributed to participants. We discussed how roles such as theme, agent, and goal can be expressed by case, particles, word order, or verbal agreement in different languages. Then we looked at how the form of a verb plays a role in determining the content and function of the sentence. We compared how this is done in English with how it is done in other languages. Verbs in some languages use inflection to mark distinctions of time and aspect. The verb is also typically involved in marking whether a sentence is a statement, an imperative, or a question.

● **TABLE 9.7**

Forms of major English sentence functions.

Function	English Form
Statement	Subject—(Auxiliary Verb)—Main Verb—(Other Stuff)
YN-Question	Auxiliary Verb—Subject—Main Verb—(Other Stuff)
Imperative	Main Verb—(Other Stuff)

Additional Exercises

1. Examples (1)–(20) in the text illustrate some typical errors that non-native speakers of English make in English. We have already discussed (1) and (8). For the remaining errors, say what the error consists of (that is, what the speaker did wrong), how to correct the error, and why you think the error occurred. In some cases, the error may show something about the speaker's language, while in other cases, the speaker may be misapplying a rule of English. Try to describe what aspect of English is being modified by the non-native speaker and what the differences are in the way that English and the other language carry out the same function. (You can say what the grammatical English variant would be, but also try to describe what the difference is in a **general** way.)

2. Choose a language other than English that you are familiar with. How is the relation expressed by the English word *afraid* expressed in this language? Does the language designate who is afraid and what she is afraid of in the same way as English?

3. Choose a language other than English that you are familiar with. How is the relation expressed by the English word *likes* expressed in this language? Does the language designate who does the liking and what that person likes in the same way as English?

4. Choose a language other than English that you are familiar with. How are the roles expressed by the arguments of words such as *give, tell, sell, send* in English designated in this language? Compare this with how English designates these arguments.

5. One of the most difficult challenges in any language is to convey the relationship between the time of speaking and the time of an event. Choose a language other than English that you are familiar with. How does this language express the future with respect to the time of speaking? Does it systematically distinguish the near future and the more distant future using grammatical form? Does English make this distinction, and if so, how?

6. Choose a language other than English that you are familiar with. As precisely as you can, describe how to make YN-questions in this language.

7. Choose a language other than English that you are familiar with. As precisely as you can, describe how to make wh-questions in this language. For example: Where does the wh-phrase go? Are there special orderings of other words in the sentence? What happens when a prepositional phrase is being questioned? What is the relationship between the form of a wh-question and the form of a YN-question in this language? Contrast how this language forms questions with how English forms questions.

8. Choose a language other than English that you are familiar with. As precisely as you can, describe how to form imperatives in this language. Compare with how imperatives are formed in English.

References

Falk, Y. N. Ditransitive constructions. Online: http://pluto.mscc.huji.ac.il/~msyfalk/ Typology/Ditransitives.pdf.

Swan, Michael, and Smith, Bernard. (2001). *Learner English*. Cambridge: Cambridge University Press.

Unbegaun, Boris. (1957). *Russian grammar*. Oxford: The Clarendon Press. 229–32.

III: Acting like a Native Speaker

The Link between Language and Culture

Introduction

*I*n the preceding chapters, we considered a number of factors that come into play in determining how a sentence of a language is understood. As we saw, the form of a sentence, along with the context in which it is spoken, provides a sentence with its literal and implied meaning. In this final section, we will look at another type of meaning that is conveyed by a sentence: **social meaning.** Acquiring the ability to understand the social meaning of an utterance is an important part of learning a new language.

Language is inherently social: we use it to interact with other people. It is also an important part of how we establish and reinforce social relations and generally define ourselves in a culture. In other words, language is more than just a way to communicate; it is a way of defining social relationships and projecting our social identity. As a result, what we say and how we say it conveys a great deal of information about our social status, gender, age, relationship to the listener, formality of the situation, and so on. This type of information can be revealed in a number of ways, such as by the pronunciation of particular words. Hearing someone pronounce the word *car* as [kɑ] rather than [kɑɹ], for example, may be a cue to the listener that the person grew up in the Boston area. The choice of grammatical construction that an individual uses can also reveal social meaning, as in the use of *May I have a coffee?* as opposed to *Give me a coffee!* or *Gimme a cup of coffee!* in making a request. Depending on the situation, the use of the command/request form instead of the interrogative form can reflect a person's educational level, politeness, emotional state, or degree of familiarity with the recipient of the command/request.

Given the interweaving of language and culture, social meaning in language can also give us information about a society's traditions, norms, and values, and therefore it provides a window into the culture of the people who speak the language. This means that learning a foreign language means more than learning new sounds, words, and grammar. It also means learning a new culture, including how social meaning is expressed in that culture. The better you understand the culture of the language you are learning, the better you will be able to interact successfully with native speakers. This knowledge will also equip you with greater control over your language usage and provide you with the ability to act like a native speaker of your new language.

In Section III, we look at some of the ways that social meaning is expressed in language. As we do this, it is important to keep in mind that the particular linguistic means by which social meaning is expressed in any language is **arbitrary.** We will see, for example, that politeness can be conveyed in a number of different ways. In some languages, words carry grammatical markers to denote differing degrees of politeness. Politeness can also be conveyed though the choice of sentence type, as in our example above: *May I have a coffee?* vs. *Give me a coffee!* Some languages may use both of these mechanisms, others may use only one, while still others may use an entirely different means of expressing politeness. The important points to remember, then, are that (a) the extent to which language is used to express social meaning depends on the language in question; and (b) the particular aspect of language that is used to convey social meaning is arbitrary.

The notion of arbitrariness in language is not, of course, limited to the expression of social meaning. In our discussion of the combinations of sounds, for example, we saw that languages can differ in the number and types of sounds that can combine to form words. It is impossible to predict that language X will use one specific set of sounds, while language Y will use another. We also saw that the link between words and properties such as grammatical gender can be arbitrary, given that the word that refers to a particular type of thing can be masculine, feminine, or neuter, depending on the language.

A particularly vivid illustration of the notion of arbitrariness can be seen by comparing the words used in languages to describe the sounds that animals make. When it comes to pigs, for instance, most native speakers of English would agree that a pig says *oink*. Yet, as shown in Figure 10.1, in Estonian, a pig says *rui rui,* in Mandarin *hulu hulu,* in Croatian *ruk ruk,* in French *groin groin,* in Japanese *buu buu,* in Korean *kkool kkool,* and in German *grunz grunz.* The fact that the sounds pigs make are described differently across languages is not, of course, an indication that pigs speak different languages or even make different sounds in different parts of the world. Rather, it makes more sense to assume that the different words that people give to the sounds of animals are simply arbitrary labels determined by the speakers of a culture, constrained by the possible sound combinations in the language. The observation that animals "speak" differently around the world is, then, a simple illustration of how similar ideas are expressed in different ways across cultures.

In Section III, we explore the link between language and culture, beginning in this chapter with a look at the place of culture in language more generally. We consider some

Figure 10.1

of the roles that language plays in social interaction, including how these roles can differ from one culture to another. In Chapters 11 and 12, we focus on two topics as a means of illustrating cultural differences in the expression of social meaning: politeness and swearing.

Language and Culture

As noted above, language is necessarily social, given its important functions in social interactions. We use language to influence the thoughts and actions of others, to request and obtain information, and to share our feelings. In general, we use language to communicate with others, and since communication is a social activity, language is also social. The fact that social structure can differ from culture to culture and from language to language makes learning a new language both fascinating and challenging.

Consider how people answer the phone, for example. American English speakers might respond with "Hello," or in a business setting, a person might simply say her name, e.g. "Julia Roberts here." Dutch speakers, by contrast, commonly respond with

Exercise 1: Using Language in Different Contexts

It is not necessary to compare two different languages in order to see that language and culture are closely linked—it is apparent from the way we use different language varieties in different social settings.

- Consider how you would (or at least should) ask each of the following people to repeat something that you did not understand: your kid brother or sister, your father or mother, your closest buddy, the instructor in a class, and an armed law enforcement officer at a sobriety check point.

med 'with,' e.g. "*med* Julia Roberts." While acceptable in The Netherlands, putting *with* before your name when answering the phone in American culture would seem very strange.

In this instance we see that a simple task such as answering the phone is accomplished in different ways in American and Dutch cultures. Notice that for this illustration we have defined culture in terms of the specific languages that the individuals speak. Yet this is not the only or perhaps the best way to define this concept.

A **culture** can be defined more generally as a group of individuals with shared attitudes about what are acceptable and unacceptable ways of performing social tasks and accomplishing social goals. Our observation that people in the United States and The Netherlands answer the phone differently indicates that there are different shared attitudes, or norms, involved in accomplishing this type of social task in each culture. In American culture, the norm is to say "Hello," while in Dutch culture, the norm is to say 'with' followed by your name. Each culture has its own set of norms, and these norms may overlap to varying degrees with other cultures. Some social norms are encoded as laws, such as which side of the street to drive on. Other norms are unwritten yet nonetheless present in the culture. Some examples of unwritten social norms of North American culture refer to the direction to stand in an elevator (facing the door), the use of cell phones in theaters (frowned upon), and the way to greet an acquaintance (extend your right hand to shake). In France, the norm is for people to greet with a kiss on each cheek, while in The Netherlands, people kiss three times (right cheek—left cheek—right cheek). So even if we consider only how people greet each other, France, The Netherlands, and North America can be defined as different cultures.

Given that language is a social phenomenon, it should not be surprising that **language norms** also exist—that is, shared attitudes about what language form to use in a particular situation. Language norms can cover topics such as what form of address to use in a particular context (for example, formal vs. informal), how politeness is expressed, what topics are considered taboo, how many people may talk at the same time in a conversation, how much you should talk during your turn in a conversation, how and when to end a conversation, and so on. Even though language norms may be unwritten, they constitute an integral part of the language and, consequently, are important for speakers to know if they want to be able to function as accepted members of the culture.

This poses an interesting challenge to the language learner: given that language norms are generally unstated and unwritten, how can a non-native speaker of a language learn what the norms of the culture are? Here are three approaches to consider. As you will see, one is considerably more effective than the others.

Perhaps the simplest way to learn about a language norm is to ask people explicitly. For example, if you are learning a language that has different forms of address for different situations, you might describe a particular scenario to a native speaker and ask her what would be the most appropriate form of address to use for that situation. Easy, right? In this particular case, perhaps, but it is probably not difficult to imagine the types of problems associated with this approach. For example, some norms may deal with

Exercise 2: Hello, Good-bye

- Investigate the different expressions that are used by native speakers of the language that you are studying:

  a. to greet someone
  b. to say goodbye.

  You can do this by observing native speakers interacting in person, in a film, or on TV. Or, if you are not living in a place where the new language is spoken, you can also ask your language instructor, watch films, look on the Internet, and so on.

- Each time you observe someone using an expression to greet or leave, jot it down in a notebook. Next to it include details such as: Who used the expression? How old was the person? What sex is the person? In what context was the expression uttered?

- As you gather more and more examples, review your notes to see if patterns are emerging. For example, is one expression used more commonly by young people, by women, or at school?

- What insights do your observations give you concerning your own use of the expressions for greeting and saying good-bye?

---

sensitive or potentially embarrassing topics, and so actually asking about them may be violating a norm in and of itself! Also, asking explicitly about a norm has a tendency to elicit a description of a stereotype rather than of normal behavior. For example, if a foreign student were to ask a native English speaker about the polite way to greet someone in English, the student might be told to shake the right hand of the person and say "Hello, nice to meet you." However, were the foreign student to visit an American college campus, he might be surprised to see the stereotypical greeting replaced by a polite, though much less formal, greeting consisting of a nod of the head and the simple expression "Hey!"

An alternative means of learning whether or not something is a norm is to violate it and see what happens. The reaction of people around you will probably be a fairly good indication of whether or not the norm exists. Of course, the major drawback of violating a potential norm is that it may trigger discomfort, embarrassment, or any number of other negative reactions.

Probably the most effective way of learning about language norms, and norms in general, is simply to observe behavior. If you are visiting a foreign country, watch people when they greet each other. What do they say? How do they say it? Do adults greet each other the same way they greet children? Do women behave differently from men? Do older people behave differently from younger people? In short, become a keen observer of human behavior, and you will learn, just as every native speaker of the language you are learning has, what form of language to use in a particular situation.

Language Varieties

In discussing language and culture, it is important to emphasize that a language need **not** define a single culture. Any one language can have many cultural groups associated with it. It may also be the case that the members of each of these cultures speak a different **variety** of the same language.

The term **language variety** refers to the language spoken by a group of people who belong to a particular social or cultural group, who communicate with other members of the community, and who share common views about linguistic norms. A "variety" of language is simply a neutral term that can include more precise classifications like "language" and "dialect." Given this, we can say that **different languages,** such as English, Italian, French, and Swahili, are also different language varieties.

A **single language** is also made up of many different varieties. English includes, among many others, British English, Cockney English, Canadian English, and Southern American English. Notice that the term "language variety" can characterize the broad distinction between British English and American English, for example. Or the distinctions can be further refined in order to refer to smaller varieties of language such as Bostonian English, New York English, Southern American English, and Valley Girl English.

Importantly, the observation that English has many different varieties is not a property just of English. All languages have multiple varieties. The French language includes Parisian French, Québécois French, and Moroccan French, among many others. In Spanish we can speak of, for example, Castilian Spanish, Puerto Rican Spanish, Chicano Spanish, and Florida/Cuban Spanish, while in Arabic we find Palestinian Arabic, Jordanian Arabic, Moroccan Arabic, and so on.

Different varieties of the same language are generally distinguished by pronunciation differences and the use of different words (e.g. *soda* vs. *pop, sack* vs. *bag*) or different grammatical structures (e.g. *he likes himself* vs. *he likes hisself*) to express the same idea. As stated in the definition of language variety above, however, speakers of different language varieties may also share different norms about language usage.

Consider the norms surrounding the use of minimal responses by male and female speakers of American English (Coates 1998). The term "minimal response" refers to communication devices such as a nod or a small comment like "yes" or "mhm." A person listening to someone speak might insert a minimal response at various points in the conversation.

Research suggests that minimal responses can have different meanings for women and men in American culture. For women, inserting a minimal response in the conversation can be interpreted as "I'm listening to you, please continue." For many men, however, the meaning tends to be stronger: "I agree with what you are saying" or at least "I follow the argument so far." The reason women use more minimal responses in conversation than men may be that women are listening more often than men are agreeing.

Yet, these different language norms can lead to miscommunication and misunderstandings. For example, a man receiving repeated nods from a woman may interpret this as meaning that the woman agrees with everything he says; she does not have opinions of her own. A woman who is getting only occasional nods from a man may interpret this as saying that the man is not listening to her, not that he does not always agree. These different interpretations of minimal responses may explain two common complaints of men and women. The first comes from men who think that women are always agreeing with them and then conclude that it is impossible to tell what a woman really thinks. The second complaint comes from women who get upset with men who never seem to be listening.

One explanation for these differences is based on the view that there are **cultural differences** between men and women (Maltz and Borker 1982). In this view, American men and women are seen as coming from different subcultures. In these subcultures, there are different norms concerning how friendly conversation is to be interpreted. There are also different rules for engaging in conversation and different rules for interpreting conversation. In other words, men and women have learned to do different things with words in a conversation, which at times can lead to miscommunication (Tannen 1990).

Each of these examples shows that how language is used in a community depends on the accepted norms or rules of that specific culture. And, as pointed out earlier, in order to become a successful language learner, it is important to learn more than the sounds, words, and grammar of a language. Understanding the language norms of the community, including how culture is expressed through the language, will help you become a better language learner and, as a result, help you to both think and behave more successfully like a native speaker.

Language Attitudes

LANGUAGE AS A REFLECTION OF SOCIAL IDENTITY

Since language is so closely linked to culture, the language variety that a person speaks also brings with it a lot of information about that person's culture, simply by association. In this sense, language is a sign of social identity; it says (rightly or wrongly) who you are. A native speaker of American English can usually determine, on the basis of listening to another speaker of English, where he is from, at least in broad terms (for example, Britain, Southern U.S., Texas, Midwest, Canada), his level of education, and his social class.

The ability of speakers to make judgments about other speakers on the basis of their speech occurs in all cultures and with all languages. Whether or not these are actual characteristics of the person speaking is another issue. They may very well be stereotypes that we have learned to associate with a particular culture. Every language variety carries with it a great deal of social meaning which generally reflects stereotypes about the group of people who usually speak the variety.

In studies of French varieties, for instance, Parisian French is generally viewed more favorably than other varieties, particularly with respect to social status. Stereotypes are also reflected in the perception of personality traits of the speakers of these varieties. In fact, studies showed that French Canadians judged a speaker of French Canadian to be more intelligent and better educated when she spoke with a Parisian accent than when she spoke with her usual French Canadian accent. Of course, the subjects in the study did not know that the same person was speaking both varieties.

A key point to remember is that the prestige and the perceived "beauty" of a language variety is determined by the cultural context in which the variety is spoken. In general, a standard variety is judged to be more prestigious and more aesthetically pleasing than non-standard varieties of the same language. Speakers of the standard variety are typically looked upon as more intelligent, as having more self-confidence, and as speaking better. Speakers of non-standard varieties are judged to be speaking a variety of language that is inferior to the standard.

It is important to emphasize that these are just stereotypes. <u>No variety is inherently better than any another.</u> All varieties are systematic and rule-governed. That is, they all have rules similar to those in English, French, Italian, Japanese, and every other language. We can see this clearly by comparing two varieties of English. Consider the following formations of reflexive pronouns in standard American English and in Appalachian English, a non-standard variety:[1]

Standard English	Appalachian English
I like myself	I like myself
you like yourself	you like yourself
he likes himself	he likes hisself
she likes herself	she likes herself
we like ourselves	we like ourselves
you like yourselves	you like yourselves
they like themselves	they like theirselves

We can describe the rules for making reflexives in the two varieties as follows:

Standard:

- 1st- and 2nd-person singular: add the reflexive suffix *-self* to **possessive** pronouns

  my + self, your + self

- 1st- and 2nd-person plural: add the reflexive suffix *-selves* to **possessive** pronouns

  our + selves, your + selves

- 3rd-person singular: add the reflexive suffix *-self* to **object** pronouns

---

1. Examples from Anouschka Bergmann, Kathleen Currie Hall, and Sharon Ross (Department of Linguistics, The Ohio State University), *Language Files*, 10th ed. (The Ohio State University Press, 2007), p. 412.

him + self, her + self

- 3rd-person plural: add the reflexive suffix -*selves* to **object** pronouns

them + selves

Non-standard:
- 1st-, 2nd-, and 3rd-person singular: add the reflexive suffix -*self* to **possessive** pronouns

my + self, your + self, her + self, his + self

- 1st-, 2nd-, and 3rd-person plural: add the reflexive suffix -*selves* to **possessive** pronouns

our + selves, their + selves

Exercise 3: Standard and Non-Standard Varieties of Language

Take this opportunity to think about your own attitudes concerning varieties of English or other languages that you know well. Here is a simple exercise to help you do this.

- Start by writing down the names of different varieties of English, beginning with the one spoken by you and your family, for example, standard American English, African American English, Bostonian English, Cockney English, Jamaican English, Texan English, or Queen Elizabeth's English.
- Next to each variety, jot down words that come to mind to describe them. Do not read the rest of the exercise until you have finished this part.

Now, below your descriptions make two scales. The first corresponds to the **prestige** associated with a given variety, with low prestige at one end and high prestige at the other end. Prestige-related adjectives describing the speakers include intelligent, sophisticated, aloof, stuffy, and so on. The second scale represents traits relating to your sense of **solidarity** with the variety and its speakers. Solidarity-related terms include friendly, kind, generous, fun-loving, down-to-earth, and so on. Locate high solidarity at one end of the scale and low solidarity at the other end.

- Based on your descriptions, situate the varieties along the two scales. Now comes the hard part: Try to think objectively about why you perceived some varieties as more or less prestigious than others. Why are some associated with positive feelings of solidarity while others are not?

Typically, descriptions correspond not to the language itself but rather to the people who speak these varieties and the experiences that we or others have had with them and their culture. Remember, however, that there is nothing inherently better about some varieties as opposed to others. Any negative or positive feelings that you associate with a variety is a learned reaction.

By comparing the two sets of rules for standard and Appalachian English, you should see that the latter variety is not any less systematic than the standard one. In fact, we could say that it is <u>more</u> systematic since it has generalized the formation of the reflexive to all possessive pronouns. As a result, for the non-standard variety there is simply one rule for the singular and one rule for the plural. On the other hand, to make reflexive pronouns in the standard variety, in some persons the suffix *-self*/*-selves* is added to the object pronoun, while in other persons it is added to the possessive pronoun. This means that two different rules are needed for the singular, and two are needed for the plural.

The point of this example is simply to emphasize that how we perceive varieties of language is tied to our perception of the culture in question. It has nothing to do with any inherent quality of the structure of the language.

Yet, if non-standard varieties are perceived so negatively, you might be wondering why everyone doesn't speak the standard variety. There are several reasons for this. First of all, we learn the language that we are exposed to as children, and the longer we are exposed to it, the more ingrained it becomes (see Chapter 1). Second, the variety of language that we use with family members and close friends and in informal situations generally triggers feelings of solidarity, group loyalty, appreciation, and attraction. If you grew up speaking a non-standard variety, you probably have the feelings noted above toward that variety, even if it may be perceived as less prestigious than the standard language. On the other hand, studies have shown that people tend to evaluate someone who speaks a non-standard variety more positively than a standard-variety speaker in terms of personality traits like friendliness and likeability.

WHAT MAKES A LANGUAGE BE PERCEIVED AS MORE PRESTIGIOUS?

We know that all languages have different varieties: both standard and possibly many non-standard varieties. We also know that the standard variety is generally associated with prestige. But what makes a language be perceived as prestigious? Some typical but **incorrect** answers given to this question are the following:

- The standard variety obeys all of the rules of grammar, while the non-standard varieties lack certain rules. [This is <u>not</u> the correct answer!]
- The standard variety does not use slang, while the non-standard varieties use a lot of slang. [This is <u>not</u> the correct answer!]
- The standard variety is more logical than the non-standard varieties. [This is <u>not</u> the correct answer!]

The **correct** answer for why a language is perceived as prestigious is the following:

- The standard variety happens to be the variety spoken by people with greater power, wealth, or education, either now or in the past.

The relative prestige of a language is a historical accident. We are taught to view one variety as better than another. Think about British English, for example. Why do you think the standard variety (referred to as Received Pronunciation, or RP) is the prestige variety? It is because that is the variety spoken by those holding power: political power, social power, or economic power. It is no coincidence that the Queen of England speaks RP. If the seat of power had been established in Glasgow, Dublin, Manchester, or Liverpool, the prestige variety today would certainly correspond to the variety spoken in one of those areas.

Just as we develop attitudes about varieties of our own language, we do the same with foreign languages. In a small study conducted by the authors of this book over several years, American college students were asked to jot down what came to mind when they thought of the following languages: French, Russian, Italian, Arabic, German, and Maltese. Before reading further, write down what comes to your mind about each of these languages, and then compare what you wrote with what the students in the experiment wrote.

The results were as follows:

- Students generally used more positive terms to describe French and Italian, for example, romantic, smooth sounding, harmonious.
- Students generally used more negative adjectives for Arabic, Russian, and German, for example, coarse, guttural, throaty, harsh.
- Students were not able to say anything about Maltese.

The perceptions of the first four languages probably reflect stereotypes that the students had acquired about these languages. French and Italian are commonly considered to be the languages of "romance" in the movies. Thinking of these languages may conjure up images of the Eiffel Tower, outdoor cafés, or a gondola on a canal. French, the language of love!

Why are negative adjectives associated with German, Russian, and Arabic? Again, these most likely reflect stereotypes that the students have learned. Some views may have derived from the media which presented speakers of these languages in a negative light. Think, for example, about how many shows you have seen where the villain spoke with a Russian, German, or Arabic accent.

The results of this study showed that the degree to which each language was described as positive or negative reflected stereotypes about some aspects of the past or present **culture** associated with the language. The expressed views did not reflect the inherent beauty or lack thereof of the language. To underscore this point, it is interesting to note that some of the properties that were viewed negatively for one language were considered in a positive light for others.

For example, some respondents described Arabic using negative-sounding terms such as coarse or guttural. This description may have been used because most Arabic languages have sounds made in the back of the mouth, like the pharyngeal [ʕ] and the uvular [q]. But English also has sounds made in the back of the mouth, such as the velar [k] which is quite similar to [q], as discussed in Chapter 3. Recall also that the French fricative 'r,' as in *rouge* 'red,' has the same place of articulation as the stop [q]. How can similar sounds lead to one language sounding coarse but another one sounding romantic?

What about Maltese? Maltese is an interesting language because the verb system and many of its sounds come from Arabic, but many of the words and other structures are related to Italian. Maltese, then, poses a serious problem for those who believe that one's perception of a language is tied to its inherent beauty or ugliness. If Maltese shares properties with both Arabic and Italian, does that make it inherently beautiful or ugly? This is clearly a problematic approach to viewing language. What we do know is that our attitudes toward a language variety, whether it be English or another language, are arbitrary and determined by the culture(s) that we are exposed to.

RELATION TO LANGUAGE LEARNING

At this point you might be wondering why it is important to know about different varieties of language when you are learning a new language. There are several reasons. The first relates to the fact that the language variety taught in the classroom will almost certainly be the standard prestige variety. However, if you go to the country where the language is spoken, you may find that the variety used in the region you are visiting is not the standard variety. Before going abroad, then, you may want to educate yourself about the variety of language spoken in the particular region you are visiting and familiarize yourself with any cultural differences that may exist.

You do not have to go very far to encounter this situation. Suppose you have been studying French at an American university and then decide to take a trip to Quebec City

Exercise 4: Linguistic Heritage

- What differences in the use of language have you noticed among the students in your classes that you would say correspond to their linguistic heritage, that is, the language of their parents or grandparents?
- How do people from different linguistic communities refer differently to each of the following:
  a. other people of the same and the opposite sex
  b. common everyday things, such as cars and foods
  c. themselves
  d. you
  e. their community
  f. the university

in Canada to practice your French. It will probably be the case that the French that you have been exposed to in the classroom only approximates what you will hear in Quebec. Not only will it sound unfamiliar, but the words and phrases that you have learned to express a particular idea may be different. Knowing that differences exist can help you prepare and get the most out of your experiences.

Another area where knowing about different varieties of language can come in handy relates to buying a dictionary. There are often different dictionaries for different varieties of a given language, so it is a good idea to find out what language variety you are studying. You will also want to keep in mind that bilingual dictionaries differ with respect to the variety of English being used. For example, a Mandarin/English dictionary that uses British English may be less helpful to you than one based on American English.

Finally, and perhaps most importantly, being sensitive to cultural differences between speakers of different language varieties will make you a better person. Really! Knowing that attitudes toward language varieties are learned and arbitrary will help you appreciate each variety for what it really is: a fascinating, complex, human phenomenon.

CULTURE IN LANGUAGE

We turn now to some of the specific ways in which culture is manifested in communicating. There are many areas where we are likely to find differences across languages:

- how men and women use language differently,
- how people use gestures,
- how people express formality or politeness in speech, and
- how people swear at and insult each other.

We introduced the first, how men and women use language differently, earlier in this chapter in the discussion of minimal responses. How people use gestures differently across cultures is outlined just below. The remaining topics make up the focus of chapters 11 and 12.

Gesture

GESTURE IN COMMUNICATION

We conclude this chapter on language and culture with some observations about the use of gesture in communication. Strictly speaking, gesture is not language. However, it is used at the same time as language is used in the course of communication. Moreover, just as we have to know something about the culture in order to use a language correctly in communication, it is useful to know something about the appropriate use of gestures.

● **TABLE 10.1**

Expressing meaning through gestures in English.

Idea	Gesture
1. Surprise	Eyes wide open, raised eyebrows
2. Ambivalence, indecision	Shoulder shrug
3. Gesturing to someone to come	Arm outstretched, hand waving back and forth toward person being beckoned
4. An angry mother beckoning to her child	Index finger curling toward herself
5. Hunger	Holding or rubbing one's stomach
6. Craziness	Index finger circling around ear Index finger tapping one's temple
7. Perfect, it's ok.	Thumb and index finger making a circle.

Gesture is a huge part of communicating. Some researchers say that more than 50% of communication is done non-verbally. Gesture is especially important if you are trying to communicate in a culture where there is a language barrier for you; when you can't find the words to say what you want to say, body language becomes even more important.

Gesture is used to communicate in all cultures, although it is used much more extensively in some cultures than in others. Brazilians and Italians, for example, seem to use gestures more than Americans do. But even in American English culture, gesture is important.

Before considering other languages, we begin by thinking about our own use of gestures. As shown in Table 10.1, without uttering a word, we can express ideas using gesture in English.

An interesting and very important part about learning to communicate in a different culture is that some of the same gestures that we use in our culture have very different meanings in others. The gesture that an angry mother might use toward her child is considered very rude in some Asian cultures. In some parts of Korea, for example, it is used only with animals.

But how do you learn the body language of a different culture? You can start by studying the gestures of your instructor or, if you are visiting the culture, by studying the people around you. There are also books available, such as Roger Axtell's *Gestures: The Do's and Taboos of Body Language around the World*. The Internet is also a rich resource. In the meantime, the important thing to remember is to be aware of the gestures that you use; do <u>not</u> assume that they mean the same thing in all cultures.

A simple example showing how gestures differ across cultures relates to greetings. When you meet someone for the first time in the United States, you probably shake the person's hand, especially if the situation is formal. If it is informal, you might just give an upward nod of the head (a sign of acknowledgment) or perhaps raise your hand and give a small wave. What about in other cultures?

In Brazil, a handshake is quite common as well, although it is often accompanied by a touch on the elbow or forearm or a pat on the back. More so than in the United States, people in Brazil shake hands when departing as well as arriving.

Kissing is also a common way to greet people in many countries, as was noted earlier. In France, people kiss on both cheeks when they meet. They also kiss on both cheeks to say goodbye. In Greece, friends also greet by kissing each other on both cheeks, though they usually do this only if they have not seen each other for some time. In Holland, people kiss three times.

Bowing is also frequently used to greet people, especially in Asian culture. In China and Korea, a slight nod of the head can be sufficient.

Regarding Japanese greetings, H. Fukuda (1993) states:

The most common mistake non-Japanese make when bowing is to bend from the neck. While you may amuse your friends with your imitation of a goose, you're better off ... if you bend from the waist. Another mistake, made by Japanese as well, is to bow more than necessary. Repeated bowing is appropriate when apologizing or making requests, but overly enthusiastic bowing ... gives the impression of being unnecessarily servile. (17)

In Japan bowing is almost an art form! Basically, the deeper the bow, the greater the respect, though there are quite a few rules governing how low you bow and who bows first. According to Fukuda, the rules are basically as follows:

- The person of lower rank bows first and lowest.
- The higher the rank of the person facing you, the lower you bow.
- The lower the bow and the longer you hold the position, the stronger is the indication of respect, gratitude, humility, and so on.
- Equals match bows.
- When unsure of status, the safest move is to bow a shade less low than the other person.

Notice that when bowing in Japan and other Asian cultures, you avoid direct eye contact. Prolonged eye contact also is avoided in Puerto Rico and in some West Indian cultures. It can be considered rude, even intimidating, and may have sexual overtones.

As this discussion has shown, the same meaning, in this case a greeting, can be expressed in many different ways across cultures. We will see additional examples in the next few pages, but we start with a look at cases where the same gesture is used to mean different things.

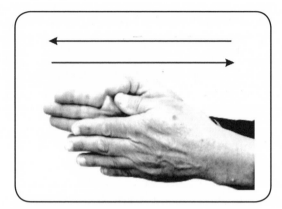

Figure 10.2

SAME GESTURE, DIFFERENT MEANING

In this section we present some cases where a gesture used in another culture is similar to one in American culture, but the meaning is quite different.

One such gesture involves the way that people indicate 'yes' and 'no.' In American culture, we nod our head to say 'yes' and shake our head to say 'no.' In Sri Lanka you would be in trouble with these gestures since in that culture you move your head from side to side to say 'yes,' and you nod your head up and down to say 'no.' The gestures used by Greeks and Turks also differ. To say 'yes,' you use a sharp downward nod. To say 'no,' you raise your chin and simultaneously click your tongue. If you shake your head in those cultures, you are saying that you do not understand.

Turkish culture also seems to differ from American culture in terms of the amount of smiling that people do. Turks may interpret too much smiling as a lack of sincerity or even a degree of deception. On the other hand, Americans should not think that just because Turks do not smile they are unhappy!

Some other gestures involving the hands that we use in the U.S. include snapping, making the "OK" sign, and making a "V" for victory or peace. In Spain, snapping a few times is used for applauding. As for the "V" sign, it is a gesture to avoid if you are visiting England, especially if you have your palm facing toward your face since this is an obscene gesture.

Exercise 5: Observing Gestures

Watch people whom you cannot hear as they interact with one another.
- What do you notice about their gestures? Do they coordinate with one another, or do they take turns?
- Do they favor one hand over another? Do they coordinate the movements of their arms and hands with the expressions on their faces?
- Do you find the same gestures across a range of different speakers?

The gesture used in American culture to denote "OK" takes on many different meanings around the world. In France, it means 'zero' or worthless, while in Japan you use it to ask for money or change in coins. In Brazil, Turkey, and Germany, it is an obscene gesture. In Brazil, for example, it is an obscene way of telling someone to get lost. And in Turkey, the symbol indicates that you are calling someone a homosexual and can be interpreted as very offensive. Obviously, it is important to know what is appropriate and inappropriate in the culture of the language that you are learning, especially if you plan to visit the country where your new language is spoken. Think about the reaction that a Brazilian might have if you used the OK gesture to say that the directions they just gave you were perfect. This stranger might not be quite as forgiving as your language instructor!

Another gesture in American culture that receives a different meaning elsewhere is the movement of rubbing your palms together back and forth as in Figure 10.2. While in North America it can mean that you are being devious or up to something, in Italian it is a positive gesture, meaning something like 'how wonderful!', 'good!', 'that's nice.'

VARIATIONS IN GESTURES

We have seen that various cultures can assign quite different meanings to similar gestures. Of course, most cultures also have a range of gestures that we do not use at all. A sampling of these is given below.

You may be interested to learn that in some cultures, mouths are used to point. In the Philippines, for example, people may shift their eyes toward the object they want to point to, or purse their lips and point with their mouth. Similar gestures are used in parts of Vietnam.

To show appreciation or admiration in Turkey, you can hold up your hand with the palm up and slowly bring your fingers toward the thumb to mean that something is good. Some French speakers also use a hand signal to indicate that something is terrific: one stretches out an arm, makes a thumbs-up sign, and then brings the thumb down a notch. Brazilians also have an interesting way of showing how much they like something such as food: a person pinches his earlobe between thumb and forefinger, and to dramatize it further, he will reach behind his head and grasp the opposite earlobe.

As for an Italian, if something is perfect, you might see him pull across an imaginary line or string with his thumb and index finger, as shown in Figure 10.3.

Clearly, Latin culture is rich in body language. Here are a few more fun gestures from Brazilian culture. To indicate that someone is stingy, tap your left elbow with your right

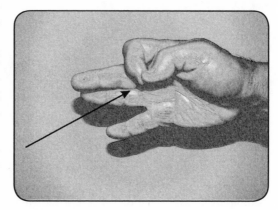

Figure 10.3

Figure 10.4

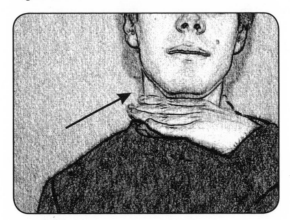

Figure 10.5

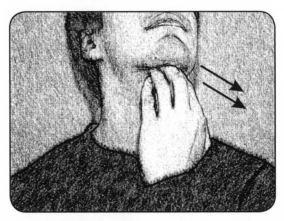

Figure 10.6

hand. Spaniards also use this gesture. If you rub your hand under your elbow in Brazil instead of tapping it, you are calling someone jealous. Brazilians and some French speakers also have a gesture to show disbelief: pull down the skin under your eye with your index finger. In English, by contrast, we might simply say a sarcastic "yeah, right!" And if you hold your palm upwards and spread your fingers, you are letting someone know that you think they are stupid. In Italy, the gesture for stupidity involves moving your hand back and forth in front of your forehead, as shown in Figure 10.4.

The chin is also a good source for body language in Italian. For example, if you want to express indifference, that you do not care, take the back of your hand and brush it up and away from your chin as shown in Figure 10.5. Or if you take the side of your hand and move it against your neck as in Figure 10.6, you are saying that you just cannot stand something.

Summary

The various gestures presented above are, of course, just a sampling of the vast number of gestures used to communicate in cultures around the world. Nonetheless, they provide a good illustration both of the ways in which languages can differ and of the idea that how a particular idea is expressed in a given language is arbitrary, determined by the speakers of that language and codified as a written or unwritten norm of the culture.

In the next two chapters we continue our look at the role of culture in language and focus on two different means of expressing social meaning: at the one end of the spectrum, politeness, and at the other end, taboos and swearing. Both provide striking examples of how much culture impacts the way that we use language.

References

Axtell, Roger. (1993). *Gestures: The do's and taboos of body language around the world.* New York: Wiley.

Bergmann, Anouschka, Currie Hall, Kathleen, and Ross, Sharon (Department of Linguistics, The Ohio State University). (2007). *Language files,* 10th edition. Columbus: The Ohio State University Press. 412.

Coates, Jennifer. (1998). *Language and gender: A reader.* Oxford, UK; Malden, MA: Blackwell.

Fukuda, H. (1993). *Flip, slither, & bang: Japanese sound and action words.* Tokyo: Kodansha International.

Maltz, D. N., and Borker, R. A. (1982). A cultural approach to male-female miscommunication. In *Communication, Language and Social Identity,* ed. J. J. Gumperz. 196–216. Cambridge: Cambridge University Press.

Tannen, Deborah. (1990). *You just don't understand: Women and men in conversation.* New York: William Morrow.

Politeness

Introduction

*T*o know your language well, you need to know the rules about how to use it, including, naturally, politeness (and rudeness) in language use. Sometimes it is very important to be polite, such as when you want to request something of someone or make a good impression on a first date or in a job interview. Politeness is useful in these kinds of situations because, among other things, it smoothes social interactions, it helps to avoid confrontational situations, it shows respect for the other person, and it can enable us to get what we want without the other person feeling as if we have imposed upon her.

Not surprisingly, knowing about politeness is also important for the language learner. As discussed in the previous chapter, the norms underlying social phenomena like politeness are determined by a given culture based on assumptions about what it means to be polite in that society. As a result, the way people express politeness differs from culture to culture. Mastering another language and knowing how to use it require an understanding of the cultural differences between your own culture and that of the language you are learning. This necessarily means that understanding the rules governing politeness is very important.

In fact, research suggests that native speakers are generally quite tolerant of mistakes in the speech of foreigners relating to pronunciation, word formation, and word order. But when foreigners violate norms relating to language usage, such as politeness, native speakers may interpret the behavior as bad manners. Here's an illustration from English and Greek. In English, politeness is closely tied to formality, while in Greek this is not the case. One result of the differences may be that since Greeks are not as formal in their social interactions, an English speaker might be led to view a Greek speaker as impolite. By contrast, Greeks might judge an English speaker as too formal and distant rather than polite.

To restate a familiar point: learning a language involves more than learning sounds, words, and sentences. It is also important to learn the rules of language usage. When it comes to politeness, you can learn to show respect for and cooperation with the person you are interacting with, or you can insult the person, even unintentionally. At least if you know the rules, you can actually choose how you want to treat people!

In this chapter we will start by getting a better understanding of how politeness is expressed in American English. With this as a basis, we will look at some other cultures and see how they differ from ours in terms of the nature of politeness and the strategies used to express it.

Solidarity and Deference

One way of looking at politeness is to consider its functions in a culture. According to P. Brown and S. Levinson (1987), the functions of politeness generally fall into one of two categories: **positive politeness** and **negative politeness.** In positive politeness, the speaker tries to treat the listener as a friend or at least to include him in the conversation. Positive politeness is used as a way of emphasizing **solidarity** with another person. Compliments are an example of this type of politeness. Another example of positive politeness is to go beyond a simple 'Hi' when you meet people. You may ask them about their family, about a recent trip they took, or about some other subject that they are interested in. A goal of this type of politeness is to make the person feel closer to you, that is, to emphasize solidarity between the two of you.

While positive politeness encourages **solidarity,** negative politeness emphasizes **deference.** By deference we are referring to a type of courteous respect, or the act of yielding to the opinion of another person. We might want to do this to preserve the other person's self-respect or to avoid making her feel bad. Suppose a friend asks you if you like her new shirt. You may tell her that you do, even though you think the shirt is completely hideous. This is a type of negative politeness since you are being polite so as not to hurt the other person's feelings. Another reason to use negative politeness might be to show respect. Responding to a dinner invitation by saying *I would be honored to come to dinner* rather than *I'll come to dinner* is one way of showing negative politeness.

Negative politeness is also used in situations to give the impression of not imposing upon the other person too much, e.g. *If it is not too much trouble. . . .* Or you might use negative politeness to create or maintain distance between you and the person you are talking to. Impersonal expressions are commonly used to achieve this goal. For example, a salesclerk, trying to be polite to a pushy customer, might say the following: *Sir, customers need to line up to the right of the counter.*

In general, politeness strategies in a language fall on a continuum, with solidarity at one end and deference at the other.

Expressing Politeness in English

Many different strategies are used in English to express politeness, including the use of questions, modal verbs, tag questions, and past tense, among others.

Framing a request in the form of a question tends to soften the impact of the request. Compare the two sentences in (1). Most English speakers would probably agree that the sentence in (b) is more polite than the one in (a):

(1) a. Give me $35 for the football tickets.
     b. Can I have $35 for the football tickets?

Use of the **modal verb** *can* in sentence (1b) is also contributing to the politeness. Other modal verbs include *would, might,* and *must* and can also add politeness to a sentence.

A small question added to the end of a sentence, called a **tag question,** is an additional device used to convey politeness, as in the examples in (2).

(2) Leave it here, will you?   vs. Leave it here.
     You can do it, can't you?   vs. You can do it.

Another way to soften the impact of a sentence is to use a **hedge.** Examples include *I was sort of wondering if . . . , maybe if . . . , I think that . . . , would you mind if. . . .* These expressions add indirectness to a request or command; indirect utterances are generally perceived by English speakers as more polite than direct utterances.

Indirectness can also be achieved by prefacing a sentence with an **apology,** e.g. *Excuse me, but I was wondering if . . . , Sorry to trouble you but. . . .* **Diminutives** such as *little, small amount of, tiny* can also soften the impact of a request or command. Examples are given in (3).

(3) Could you give me a <u>little</u> milk?
     I need <u>a few</u> minutes of your time to help me with something.

The expression *real quick* is also a popular expression used by speakers in some varieties of American English, especially young adults. It too can be interpreted as a type of diminutive, intended to attenuate or downplay the imposition that the request may have on the person being asked.

(4) Can you give me that <u>real quick</u>?

The choice of **verb tense** is also used to convey politeness in English, contributing, once again, an indirectness to the sentence. Most speakers would likely judge the sentence in (5a) with the past tense verb *were* as more polite than the one in (5b) with the present tense *are:*

(5)   a. <u>Were</u> you looking for something?
       b. <u>Are</u> you looking for something?

A final strategy worth mentioning is the use of **pre-statements,** again adding indirectness to a phrase as shown in the examples in (6).

(6)   a. You (pre-request):   Do you have a minute?
             Response: Sure, what's up?
             You (actual request):   Would you read over my homework for me?

       b. You (pre-invitation):   Are you going to be in town this weekend?
             Response: Yup.
             You (actual invitation):   Do you want to go out to dinner?

In (6a) the request is softened by the pre-statement (or pre-request), while in (6b) a pre-invitation is used before the actual invitation. One of the functions of a pre-statement is to give the person being addressed an easy way to say *no* while at the same time preserving the self-respect of both the addressee and the person making the pre-statement. Pre-statements, then, are examples of negative politeness.

If you are a speaker of American English and are able to judge a particular sentence as more polite than another, you have learned the rules of politeness in your culture, as well as the different strategies used to convey politeness.

In addition to the particular device used to express politeness, there are many factors that need to be taken into account in order to know when politeness is in order. Age, for example, is a common consideration. Is the person you are addressing older than you or younger than you? The social distance between you and the other person, the context in which the interaction occurs, and your familiarity with the other person may all be relevant. In addition, the urgency of the message also factors in. For example, the command *Get away from there!* would probably not be interpreted as being rude and

Exercise 1: Politeness

Think of ten or more ways to get someone to turn down loud music. Rank them in order of decreasing politeness. What factors seem to make the more polite versions more polite, and the ruder versions ruder?

offensive when yelled by a firefighter trying to keep you away from a car that is about to explode compared to its being yelled in some less urgent situation.

If you are able to determine, based on these kinds of factors, how polite you would need to be in a given situation, you have been successful in acquiring an amazing amount of information regarding the use of English in social interactions. First do Exercise 1 in the box at the bottom of p. 197. Then we will consider how other cultures may differ from ours in expressing politeness.

Politeness across Cultures

In this section we focus on three ways that languages differ from English in expressing politeness. The first involves situations in which the same type of politeness strategy is used, but the responses to the strategy differ in the two cultures. In the second, the same type of politeness is conveyed in different ways among different language varieties. And finally, we touch upon cases in which politeness has become an integral part of the language's grammar.

SIMILAR STRATEGY, DIFFERENT RESPONSE

The use of compliments and requests is a fruitful area of study to discover differences among cultures. Comparative studies of politeness between Chinese and American speakers, and between Japanese and American speakers, have shown that while both cultures use negative and positive politeness strategies, their responses to compliments and requests are quite different. In both cultures, compliments are recognized as compliments and requests are recognized as requests. What differs is the way that speakers are expected to respond.

R. Chen (1993), for example, found that Chinese speakers frequently responded to compliments either by rejecting the compliment completely or by thanking the speaker and then denigrating or putting themselves down. Results of this survey are shown in (7).

(7) **Differences in American English Speakers and Chinese Speakers**[1]

	American:	*Chinese:*
Accepting the compliment	Yes (39.3%)	Yes (1.0%)
Returning the compliment	Yes (18.5%)	No
Thanking and denigrating	No	Yes (3.4%)
Deflecting	Yes (29.5%)	No
Rejecting the compliment	Yes (12.7%)	Yes (95.7%)

1. R. Chen, "Responding to Compliments," 1993, pp. 49–75.

You can see that Americans accepted a compliment about 39% of the time compared to 1% for the Chinese participants. Americans were also more likely to return a compliment than Chinese. While the Chinese speakers thanked the person for the compliment and then put themselves down about 3% of the time, their overwhelming response was to completely reject the compliment.

To illustrate, consider the example where someone says, "Wow, you look absolutely fantastic in that outfit!" A typical American response would be along the lines of "Thanks" (39.3%), "You look good too!" (18.5%), or "Really? I think it makes me look like a dork" (12.7%). For Chinese, by contrast, the first two responses would be either nonexistent or very rare. Rather, while they might say something like "Thanks, I really do not deserve to wear such nice clothes" (3.4%), a response such as "Really? I think it makes me look stupid" would occur an astonishing 95.7% of the time. This difference appears to be related to social value differences between the two cultures, particularly in their respective beliefs regarding what constitutes self-image (Hondo and Goodman 2001).

Japanese speakers respond similarly to the Chinese. A study by M. Daikuhara (1986) found that 95% of Japanese responses to compliments were "self-praise avoidance," and only 5% showed appreciation. By contrast, "thank you" was the most frequent response for Americans. It is interesting that Daikuhara also found that Japanese speakers rarely compliment their own families, while it is not uncommon for Americans to do so. Junko Hondo and Bridget Goodman (2001) suggest that this could be an indication of the function of downgrading oneself in Japanese culture, since in Japan the family is often considered to be a part of one's self.

It is not hard to imagine how miscommunications could arise because a speaker of one language is not familiar with the ways in which compliments are interpreted in the other language. Hondo and Goodman give a few examples. The first one involves an American speaker giving a compliment to a Japanese speaker. The American says: "Your

Exercise 2: Giving a Compliment

In the United States people tend to be very much aware of how they look, and they want others to think that they look good. What sort of relationship could be assumed between you and another person in order for each of the following to be appropriate?

a. You look nice.
b. You are very nice-looking.
c. You look great—have you lost weight?
d. That hat looks great on you!
e. I've never seen you looking so good.
f. I like the way you look.

What determines what you would say to someone else?

child is one smart girl," by which she means exactly what she says: the girl is smart. The Japanese speaker replies: "Oh, no, she is not." She says this because she has learned in her culture that it is not good to praise one's own child too much. The result is that the American is left thinking that the Japanese woman does not think her own child is very smart.

In the second scenario, a Japanese woman gives a compliment to an American. She says: "Your presentation last week was spectacular," and she means it. The American does not really think her presentation was that great but does not want to argue, so she says: "Why, thank you." Since in Japanese culture accepting a compliment is considered inappropriate, the Japanese speaker is left thinking that the American is full of herself; according to Japanese culture, the American should have said something like "No, it was awful" (Chen 1993).

These two examples show just how important it is to understand the rules of conversation of another language. Both miscommunications could have been avoided had the speakers been aware of and sensitive to cultural differences in their language usage.

THE NATURE OF A COMPLIMENT

We continue our look at compliments, turning to the nature of compliments and some additional ways in which languages express politeness differently from English.

Interestingly, **the focus and content of a compliment** can differ from culture to culture. Egyptians, for example, tend to offer compliments about a person's appearance and personal traits, but not about what the person does or has (Nelson, Bakary, and Batal 1993). They do so apparently to avoid harm caused by the "evil eye": when seeing something attractive and beautiful belonging to someone else, one must say "God preserve you from the evil eye." If not, something bad could happen to the owner of the beautiful object.

Elsewhere in the Middle East, Farsi speakers use other culture-specific devices to express politeness (Akbari 2002). Many speakers, mostly older or uneducated ones, use positive politeness strategies that are rooted in religious beliefs, such as "if God wishes" and "God preserve you from the evil eye." Referring to God when making a request is based on the belief that if they are talking about doing something in the future, they must say "if God wishes"; otherwise they will not be able to do it when they intend to.

The study also found that "prayers" are used by a speaker to encourage the listener to do something for her. Zahra Akbari (2002) gives the following example of a mother asking her daughter to do her a favor: "My dear daughter, may your life be blessed. Would you please hang these clothes up upstairs? My legs hurt and I cannot go up the stairs."

While compliments are strongly influenced by religion in Arab cultures, at least one type of compliment in Hispanic culture is influenced by romance and art. These compliments, called *piropos,* are considered by some Spanish speakers to be a type of verbal artistry. According to Z. Moore (1996), *piropos* are commonly used by a young man toward a young woman. Some examples from Moore's study are given in Table 11.1, with the cultural meanings added by Hondo and Goodman.

> **● TABLE 11.1**
>
> **Examples of *piropos.***
>
> | | |
> |---|---|
> | Spanish Form: | ¡Vaya usted con Dios y su hija conmigo! |
> | (Direct Translation:) | ('May you go with God and your daughter with me!') |
> | *Cultural Meaning:* | *You have a beautiful daughter.* |
> | Spanish Form: | ¡Dios mío! Tantas curvas y yo sin freno! |
> | (Direct Translation:) | ('My God! So many curves, and me without brakes!') |
> | *Cultural Meaning:* | *You are sexy.* |
> | Spanish Form: | Dejaran el cielo abierto y se voló un angelito. |
> | (Direct Translation:) | ('Heaven was left open, and out flew an angel.') |
> | *Cultural Meaning:* | *You are beautiful.* |

Source: Moore (1996) and Hondo and Goodman (2001).

In American culture, there is a good chance that *piropos* would not be interpreted as compliments but instead as sexist—maybe even harassment. In Hispanic cultures, however, there is good reason to believe that they are intended to be compliments, since they can be said to children as well as adults. As Hondo and Goodman (2001) point out:

> One Spanish speaker consulted in this regard pointed out that the phrase, "¡Vaya usted con Dios y su hija conmigo!" "(May you) go with God, and your daughter (go) with me" may be uttered to a little child. . . . In that context, the statement is no more an invitation to sex than the American English expression to a child "he's so cute I could just eat him up" is a display of cannibalistic tendencies.

The appropriate **number of compliments** can also differ from culture to culture. Egyptians tend to offer fewer compliments than Americans. The reason is, of course, cultural, related to the Arab belief in the "evil eye": too many compliments can bring bad luck (Nelson, Bakary, and Batal). In North American culture, this could be viewed as similar to the "knock on wood" superstition.

DIFFERENT RESPONSES TO REQUESTS

Languages also differ in the types of sentences used to express politeness. As we saw for English, questions are more polite than declaratives. This is not the case in all cultures, however. An interesting example comes from Wes Collins,[2] an expert on the Mam

---

2. Personal communication.

language of Guatemala. There are approximately 500,000 Mam speakers spanning five major dialects. While Wes was learning to speak Mam, he also learned, sometimes unintentionally, how his American culture differed from Mam culture. For example, when Wes was working in a Mam village, he asked his language consultant in what he thought was a polite manner, "Would you like some coffee?" Every time he asked this the language consultant just looked embarrassed and never quite knew what to say. When she did finally answer, she said, "Perhaps, yes."

The reason for the Mam speaker's hesitation is that Wes's request was interpreted as "Is it possible that you might want some coffee at some point in the future?" This is because any reference to the future in Mam is cast in **dubitative** aspect, which associates doubt with a sentence. This reflects the belief in Mam culture that the future is unknowable. So if an English speaker asks a Mam speaker if she would like some coffee, she interprets it as meaning "at some point in the future." How would she know how to answer such a question? As a result, the response is usually a simple "Perhaps, yes." Since, for a Mam speaker, the future is in such doubt, it would be presumptuous to know the future and to assume that there would be coffee at some point in the future. Consequently, while Wes was using politeness strategies that he had learned in English, he was actually being rude. What Wes should have said was "Here, take this." It is inconceivable that a Mam would be offered a cup of coffee and not accept it.

Greek and American cultures also differ in how one makes a request. In Greek society, imperative constructions, or commands, are appropriate forms for making a request in many more contexts than in American culture. In American culture, making a command is generally perceived as impolite. As a result, an American might interpret Greeks as "impolite" or "bossy."

The Expression of Politeness in Grammar

In this section we look at additional examples where politeness has been encoded into the grammar. In these languages, different words are used to express degrees of politeness.

Many languages use different pronouns to express differences in respect, including French, Greek, Spanish, Italian, Russian, and German, to name a few. In French, for example, there are different forms of the second-person pronoun 'you,' as shown in (8).

(8) **French 'you'**

Singular, informal:	Tu vas au cinéma?	'Are you going to the movies?'
Plural; formal singular:	Vous allez au cinéma?	'Are you going to the movies?'

In very general terms, the singular pronoun *tu* is used when talking with someone you know or someone who is younger than you, and in casual speech. The pronoun *vous* is used if addressing someone you do not know or a superior, or if the situation is rather formal. The *vous* form is also used when referring to more than one person, regardless of how well you know the people or how formal the situation is. *Vous* is both singular and plural.

What happens if you use the wrong form? For instance, what if you are meeting your new girlfriend's or boyfriend's mother for the first time and you use the *tu* form? Let's just say that you probably would not make a very good first impression. In fact, you would probably be thought of as rude.

There is also a flip side to this. In some cultures, people do not really expect foreigners to master their language, so they are more sympathetic to the blunders that a nonnative speaker might make. This apparently is the case with Russian. According to D. Offord (1996):

> There are particular advantages for the foreign student of Russian in deploying the correct formulae in a given situation. . . . Russians are aware of the difficulty of their language for the foreign student and have little expectation that a foreigner will speak it well, let alone that a foreigner would be sympathetic to their customs. . . . They therefore tend to be more impressed by and favourably disposed toward the foreigner who has mastered the intricacies of their language and is prepared to observe at least their linguistic customs than are perhaps the French toward foreign French-speakers. (179)

For the language learner, then, it can be a win-win situation to learn to try to use the appropriate forms in a given context. If you make a mistake, you will not be misperceived as rude, and you might even impress the people that you are speaking to!

It is therefore useful to know what the appropriate form is for a given situation. However, it is also important to keep in mind that the choice of which form is used to express familiarity or formality is arbitrary and can differ from culture to culture. We saw in French, for example, that the second-person singular is the familiar form, while the second-person plural is formal. In Italian, by contrast, the polite form is the third person, not the second person. So instead of saying "How do <u>you</u> do?" you would say "How does <u>he</u> do?" But both sentences would still be interpreted as meaning "How do you do?"

As seen above, English also uses grammatical devices to express politeness; the past tense can sometimes be perceived as more polite than the present tense. Some additional examples are given in (9).

(9) | **More polite?** | **Less polite?** |
|---|---|
| Did you want something? | Do you want something? |
| I was thinking of borrowing your car. | I am thinking of borrowing your car. |
| I didn't understand what you were saying. | I do not understand what you are saying. |

The differences between the sentences in (9) are very subtle, and not all speakers will have the same judgments. If, on the other hand, the differences between the two tenses were systematic and all instances of the past tense were always interpreted as more polite, we would say that politeness is an integral part of a particular word or phrase. In this sense, it has been **grammaticalized,** such as the *tu* vs. *vous* forms in French. That is, it is part of the rules governing the form and structure of words and sentences in the language. This is not the case in English. Instead, our strategies for expressing politeness are rules of language **usage.**

In some languages, the grammaticalization of politeness has been raised to an art form. This is the case in languages like Korean and Japanese where forms of language called **honorifics** are used to express different degrees of politeness and respect. An honorific is a type of prefix or suffix that is added to a word to show respect for the person you are talking to. Here is an example of the same sentence in Japanese, first without an honorific, and then with an honorific:[3]

(10) **Without honorific:**
Yamada ga musuko to   syokuzi o tanosinda.
Yamada   son   dinner   enjoyed
'Yamada enjoyed dinner with his son.'

With honorific:
Yamada-san ga musuko-san to o-syokuzi o   tanosim-are-ta.
yamada-HON   son-HON   HON-dinner enjoyed-HON
'Yamada enjoyed dinner with his son.'

In Japanese, there are different types of honorifics, and the one that you use depends on a number of different factors, including, for example, the social relationship between you and the person you are talking with, the place where the conversation is taking place, and the activity involved. According to Masayoshi Shibatani (1990), the honorific system "functions to indicate the relative social and psychological distance" between the speaker and the addressee. Every person has an "intuitive personal sphere," and politeness is a way of managing the positions of other individuals with respect to this sphere (p. 380).

We can illustrate how this distance can vary through the use of spheres as shown in Figure 11.1. The size of the sphere indicates the social status of the two people, where the bigger sphere means higher social status, and the smaller indicates lower status. Note that age is a very important factor determining status: the older you are, the more status you have and the more respect you should be shown. Showing intimacy indicates your belief that the other person is within your sphere (and that you are in his or hers), while showing respect indicates your beliefs about the distance between the spheres, as well as your social levels relative to one another.

---

3. Examples from Nancy Bonvillain, *Language, Culture, and Communication,* 2002.

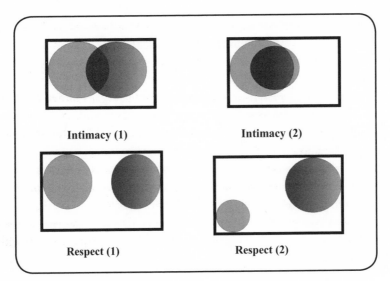

Figure 11.1

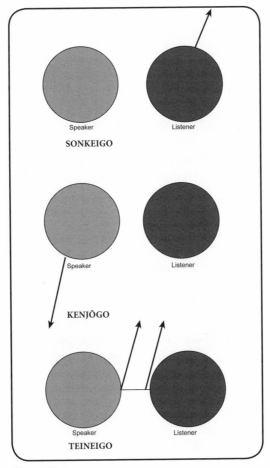

Figure 11.2

One class of honorifics, or *keigo* as they are called in Japanese, is called *sonkeigo,* illustrated in Figure 11.2. This literally means 'respect language' and is used to raise the relative level of the person that you are talking to. Another one, called *kenjōgo,* means 'humble language.' It lowers the level of the speaker so that it makes the person talking seem more humble. A third type is called *teineigo* which generally means 'polite language.' It is used to raise the level of the speech as a whole (Hendry 1993).

The level of speech used is controlled in large part by the formality of the situation. Polite language is always used in formal situations. If a situation is informal, honorifics might not be used, but again it depends on the social relationship between the speaker and addressee, the topic under discussion, and so on. Just because a situation is informal does not mean that an honorific is not used!

We provide an example from Shibatani's book (pp. 377–78), illustrating many different levels of politeness:

(11) a. *Vulgar:*
Ore aitu   ni au yo.
I   that fellow to meet
'I'll see that fellow.'

b. *Plain, informal:*
Boku kare ni au   yo.
I   he   to meet
'I'll see him.'

c. *Polite, informal:*
Boku kare ni ai-masu   yo.
I   he   to meet-POLITE
'I'll see him.'

d. *Polite, formal:*
Watakusi kare ni ai-masu.
I   he   to meet-POLITE
'I'll see him.'

e. *Polite, formal, object honorific:*
Watakusi kare ni o-ai-si-masu.
I   he   to HON-meet-POLITE
'I'll see him.'

f. *Polite, formal, object honorific, honorified 'he':*
Watakusi ano   kata ni o-ai-si-masu.
I   that   person to HON-meet-POLITE
'I'll see that person.' (lit. 'yonder')

g. *Polite, formal, super object honorific, super-honorified 'he':*
Watakusi ano o-kata   ni o-me   ni kakari-masu.
I   that HON-person to HON-eye to involve-POLITE

'I'll see that person.' (lit. 'I'll be humbly involved in the eye's (seeing) that honorable yonder.')

The expression in (11a) might be said by some drunken working-class men. The final particle *yo* means something like 'all right?' and adds to the informality of the sentence. The second sentence is also informal. The difference is that it is not vulgar. Note that although there are only two informal examples, there are at least five different levels of politeness. The level of respect and formality increases through the addition of politeness endings like *-masu* and honorifics like the prefix *o-*. The final, super-respectful sentence is especially interesting. Literally, it means 'I'll be humbly involved in the eye's (seeing) that honorable yonder,' though the actual translation is just an extremely polite and respectful way of saying "I'll see that person."

Summary

From this brief discussion of politeness across cultures, we hope that you can appreciate that how a particular culture shows respect and politeness is arbitrary. The norms are defined on a culture-to-culture basis. Note again that we say "culture," not "language." This, of course, is because different varieties of the same language can have different rules about politeness. In French Canada, for example, it is quite common for college students to refer to each other with the singular *tu* 'you' form even if they do not know each other. In Paris, however, a higher degree of formality is maintained, and *vous* 'you' is more commonly used for someone you do not know, even if that person is the same age and social class as you.

References

Akbari, Zahra. (2002). The realization of politeness principles in Persian. Isfahan, Iran: Department of Foreign Languages, Isfahan University. Manuscript online: http://www3.telus .net/linguisticsissues/persian.pdf.

Bonvillain, Nancy. (2002). *Language, culture, and communication: The meaning of messages,* 4th edition. London: Prentice Hall.

Brown, P., and Levinson, S. (1987). *Politeness: Some universals in language usage.* New York: Cambridge University Press.

Chen, R. (1993). Responding to compliments: A contrastive study of politeness strategies between American English and Chinese Speakers. *Journal of Pragmatics* 20(1): 49–75.

Daikuhara, M. (1986). A study of compliments from a cross-cultural perspective: Japanese vs. American English. *Working Papers in Educational Linguistics* 2(2): 103–34.

Hendry, J. (1993). *Wrapping culture.* Oxford: Clarendon Press.

Hondo, Junko, and Goodman, Bridget. (2001). Cross cultural varieties of politeness. *Texas Papers in Foreign Language Education: Selected Proceedings from the Texas Foreign Language Education Conference 2001.* Austin: University of Texas at Austin.

Moore, Z. (1996). Teaching culture: A study of *piropos. Hispania* 79(1): 113–20.

Nelson, G., Bakary, W., and Batal, M. (1993). Egyptian and American compliments: A cross-cultural study. *International Journal of International Relations* 17: 293–313.

Offord, D. (1996). *Using Russian: A guide to contemporary usage.* Cambridge: Cambridge University Press.

Shibatani, Masayoshi. (1990). *The languages of Japan.* Cambridge: Cambridge University Press.

Swearing, Insults, and Taboos

Introduction

*J*ust as languages can differ in terms of their rules of politeness, it is perhaps not surprising that they can also differ when it comes to the specific terms and topics that form the basis of swearing and insults. In this chapter you will be introduced to some of the ways in which languages differ in this regard. You will learn how cultural views influence swearing and insults in a given language. To begin, however, let's consider why one might swear in the first place. In other words, what is the function of swearing?

As you are well aware, swearing is generally used as a means of expressing frustration, anger, excitement, pleasure, or some other strong emotion, whether it be positive or negative. For example, when seeing an old college roommate at a party after not seeing him for ten years, a man might exclaim: "Hey, how the *hell* are you! What the *f**** are you doing in town?" In a situation like this, swear words can be used in conversation among friends without a negative or confrontational meaning. Swearing is a way of signaling in-group membership, friendship, and solidarity. By contrast, it is not hard to imagine a situation where these same swear words would be used to express anger or some other negative emotion.

As Lars-Gunnar Andersson and Peter Trudgill (1990) point out, swear words are not intended to be taken literally. So, for example, if a person yells "This paper is full of shit!" he probably is not referring literally to human excrement.

Swearing is also used to denigrate someone or something. Referring to a person as an animal, e.g. *bitch, cow, pig,* is a good example. This is because in American and many other cultures, humans are more highly valued than animals given their higher position

209

on the evolutionary scale, greater intelligence, and so on. As a result, referring to a person as an animal, that is, a lower life form, can be interpreted as an insult. Denigration thus involves associating someone or something with a lower position on some scale as defined by a given culture. Other common scales used in American culture for the basis of denigration include, for example, manliness (strength, virility), chastity (for women), sexuality, and social status.

For each of the cases of swearing and insults mentioned above, the words used can have a very strong impact, particularly if used in a negative context. But what gives them such power? The answer is that they refer to taboos. Taboos are topics governed by written or unwritten rules about what is or is not appropriate to talk about in a given context. Taboos are not necessarily prohibited topics; rather, they are topics associated with social norms relating to their appropriate and inappropriate usage. In English, these include topics such as bodily functions, body parts, sex, mothers, animals, religion, race, and ethnicity. There is nothing inappropriate, for example, about discussing bodily functions in a college biology course, though the same discussion would be considered taboo if discussed in most other contexts, even though these are important functions needed to live. This is also illustrated by the use of euphemisms in English to refer to the room used for these functions. There is the *restroom,* though one rarely "rests" in the room, and the *bathroom,* even if it doesn't have a "bath." In Canada, it is called a *washroom,* evidently because it is more polite to talk about "washing" than about bodily functions, and in England, it is referred to as the *WC* or the *loo.*

The key point about swearing for our purposes, and illustrated by many of the examples above, is that what defines swearing can differ from culture to culture. This is because the topics forming the basis for swearing directly reflect the attitudes and social structure of a particular community. If a society is not religious, then using a religious term in an inappropriate context will not provoke a reaction. Similarly, if the particular scale used as the basis for denigrating someone is not understood by the members of a community, it will not be an effective basis for swearing. In other words, the word used for swearing will have no power.

Swearing, Insults, and Language Learning

Just as learning about politeness is important when you're learning another language, so too is learning about the nature of swearing and insults. Since swearing (and insults) is so tightly intertwined with the values of a particular culture, it can pose a problem for you if you do not know the rules. This is also the case if you are using a swear word from a foreign language. The word will most likely not arouse the same strong emotions for you as it would for a native speaker. For this reason, use swear words in a foreign language with care (even if you're interjecting them in your own language)! In Canadian French, for example, almost any religious term can be made into a swear word. However, the term *fucké,* meaning 'broken, screwed up,' is considerably less strong than it is in English, even though it was borrowed from English.

Knowing when, how, where, and why to use swear words (or not to use them!) gives you more power over your interactions with native speakers.

So how can you find out what the swear words are in Spanish, Mandarin, Swahili, or whatever language you're learning? Obviously, one place to look would be in a dictionary. You can always look up a swear word in English and see what the translation is. For example, if you were to look up *shit* in a French, German, Swedish, or Spanish dictionary, you'd probably be given the terms *merde* (French), *Scheisse* (German), *skit* (Swedish), and *mierda* (Spanish).

That is a good start, but unless you have a <u>good</u> dictionary, it may not tell you how vulgar the term is in that particular language. Is it all right to use *merde* with your friends as well as with your mother or your professor? Using a dictionary is a start, but be sure that it is up-to-date since the most recent version reflects the current state of the language better than older versions do. Taboos, like swear words that violate them, change over time. We can see this in American culture with regard to religion as a basis for swearing. The shock value of religious swear words is less severe than it was even a few decades ago due to the rise in secularization. *Damn* and *hell* are now considered fairly mild, while most of the blasphemies used by Shakespeare—exclamations like *Zounds!* (God's wounds) and *marry!* (by the Virgin Mary)—disappeared long ago.

Another source for swear words is obviously your language instructor, if she feels comfortable talking about taboo words and topics. Some language grammars also include sections on swearing. For example, the textbook *Using Russian: A Guide to Contemporary Usage* by Derek Offord includes a section on profanity in Russian.

Needless to say, the Internet is also a rich resource for swearing terms in foreign languages. By typing "swearing," "curses," or "profanity" in most search engines, you'll come up with more links than you'll probably ever have time to look at!

Finally, there is a journal of vulgarities called *Maledicta,* available online at http://aman.members.sonic.net/.

Common Bases for Swearing and Insults across Cultures

As we stated above, swearing mirrors the values of society, and since social values vary from culture to culture, so do swear words and insults. This affects the topics used as well as who uses them. In some cultures, men and women both use swear words, while in others, such as Russian, it is considered more shocking for a woman to use vulgarities. In this section we review some of the common bases for swearing and insults in languages.

SEX

In many languages, English included, one of the main topics of swearing has to do with sex. For English, the sexual taboos of Victorian English are to blame, though they became even more severe in America. Hollywood played a big role in this. In 1934, the film industry enacted a code of ethics that laid out what was and was not appropriate behavior on-screen. Inappropriate behavior included lustful kissing and embracing, and suggestive postures and gestures. Profane language and expressions were also censored, and, as a result, words like *God, Lord, Jesus,* and *Christ* were strictly prohibited unless used for religious purposes.

The situation has clearly changed. Between the 1950s and 1970s there was a dramatic shift in attitudes and, consequently, an increase in use of vocabulary that had previously been considered profane. Media outlets were partly responsible for this change, in particular, competition between the movie industry and TV. As a way of attracting viewers away from TV, which was more family-oriented and sanitized than the movies, film studios incorporated riskier language and behavior into movies.

The 1960s contributed a great deal to the change in attitudes. This was a time of social division and sexual liberation, and a strong, sexual vocabulary became linked to the movement. Many of the protest movements that developed at this time exploited this language to get attention and stress their radical nature, such as Berkeley students' "Filthy Speech Movement" (Hughes 1991). Many other influences can be noted as well, including the publicity surrounding comedian George Carlin and his "shocking discourse" monologue. His famous "Seven Words That You Can't Say on TV" and other monologues that he gave on his "Filthy Words" radio program led to charges against him, charges that were ultimately upheld by the Supreme Court.

Of course, nowadays, even television shows billed as family entertainment contain words and phrases that would have been completely banned by Hollywood's earlier Code of Ethics. In fact, the use of profanity on TV is increasing every year. According to David Bauder (2002), during four weeks of viewing in 1989, Parents Television Council researchers counted 108 uses of *hell* and *damn.* By 1999, there were 518.

RELIGION

In other cultures, some of the most common types of words used for swearing have to do with religion, including languages such as Italian, Spanish, French, and Catalan.

Consider Catalan, a Romance language related to Spanish and Provençal spoken by about 6 million speakers, mostly in the northeast region of Spain (Vinyoles 1993). The most common and severe swear words in the language relate to God; Christ; the body parts of God (for example, the head, the heart, the liver of God); the Virgin Mary and other saints; the body parts of Mary and other biblical persons; and liturgical objects (unleavened bread, host).

Québec French is similar. Josh Freed and Jon Kalina (1983) present a comical look at swearing in Québec in their book, *The Anglo Guide to Survival in Québec.* Table 12.1 gives examples from Freed and Kalina's book. This listing provides a rich assortment of religious terms that share a single idea in English: *son-uv-a-gun* or, more commonly, the stronger version, *son-of-a-bitch.*

● **TABLE 12.1**

Québec French swear words for *son-of-a-bitch*.

Québec French	Literal Translation	Meaning
hostie	host; small delicate water representing the body of Christ	son-of-a-bitch!
calvaire	Calvary, the place where Christ was crucified	son-of-a-bitch!
sacrifice	holy sacrifice	son-of-a-bitch!
esprit	the Holy Spirit	son-uv-a-gun

Source: Freed and Kalina, 1983.

Table 12.2 gives an interesting look at how swear words are attenuated in both French and English. On the left we find different variations of the word *tabernacle*. Looking down the list of English translations on the right, you can see the impact of the swear word also decreasing, with *shit* (or something stronger) at the top and the innocent term *shucks* at the bottom. An English parallel would be the use of the euphemisms *jeez, jeepers,* and *sheesh* for the name *Jesus*.

● **TABLE 12.2**

Attenuation of the Québec French swear word *tabernacle*.

Québec French	Literal Translation	Meaning
tabernacle	tabernacle; altar	shit!
taberouette	tabernacle	shoot!
tabernouche	tabernacle	sugar!
taberslaque	tabernacle	shucks!

Source: Freed and Kalina, 1983.

Religious terms are so commonly used for swearing in these cultures because the Catholic Church has traditionally been a very strong presence. For any culture that places importance on religion, a powerful insult involves referring to aspects of the religious belief in a negative manner. While sexual terms still figure into swearing in French, Spanish, and other traditionally Catholic societies, they are generally less common and typically less powerful than religious terms.

MOTHERS

Reverence toward motherhood as a basis for swearing is not uncommon cross-culturally. Thus, in Macedonian and Serbian, referring to someone's mother in an inappropriate manner, for example, in sexual terms, can be considered one of the worst types of profanity.

Using motherhood as a basis for swearing is considered by some scholars to reflect cultural views regarding the categorization of women as, on the one hand, angelic objects to revere and worship like the Virgin Mary and, on the other hand, the wild temptress such as Eve. This is often referred to in the literature as the angel vs. whore dichotomy. Geoffrey Hughes (1991) suggests that this has traditionally been reflected in English through the use of terms of praise and abuse when referring to females:

- *Abuse:* slut, whore, hussy, broad, bitch, hag, witch
- *Praise:* honey, sweetheart, darling, dear, angel, baby, sweetie

There have traditionally been few neutral terms that refer to women besides *woman*. Even seemingly neutral terms like *lady* and *girl* can have strong negative connotations depending on the context. In fact, most terms used for women have strong connotations, in either moral or emotional terms. For men, by contrast, there have been (at least in the past) a larger number of neutral terms, for example, *guy, bud, fellow, man, dude, dog*.

SOCIAL STATUS

Cultures with strong social hierarchies regarding, for example, class, gender, sex, race, and ethnicity, frequently base insults and swearing on these scales.

In many Asian cultures, great emphasis is placed on hierarchical social relations, for example, male vs. female, older vs. younger, superior vs. subordinate, learned vs. illiterate. Not surprisingly, there are strict norms governing appropriate behavior in each of these relations. Deviating from this behavior through either words or actions is a serious offense and the focus of many insults and swear words. In Chinese culture, one's elders and those who went before are held in high regard, so any negative reference to them is considered derogatory. One such insult translates as "forgotten origin" which would be used to refer to a person who has forgotten his or her own ancestry.

Hierarchical relations based on sex are also common themes for swearing in cultures where one sex is valued less highly than the other. We see this in American English where women have traditionally been considered to have lower social status than men. Most women runners would not be offended were someone to tell them that they "run like a man"; in fact, it may even be taken as a compliment. However, telling a man that he "runs like a woman" would be less well-received by most men. Differences in the use of positive and negative terms for men and women noted just above can be viewed as a reflection of these differing roles in society. The lower status of women in traditional

Chinese culture, and other cultures where men typically occupy a higher social level than women, is similarly reflected in swearing, where there are more negative terms focusing on the behavior of women than the behavior of men.

ANIMALS

Finally, as we noted at the beginning of this chapter, reference to animals is used in some cultures as a basis for swearing. In traditional Chinese culture, for example, the division between humans and animals is very clear-cut, and to cross this line is a way of degrading a person. Some insults include *bald donkey* 'a bald man who looks like a donkey'; and *well-bottom frog* 'a person who has narrow views regarding some things, like a frog who sits at the bottom of a well; an ignorant or arrogant person.'

Summary

It should be clear that the terms people use for swearing and insults reflect the values of their culture. Learning a new language means more than learning to say words and sentences: it also means learning how to use, and not to use, the language. Learning about politeness or swearing in another language is important because it gives you power. If you know when, how, where, and why to use rude or polite terms, you will have more power over your interactions with native speakers and, as a result, be closer to acting like a native speaker.

References

Andersson, Lars-Gunnar, and Trudgill, Peter. (1990). *Bad language.* London: Penguin.

Bauder, David. (2002). A red-letter day for TV swearing. Monday, March 11, 2002. *The Associated Press.*

Freed, Josh, and Kalina, Jon. (1983). *The Anglo guide to survival in Québec.* Montreal: Eden Press.

Hughes, Geoffrey. (1991). *Swearing: A social history of foul language, oaths and profanity in English.* Cambridge, MA: Basil Blackwell.

Maledicta. Online: http://aman.members.sonic.net/.

Offord, Derek. (1996). *Using Russian: A guide to contemporary usage.* Cambridge: Cambridge University Press.

Vinyoles, J. J. (1983). Catalan blasphemies. *Maledicta* 7: 99–107.

Conclusion

Let's review where we have been and what we have learned.

Language Is a Human Phenomenon

Young children are remarkably successful in acquiring language. The human mind is uniquely adapted for this purpose. Children are able to identify the general properties of the language or languages that they are exposed to and use this knowledge to speak and understand. For various reasons, this capacity is gradually lost as children grow older and acquire their first language.

Language Is a Skill, and Practice Is Essential

A child learning a first language has ample opportunities for practice. The speech directed to children is generally very simple, the concepts are basic, the sentences are short, and there is considerable repetition and feedback. The child gets to practice this very fundamental skill all day long from a very early age.

The task for the adult learner is similar to the task for the child, but there are some important differences. The main similarity is that it is a skill for the adult just as it is a skill for the child. The key to success for both is PRACTICE, PRACTICE, PRACTICE.

But the differences are significant:

- The child's 'universe of discourse' is very limited and simple; the adult's is very broad and often complex.

- The child gets to practice the same things over and over again for most of her waking day; the adult has other things to do and thus limited time for practice. In addition, practice may become boring for the adult.
- Practice for the child is mixed in with learning to do other things, such as playing, eating, and interacting with other people; for the adult learner, language practice is an activity that is often distinct from other activities.
- The first language that a child learns is not competing with another language; a second language that an adult learns is competing with a first language that has been very well learned and intensely practiced for many years. The linguistic habits associated with the first language often interfere with the capacity to perform flexibly and spontaneously in the second language, especially in the early stages of learning.
- An adult learner is able to reflect on the structure of his own language and that of the language to be learned.

There Is a Social Aspect to Language

When we learn a language, we must learn not only what to say and how to say it, but also when to say it. The 'when' has to do with the social situation, including what is appropriate in a given situation. Appropriateness has to do with choice of words, use of particular grammatical constructions, and even accent.

Children learning a first language are usually very good at identifying the social aspects of languages and figure out what is appropriate in a range of situations. However, the task is a complex one, and the rules are sometimes difficult to figure out, even given ample evidence.

For the adult learner there are cultural differences that have to be understood and internalized in order to use a language properly in social contexts. These differences are usually difficult to describe in concrete terms. While it is sometimes possible to state clearly what the linguistic differences are between two languages (for example, in terms of the sounds or the order of words), the cultural differences are very subtle and often not understood consciously by native speakers. Nevertheless, sensitivity to the existence of these differences is an important part of learning another language.

Look at Your Own Language

Adult learners typically do not have the time that young children do to focus on the problem of language learning. This, and the fact that the first language interferes with the second language, suggest that adult learners need to adopt certain strategies to make their task more manageable and increase the likelihood of success. One is to understand as well as possible the differences between the two languages. For some people, a conscious recognition of the differences is an important step toward isolating where problems lie and for dealing with them.

The main areas that we have looked where there are significant differences among language are the following:

> *Word order:* Different languages order the main verb and other important words differently with respect to other parts of the sentence than does English.

- *Word forms:* Some languages mark the function of words and phrases using inflection (such as case, tense, and aspect), while for the most part English does not.
- *Sounds:* The sound inventories of languages differ dramatically, as do their phonotactics.
- *Getting people to do things:* What counts as a polite request in one language sounds rude in another language, and doesn't sound like a request at all in yet another language.

How to Use This Knowledge

Observations such as these can be used to structure one's learning to make the best use of the available time and energy. Here are some of the strategies we have suggested in this book:

- *Keep it simple.* Don't try to master something complex until you've mastered the parts.
- *Keep in mind that structure matters.* Language has structure. It is possible to take advantage of the structure to understand the differences between languages more effectively and focus on what needs to be learned and practiced.
- *Play the odds.* The best strategy is to focus one's time and energy on those aspects of the language that are most frequent. This includes the words, the forms, the structures, and the set phrases.[1]
- *Practice, practice, practice.* Learning a language is like any skilled activity that requires physical and mental coordination—practice makes perfect.

---

1. We do not recommend this strategy if you are going to be tested on a large number of items that are used relatively infrequently.

Subject Index

A

Absence of Speech Sounds: 25
Accusative Case: 145
Active/Passive Rule for English: 150, 151
Active Voice: 148–52
Adam's Apple: *See* Larynx.
Adjective: 118
Adjective Rule for English: 119, 121
Adverb: 157
Affricate Speech Sounds: 43, 63
Age: 197
Agent: 136, 137, 138, 141, 147, 148, 149
Agent/Theme Rule for English: 148
Agreement: 110, 118, 145, 146
Air Flow: 24
Air Passage: 41–45
Alveolar Ridge: 35. *See also* Alveolar
    Speech Sounds.
Alveolar Speech Sounds: 33, 37, 42,
    77–80
Animals:
    Cognition: 6
    Topic for Insults: 215
    Words for Animal Sounds: 176–77
Apologies: 196
Appositive: 128
Approximant Speech Sounds: 44

Arbitrariness: 73, 176–77
Article: 105, 108
Aspect: 154–56, 158–61, 202
Aspirated Speech Sounds: *See* Aspira-
    tion.
Aspiration: 46, 74–77, 79
Attenuation of Swear Words: 213
Attributive Modification: *See* Modifica-
    tion.
Auxiliary Verb: 135, 157, 161–62, 164,
    165. *See also* Modal Verb.
Auxiliary Verb Rule for English: 162, 165

B

Babbling: 9
Back Vowels: 53, 84–85
Bare Form: 153
Bilabial Speech Sounds: *See* Labial
    Speech Sounds.
Body Language: *See* Gesture, Commu-
    nicative.
Bowing: 189

C

Carlin, George: 212

Case: 142, 143–45
Case Marker: 144
Categories (of words): *See* Lexical Categories.
Central Vowels: 53
Child Language Acquisition: *See* First Language Acquisition.
CHILDES: 5, 6, 7, 8, 11
Click Speech Sounds: 32–33
Commands: 91, 156, 175. *See also* Imperative.
Completed Event: 158
Compliments: 198–201
Conjugation: 3, 154
Consonant: 31–50. *See also* Manner of Articulation; Place of Articulation; Voicing.
Consonant Length: 47–48
Content: 91, 132, 143
Context of an Utterance: 91, 92
Contrastive Modification: *See* Modification.
Count Noun: 107, 120, 126
Critical Period: 13
Culture: 175, 177–80, 185
    Definition: 178
    Customs: 178

D

Dative: 145
Declarative: 91, 163
Deference: 195
Definiteness: 105, 108
Dental Speech Sounds: 37, 40, 77–80
Descriptive Modification: *See* Modification.
Determiner: 105, 108, 109–10, 116–17
Determiner Rule for English: 110, 119, 121, 135
Dialect: 28, 94, 180
Dictionary: 74, 111, 187, 211
Diminutive: 196
Diphthongs: 57–58, 83–84
Direct Object: 136, 145, 151, 156
Distinctive Sounds: 8, 23
Doubly-Articulated Consonants: 40
Dubitative Aspect: 202

E

Epiglottis: 35, 36, 39
Errors in Child Language: 12
Euphemisms: 212
Experiencer: 147, 150
Explicit Knowledge (of a language): xii, 17
Eye Contact: 189

F

Familiarity: 175, 197. *See also* Social Distance.
Feedback: 5
Feminine: *See* Gender.
"Filthy Speech Movement": 212
First Language Acquisition: 1, 4–13, 216–17
Flap Speech Sounds: 42, 80–81, 82
Flow of Air: *See* Air Flow.
Force of a Sentence: 91, 92–94
Foreign Accent: 22, 89
Form of a Sentence: 89, 92–94, 95–96, 135
Fricative Speech Sounds: 24, 42, 43, 63, 79
Front Vowels: 32, 53
Full Vowels: 82–83
Function of a Sentence: 89, 92–94, 132
Future: *See* Tense.

G

Gap: 127
Gender:
    Grammatical: 3, 105, 111, 112–14
    Language Behavior: 180–81, 211
Genitive: 145
Gesture:
    Articulatory: 32, 85
    Communicative: 187–93
Glide Speech Sounds: 44, 63
Glottal Speech Sounds: 39
Glottal Stop: 39, 45
Glottis: 35, 36, 39. *See also* Glottal Speech Sounds.
Goal: 141, 143, 147
Governance (of a verb): 147

Grammar: 4, 95–96
Grammatical Competence: 10
Grammatical Expression of Politeness: 202–7
Grammatical Function: 139
Grammatical Gender: *See* Gender, Grammatical.
Grammatical Rules: 94, 96, 102
    For English: 110, 119, 137, 148, 150, 165
Greetings: 177, 179, 189

H

Hard Palate: 35, 37. *See also* Palatal Speech Sounds.
Hedge: 196
High Vowels: *See* Vowel Height.
Hollywood: *See* Media.
Honorific: 204–7

I

Imperative: 91, 95, 150, 163, 168–69, 175
Imperfective: 160
Indirect Object: 141
Inflection: 154, 156, 218
-ing Form: 153
Input in Child Language: 10–12
Insertion (of speech sounds): 26
Instrument: 139, 147
Instrumental Case: 145
Insults: 209, 211–15
Intention (of a speaker): 9
Interdental Speech Sounds: 36
Interrogative: 91, 163, 175
Intonation: 27, 28
Intransitive Verb: *See* Transitivity.
IPA: 33, 36, 49–50, 61

L

Labial Speech Sounds: 23, 36, 40, 43
Labialized Consonants: 40
Labiodental Speech Sounds: 36
Language Attitudes: 181–84
Language Capacity: 6–9

Language Development: 9–10
Language Norms: 178–79, 181, 217
Language Variety: 180–81, 186–87. *See also* Dialect; Prestige; Standard Variety of a Language.
Larynx: 35, 36
Length: *See* Consonant Length; Vowel Length.
Lexical Categories: 97, 98–102, 106. *See also* Adjective; Article; Adverb; Determiner; Noun; Pronoun; Verb.
Lips: 23, 35. *See also* Labial Speech Sounds.
Liquid Speech Sounds: 44, 63
Literal Meaning: 91, 92–94, 96, 132, 143
Low Vowels: *See* Vowel Height.

M

Main Verb: 135, 161–62
Making a Consonant Sound: 34
Making a Vowel Sound:
    Overview: 52
Manner of Articulation:
    Overview: 41–45
Manners: *See* Politeness.
Masculine: *See* Gender.
Mass Noun: 107, 126
Meaning: 8, 89, 98, 106, 120, 135, 140, 155. *See also* Literal Meaning; Social Meaning.
Media: 185, 212
Melody: *See* Intonation.
Metaphor: 120
Minimal Pair: 8, 21, 23
Minimal Response: 180–81
Misformed Sentences—Common Errors: 89–90
Mispronunciations—Common for English Speakers: 73–85
Modal Verb: 162, 196
Modification: 121, 128
Monophthongs: 57–58, 83–84
Morphology: 144, 153, 155, 218. *See also* Inflection.
Motherese: *See* Parents' Speech to Children.
Mothers (as topic for insults): 214

Motivation: 13

N

Nasal Cavity: 34, 35. *See also* Nasal
    Speech Sounds.
Nasal Speech Sounds: 44–45, 63, 79
Negative Politeness: 195, 197
Neuter: *See* Gender, Grammatical.
Nodding: 190
Noun Classes: 115–16, 124
Noun Phrase: 110, 136
Noun: 3, 104, 105–9, 135
    Examples: 107
Number: 105, 107, 108, 109–10, 111

O

Object: 136, 137, 139, 140, 142–43. *See
    also* Direct Object; Indirect Object.
Obstruent Speech Sounds: 63
Omission of unfamiliar sounds: 24
One-Word Stage: 10
Ongoing Event: 158
Order of Words: *See* Word Order.
Orthography: *See* Spelling.
Overview of the Book: 1–4

P

Palatal Speech Sounds: 37
Palatalized Consonants: 40–41
Palate: *See* Hard Palate; Velum. *See also*
    Palatal Speech Sounds.
Palato-Alveolar Speech Sounds: *See*
    Palatal Speech Sounds.
Parents' Speech to Children: 5, 10–12,
    216
Particle: 99, 143
Parts of Speech: *See* Lexical Categories.
Passive Participle: 149
Passive Voice: 148–52
Past: *See* Tense.
Perceptual Biases: 16
Perfect: 158
Perfective: 160
Pharyngeal Speech Sounds: 39

Pharynx: 39. *See also* Pharyngeal Speech
    Sounds.
Phonetics: 34
Phonology: 34
Phonotactics: 25, 27, 64, 218
Phrase: 97. *See also* Noun Phrase; Verb
    Phrase.
Place of Articulation: 36–41, 42
Plural: *See* Number.
Politeness: 91, 176, 194–208. *See also*
    Grammatical Expression of Polite-
    ness; Positive Politeness; Negative
    Politeness.
Positive Politeness: 195
Possession: 145
Pre-Invitations: 197
Prenatal Language Learning: 6
Prepositional Case: 145
Prepositions: 146–47
Pre-Requests: 197
Present: *See* Tense.
Pre-Statements: 197
Prestige: 182, 184–86
Primitive Languages (lack of): 94
Producing a Consonant Sound:
    Overview: 34
Producing a Vowel Sound:
    Overview: 52
Progressive: 158, 161
Pronoun: 105, 202–3
Proper Noun: 107
Puberty: 13

Q

Question: 91, 164–68. *See also* Interrog-
    ative; Tag Question; Wh- Question;
    Yes-No Question.
Question Marker: 28

R

Recipient: 150
Reduced Vowels: 82–83
Redundancy in Language Input: 11, 16
Relative Clause: 118, 126–30
Relative Phrase: *See* Relative Clause.
Released and Unreleased Stops: 81–82

Religion: 200, 211, 212–13
Replacement of unfamiliar sounds: 22
Request: 175, 196, 201–2
Restrictive Modification: *See* Modification.
Retroflex Speech Sounds: 37–38
Roles: 98, 134, 135, 138–41. *See also* Agent; Experiencer; Goal; Instrument; Patient; Source; Theme
Rounded Vowels: *See* Rounding.
Rounding: 2, 32, 56–57, 84–85

S

Sagittal Section: 35
Scrambling (of words): 97, 98
Second Language Acquisition: xi, 2, 13–18
Sentence:
    Force: 91, 92–94
    Form: 89, 92–94, 95–96, 135
    Function: 89, 92–94, 132
    Misformed—Common Errors: 89–90
Sentence Diagramming: 97–98
Sequences of Sounds: *See* Sound Sequences.
Sex: 112, 211–12. *See also* Gender.
Singular: *See* Number.
Smiling: 190
Social Distance: 197, 204
Social Identity: 181–84
Social Meaning: 175
Social Norms: 178, 210
Social Status: 214–15
Soft Palate: *See* Velum.
Solidarity: 184, 195
Sonorant Speech Sounds: 63
Sound Inventory: 22, 27
Sound Sequences: 21, 25, 62–72
Sounds: *See* Speech Sounds.
Source: 147
Speakers' Intentions: 9
Speech Sounds: See *names of kinds of speech sounds*. *See also* Consonants; Vowels.
    Absence of: 25
    In combination: *See* Sound Sequences.
    Inventory: 22, 27

Sequences: 21, 25, 62–72
Spelling: 23, 25, 33, 48, 63, 73, 85
Standard Variety of a Language: 182, 184–85
Statement: 91
Status: 204, 210
Stereotypes: 181–82, 185
Stop Speech Sounds: 24, 42, 63, 79, 81–82
Strategies for Dealing with Non-native Sound Systems: 22, 24, 26, 29
Stress: 27, 83, 121
Structure: 97–98
Subject: 139, 140, 142–43, 148, 156
Swear Words: 209, 210–15
    Attenuation of: 213
Syllable: 27
Syntactic Categories: *See* Lexical Categories.

T

Taboo: 210, 211–15
Tag Question: 196
Teeth: 35. *See also* Dental Speech Sounds; Interdental Speech Sounds; Labiodental Speech Sounds.
Telephone Behavior: 177–78
Tense: 3, 154–56, 159, 161, 196, 203–4
Theme: 139, 141, 147, 148
Time and Truth: 152–53
Tone: 27, 28
Tongue: 35, 36, 52
Transfer Errors: 94
Transitive Verb: *See* Transitivity.
Transitivity: 136, 137, 140, 156
Trill Speech Sounds: 80
Two-Word Stage: 10

U

Unaspirated Speech Sounds: *See* Aspiration.
Unreleased Stops: 81–82
Unrounded Back Vowels: 84–85
Unrounded Vowels: *See* Rounding.
Unvoiced Speech Sounds: *See* Voicing.
Uses of Language: 177

Uvula: 35, 38. *See also* Uvular Speech
  Sounds.
Uvular Speech Sounds: 38–39

V

Varieties of Language: *See* Language
  Variety.
Variety, Standard: *See* Standard Variety
  of a Language.
Velar Speech Sounds: 24, 38, 40
Velum: 35, 44. *See also* Velar Speech
  Sounds.
Verb: 3, 134–37. *See also* Auxiliary Verb;
  Main Verb; Modal Verb; Transitiv-
  ity.
Verb Phrase: 97, 134–37
Verb Phrase Rule for English: 137
Verbal Cluster: 161
Vocal Cords: *See* Vocal Folds.
Vocal Folds: 34, 36, 45–47

Vocal Tract: 34, 35
Voiced Speech Sounds: *See* Voicing.
Voiceless Speech Sounds: *See* Voicing.
Voicing: 45–47, 59
Vowel: 32, 44, 51–61, 82–83
Vowel Height: 54–56
Vowel Length: 2, 59–60

W

Wh-Questions: 92, 95, 164, 167–68
Word Forms: *See* Inflection.
Word Order: 89, 97, 98, 100, 118, 119,
  135, 143, 156, 218
Word-Final Sound Sequences: 68–70
Word-Initial Sound Sequences: 64–68
Writing: 73, 96. *See also* Spelling.

Y

Yes-No Questions: 92, 164–67

Language Index

A

African American Vernacular English:
See English, African American Vernacular.

Algonquian languages: See *names of specific languages.*

Ancient Greek: *See* Greek, Ancient.

American English: *See* English, North American.

Appalachian English: *See* English, Appalachian.

Arabic: 38, 56, 57, 67, 84, 133, 159, 180, 185–86

Egyptian: 200–201

B

Bantu languages: See *names of specific languages.*

Bella Coola: 41

Berber: 41

Boumaa: *See* Fijian.

British English: *See* English, Received Pronunciation.

Bulgarian: 56, 57, 84, 99, 115, 116, 122

C

Canadian French: *See* French, Canadian.

Catalan: 212

Chinese: 28, 32, 54, 67, 108, 101, 115, 122, 130, 133, 157, 165–66, 167, 176–77, 198–99, 214–15

Chipewyan: 41

Croatian: 176–77

Czech: 27, 83

D

Dravidian languages: See *names of specific languages.*

Dutch: 56, 132, 134, 177

E

Egyptian Arabic: *See* Arabic, Egyptian.

English:
African American Vernacular: 28
Appalachian: 182–84
Dialects of: 180
North American: 63, 80–81, 85, 177, 214

Received Pronunciation 29, 185
   Shakespearean: 211
   Victorian: 211
Eskimo, Siberian: *See* Siberian Eskimo.
Estonian: 176–77
Ewe: 43, 57, 84

F

Farsi (also called Persian): 56, 133, 200
Fijian: 67, 69
Finnish: 28
French: 24, 27, 32, 37, 38, 39, 56, 57, 59,
   73–74, 76, 78–79, 84, 108, 111, 112,
   114, 115, 116, 120, 121, 122, 128–29,
   133, 142, 154, 168, 169, 176–77, 180,
   185, 202–3, 212
   Canadian: 210
   Parisian: 39, 57
   Québec: 212–13

G

German: 2, 24, 32, 56, 57, 82, 84, 113,
   114, 115, 122, 128, 130, 133, 138,
   144, 153, 162–64, 168, 176–77, 185,
   202
Greek: 22, 56, 57, 67–68, 69, 76, 83, 84,
   195, 202
   Ancient: 41

H

Hausa: 41
Hawaiian: 56, 57, 84
Hebrew: 38, 56, 57, 84
Hindi: 47, 76–77
Hungarian: 32, 56, 57, 84

I

Igbo: 41
Indonesian: 29
Italian: 37, 48, 56, 57, 76, 78–79, 84, 95,
   111, 115, 121–24, 129–30, 133, 134,
   185–86, 202, 203, 212

J

Japanese: 56, 57, 69, 84, 99, 126, 128,
   130, 143–44, 166–67, 168, 177,
   198–200, 204–7

K

Kinyarwanda: 143
Korean: 22, 23, 27, 54, 56, 67, 82, 84,
   129–30, 133, 168, 176–77, 204
Kwamera: 115, 116

L

Latin: 56

M

Macedonian: 214
Malayalam: 44–45, 80
Maltese: 39, 185–86
Man: 201–2
Mandarin Chinese: *See* Chinese.
Maori: 108

N

Navaho: 41, 57, 84
North American English: *See* English,
   North American.

O

Ojibwa: 142

P

Palauan: 143
Parisian French: *See* French, Parisian.
Persian (also called Farsi): 56, 133,
   200
Polish: 26–27, 56, 58–59, 67–68, 70, 73,
   133, 168
Portuguese: 59, 73–74
Provençal: 212

Q

Québec French: See French, Québec.
Queen's English: *See* English, Received
   Pronunciation.

R

Received Pronunciation: *See* English,
   Received Pronunciation.
Russian: 40, 41, 56, 114, 115, 122, 133,
   144–45, 157, 160, 185, 202, 203, 211

S

Serbian: 214
Serbo-Croatian: 56
Shakespearean English: *See* English,
   Shakespearean.
Siberian Eskimo: 41
Spanish: 22, 26–27, 37, 42, 43, 56, 57,
   76, 78, 80–81, 83, 84, 99–100, 111,
114, 121, 122, 133, 156–57, 180, 200,
   202, 212
Swahili: 56, 57, 67, 84, 115, 121, 122, 146
Swedish: 24, 32, 56, 115, 116, 122, 124–25

T

Turkish: 24, 32, 54, 56, 59–60, 84

V

Victorian English: *See* English, Victorian.

Y

Yiddish: 56

Z

Zulu: 32–33, 57, 67, 84

Consonants of Standard American English

The consonants of Standard American English, written with IPA symbols, classified by voicing, place of articulation, and manner of articulation:

		Bilabial		Labio-dental		Inter-dental		Alveolar		Palatal		Velar		Glottal	
Manner of Articulation	Stop	p	b					t	d			k	g	ʔ	
	Fricative			f	v	θ	ð	s	z	ʃ	ʒ			h	
	Affricate									tʃ	dʒ				
	Flap								ɾ						
	Nasal		m						n				ŋ		
	Lateral Liquid								l						
	Retroflex Liquid								ɹ						
	Glide	ʍ̥	w								j				

Place of Articulation (column header spanning the above)

State of the Glottis: | Voiceless | Voiced |

Vowels of Standard American English

The vowels of Standard American English, written with IPA symbols, presented using the traditional American classification system:

Monophthongs: Diphthongs:

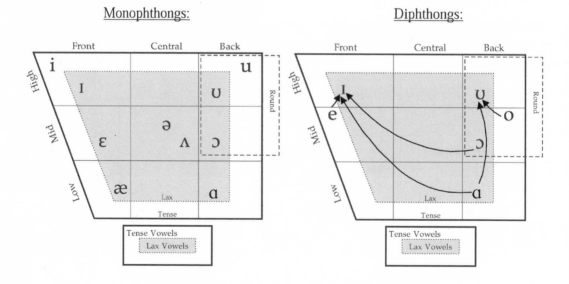

La Cucarachita Martina
y el terrible huracán

Escrito/Ilustrado
Tere Marichal-Lugo

Tere Marichal-Lugo es escritora,
ilustradora, dramaturga, contadora
de cuentos y titiritera.

Otros títulos de la autora:
La Granja global
El nacimiento global
El nacimiento boricua
María Chucena techaba su choza
María Magañas
¡Hagamos títeres!
La fiesta de las abejitas
Generosa, la gallinita agricultora
La fiesta global
Mangú y Mofongo
El huerto de mi casa
Juan Bobo aprende a leer
¡Mamá, debajo de mi cama hay un dragón!
Ánade Real o Azulón
ReArte: Crea personajes fantásticos
con latas de aluminio
Tres tristes tigres
Pancha la planchadora
El cielo está encancaranublado
¡Yo hago composta!
La gallinita Colorá, Colorá
Los cuentos de Doña Gramática
Chanda Candela
Tragedia en el Golfo
Los derechos de los animales
La Chivita
El sol taíno
La vaca de Juan Gandules
Los derechos de las niñas y de los niños

© Texto: Tere Marichal-Lugo
© Ilustraciones: Tere Marichal-Lugo
© Primera edición 2019:
Colección La mancha de plátano
email:maria.marichal@gmail.com

978-1-64606-211-9

Primera edición: 2019
San Juan, Puerto Rico

Colección
la mancha de plátano

Dedicatoria

A todos los que
guardaron en su memoria
y contaron,
recopilaron, protegieron,
investigaron, escribieron, publicaron
y dieron a conocer
los cuentos, las leyendas,
los juegos, las canciones
los refranes, y las adivinanzas
del folclor puertorriqueño,
especialmente a:

John Alden Mason
Ricardo Alegría
Pura Belpré
María Cadilla de Martínez
Marcelino Canino
Cayetano Coll y Toste
Monserrate Deliz
Elsa Escabí
Pedro Escabí
Aurelio M. Espinosa
Roberto Fernández Valledor
Yvette Jiménez de Báez
Francisco López Cruz
Walter Murray Chiesa
Néstor Murray Irizarry
Julia Cristina Ortiz Lugo
Ángeles Pastor
Flor Piñero de Rivera
Rafael Ramírez de Arellano
Calixta Vélez Adorno
Teodoro Vidal

¡Larga vida al folclor
puertorriqueño!

1.
¡Ay bendito!

Hace un reguerete de años había una hermosa comunidad muy diversa y alegre que se llamaba: "La folclorriqueña". Allí vivían todos los personajes de los maravillosos cuentos, las canciones y los divertidos juegos folclóricos de Puerto Rico.

La Cucarachita Martina era la líder de aquella comunidad. Ella era una gran agricultora y vivía en medio de un valle muy oloroso que estaba sembrado con exquisitas hierbas aromáticas; otras eran culinarias y también había medicinales.

Un día del mes de septiembre, Martina salió al patio de su casa y de momento sintió un chipichipi, esa lloviznita fina, muy fina que cae en las Antillas.

Inmediatamente escuchó el suave arrullo de una blanca palomita que se posó sobre un tronco. Estaba temblando y exclamó:

—¡Ay bendito! —.

—¡Ay bendito! ¡Ay bendito! ¡Martina, el cielo se está cayendo! ¡Lo que viene no es un mamey! —explicaba muy exaltada la Palomita Blanca. —¡Lo que nos espera es terrible! ¡Se acerca! ¡Se acerca!

—Palomita Blanca, ¿qué se acerca? ¡Estás temblando! Vamos a casa, te secaré y te prepararé un plato de harina de maíz bien calientita —le dijo Martina mientras la palomita sacudía sus alas.

—¡No tengo tiempo! ¡Se acerca! Tengo que ir a proteger mi nido. Acabo de ver y sentir el aguacero, la ventolera fuerte y gigantesca del terrible huracán que viene directo para acá. ¡Se acerca! ¡Ay bendito! ¡Me va a dar un yeyo! —le explicó la Palomita Blanca.

—¿Un terrible huracán? No he escuchado nada, nadita. ¿Estás segura? —le preguntó la Cucarachita Martina.

—¡Segurísima! —respondió a la soltá la palomita. —Esta comunidad ha sido olvidada y aquí no llegan las noticias. ¡Te digo y te repito que es un huracán! ¡Ay bendito! —le dijo finalmente y salió volando más rápido que ligero.

—¡Cuidado con los truenos y relámpagos! Tengo que organizar a todos mis vecinos enseguida —pensó Martina mientras veía como el cielo se iba oscureciendo. —Llamaré al magnífico Compay Araña para que me ayude a avisar a los vecinos.
—Una, dona, tena, catena,
saca, mulaca, vira, virón,
cuéntalas bien que las ocho son.
¡Magnífico Compay Araña,
venga con sus ocho patas
y su telaraña!

—¿Qué sucede? ¿A qué se debe este sorteo? ¿Qué juego vamos a jugar?¿A quien tengo que enredar en la telaraña? —preguntó el Maravilloso Compay Araña y Martina enseguida le explicó lo que sucedía y le pidió su ayuda para avisar a los vecinos.

El maravilloso Compay Araña avisó al Pájaro que habla para que lo ayudara en la tarea. Martina hizo una lista con los nombres de sus vecinas y vecinos y se dividieron el trabajo. En medio de la lluvia salieron a avisar a los vecinos y los invitaron a una reunión de emergencia. Esta fue la primera lista que hicieron:

Ratoncito Pérez
El Esclavo
Catilangua Lantemué
Pedro Animala
María Sabida
Siño Goyo
El Gallo Pelón
Bartolo
El Pescador y sus hijos
Los Cisnes Encantados
Las Tres Hermanas
Las Dos Brujas
Cenisosa
Los Niños Abandonados
La Princesa Adivinadora
El Loro charlatán
Compay Conejillo
Compay Araña
La Pájara Pinta
Así
Doña Ana
El Príncipe Negro
La tía Miseria
El Chivo
La Hormiguita
El Múcaro
El Principe Encantado
Mambrú
Antón Pirulero
Las Encantadas
Arroz con leche

Todos los Juanes: Juan bobo, Juan Gandules. Juan Pelao, Juan Calalú, Juan Soldado, Juan Periquito, Juan Paleta y don Juan Bolondrón
Saturnino
La Vaca del Rey
El Pavero
El Gato de Trapo
El Soldado
El Preso y su hija
El Zapatero
La Puerquita
El Loro que come chorizos
El Rey Ciego y sus tres hijas
El Gigante
Mercedes
San Isidro Labrador
Pico Pico Mandorico
El Gallo Pelao
El Conde de Fe, Esperanza y Caridad
El Hijo del Conde
La Novia Tonta y Pepe
Sol Divino
La Jicotea y el Caballo
El Grillo y La Changa
Los Tres Consejos
El Caballo de los Siete Colores
Los Tres Gallegos
Tía Miseria

Algunos vecinos llegaron enseguida a la reunión. ¡Hablaban hasta por los codos!

—¿Es cierto que viene un dragón gigantesco que bota fuego por los ojos, la boca y los oídos? —preguntó Juan bobo

—Lo que viene es un terrible huracán —le contestó Martina.

—¡Eso es imposible! ¡No he escuchado noticia alguna sobre ese evento natural! —gritó el altanero Rey quien había llegado con su hija la Princesa Adivinadora.

—Le digo que la Palomita Blanca llegó empapada y alterada porque voló cerca del terrible huracán —le explicó Martina mientras los demás observaban sin decir ni pío.

—La Palomita Blanca está exagerando. ¡Se los aseguro! Seguramente lo que vio fue un aguacero. Vivimos en el trópico y aquí llueve todo el tiempo. Me marcho ahora mismo. Tengo cosas más importantes que hacer —contestó el Rey desafiando a Martina con la mirada.

En ese preciso momento se escuchó un trueno tan fuerte que hizo temblar el techo de la casita de Martina y de momento se vio el inmenso reflejo del relámpago. Inmediatamente comenzó un viento fuerte y otro trueno y otro más poderoso que el primero. Entonces el Rey se asustó y gritó:

—¡Huyy!¡Es cierto lo que dijo la Palomita y lo que dice Martina! ¡Viene un terrible huracán! ¡Viene un terrible huracán! ¡Auxilio! ¡No me atrevo a salir de aquí! ¡Le tengo miedo a los truenos y a los relámpagos!

—¡Cálmese! Deje de gritar porque necesitamos conservar la calma —le dijo Martina y el Rey se sentó en una esquinita sin chistar.

—¡Huyyy! ¡Viene el terrible huracán! —exclamaron todos a la vez.

—No podemos perder tiempo. Tenemos que prepararnos y buscar alimentos, agua potable y todo lo que necesitemos porque viene mucha lluvia y viento —les aclaró Martina.

—En mi casa tengo queso del país, casquitos de guayaba, papaya en almíbar y besitos de coco para endulzarnos la vida. Los compartiré con todos —dijo el Ratoncito Pérez con su suave y apacible voz.

—Debemos buscar un refugio donde quepamos todos —señaló doña Juana.

—Me encantaría ofrecerles mi casa, pero está destartalada. ¡Es una ruina! —explicó la Tía Miseria.

—La mía es muy pequeñita y ya siento tristeza porque me la va a llevar el huracán —dijo llorosa La Hormiguita.

—¡Yo buscaré un refugio! —les propuso El Esclavo. Conozco una cueva donde se esconden los cimarrones y me parece que es el lugar ideal

—¡Pues vamos a trabajar! ¡Juntos enfrentaremos a este terrible huracán! No podemos perder tiempo. Tenemos que avisar a todos antes de que sea tarde. Vamos a dividirnos las tareas —dijo Martina con mucha energía y todos la aplaudieron con entusiasmo. Definitivamente Martina había nacido para ser líder de aquella comunidad.

Poco a poco aquella casita fue llenándose de personajes que se iban uniendo a los grupos que se habían formado para enfrentar al terrible huracán.

—¡Comadres! ¡Compadres! vamos a buscar comida. ¿Quién me quiere ayudar? —preguntó Compay Araña y enseguida el Compay Conejito, el Gallito Quiquiriquí y el Loro Charlatán se ofrecieron para ayudarlo.

—Por favor recojan pomarrosas, muchas acerolas y carambolas. Que no falten las guanábanas, las guayabas y los lerenes. Además traigan batatas y plátanos —les pidió La Cucarachita Martina.

—¡Camarón que se duerme se lo lleva la corriente! ¡Vamos a trabajar! Cada vez que hablan de alimentos me da mucha hambre. Mucha,mucha hambre —exclamó Compay Conejito.

—¡No se nos puede olvidar el jengibre, ni la menta por si nos da catarro!

—¡La planta de huaco! ¡El limoncillo y la canela! ¡Las hojas de plátano pa' hacer los pasteles!

—¡El pilón para hacer mofongo y la tostonera para hacer tostones!

—¡El abanico de mano! Eso sí que no se puede quedar.

—¡Los mosquiteros! ¡Los mosquiteros no pueden faltar!

—¡Ni la cuica! ¡Ni el trompo, ni la muñeca azul! ¡Tampoco olviden las canicas!

—¡Traigan un chinchín de pimienta pa' echarle al huracán! ¡De esa forma lo espantaremos! —dijo Juan bobo y todos empezaron a reír.

—¡Que nadie se ponga kikirimiao y salga pitao! Todos nos enfrentaremos a este huracán. Y como diría mi abuelita doña Marina: *Uno para todos y todos para uno* —exclamó con mucho ánimo La Cucarachita Martina.

—Cenisosa, Tía Miseria y Princesa Adivinadora, vengan conmigo por favor. LLenaremos los baldes con agua potable —les pidió Martina.

—Tenemos que buscar mantas, toallas y muchas sábanas. ¿Quién me quiere ayudar? —preguntó María Sabida y enseguida Juan Pelao se ofreció para ayudarla.

Doña Ana se ocupó de guardar en un cofre todos los juegos sueltos que había por allí: las canicas, los yo-yos, los trompos de corozo, las chiringas y hasta el asiento de un columpio con las sogas.

—En el refugio podremos jugar a El Chico Paralizado o Ambos a dos. A mi me encanta jugar A la limón y también La cebollita —les dijo Doña Ana.

—Aunque yo soy grande me gusta jugar a Las estatuas. Siempre se me ocurren poses bien graciosas —le comentó Juan Pelao.

—Podremos jugar Matarile, A la víbora, entre muchos otros juegos como Chequi Morena, la Papa Caliente y Gallinita Ciega —les recordó María Sabida.

—¡Vamos a enfrentar este terrible huracán juntos! ¡Él no puede más que nosotros! Tenemos que mantenernos unidos y como decía mi abuelita doña Marina: *¡En la unión está la fuerza!* —exclamó Martina y todos se fueron a trabajar para poder enfrentarse a ese terrible huracán.

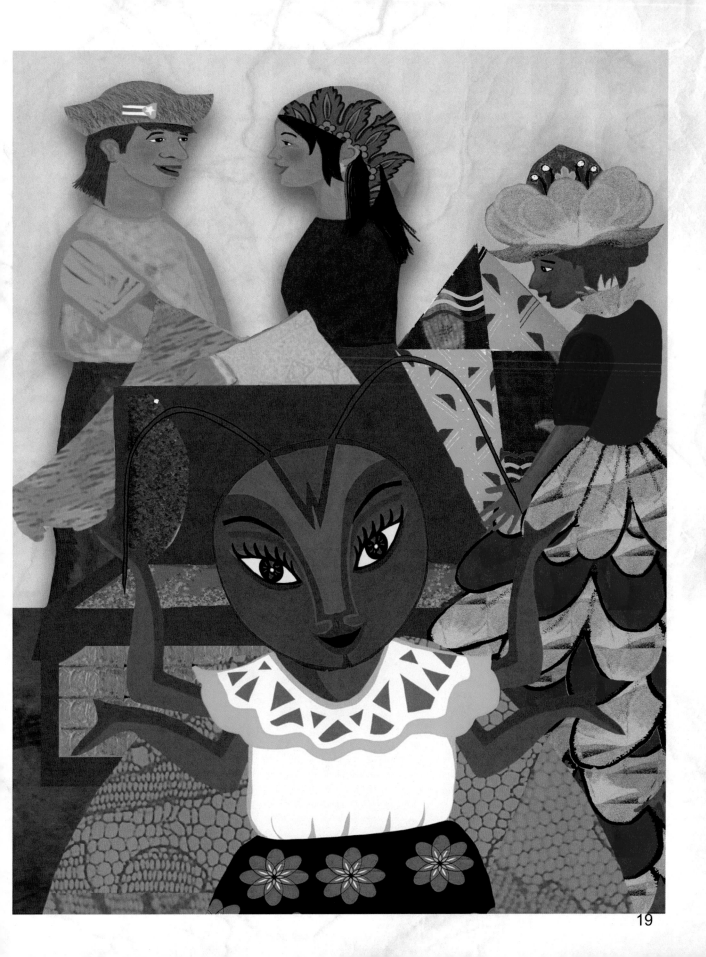

2.

*No dejes para mañana
lo que puedas hacer hoy*

Aquella tarde, todos los habitantes
de la comunidad "La Folclorriqueña",
comenzaron a prepararse
para la llegada del
terrible huracán.

Había un corre y corre
que no paraba
y entre llovizna y llovizna
se contaban un cuento,
una adivinanza o cantaban.

La Princesa Adivinadora, Cenisosa, Tía Miseria y Martina fueron a llenar envases con agua potable.

—Mi querida abuelita doña Marina nos contaba historias sobre los terribles huracanes San Felipe y San Ciriaco. Ambos fueron muy fuertes —les contaba La Cucarachita Martina mientras llenaban los baldes con agua potable.

Entonces La Princesa Adivinadora les hizo una adivinanza:

—Viento va,
viento viene,
con el aguacero
nada lo detiene.
Suenan sus truenos,
se alumbra con rayos
rompe techos y derrumba paredes
Dime a ver si adivinas
¿Qué es?¿Qué es lo que viene?

—¡El huracán! ¡El huracán!—dijeron todas a la vez y se echaron a reír. Catilanguá Lantemué comenzó a bailar y a cantar:

—Temporal, temporal
por ahí viene el temporal
¿Qué será de mi Borinquen
cuando llegue el temporal?
¿Qué será de Puerto Rico
cuando llegue el temporal?

Entre adivinanzas y canciones fueron llenando de agua todos los baldes. Todos en aquella comunidad trabajaban con afán para enfrentar al huracán mientras Martina les recordaba:

*—¡A mal tiempo, buena cara!.*Así decía mi abuelita doña Marina.

—Si el agua del río sube, destruirá nuestras casitas y como la mía está tan y tan y tan destartalada, desaparecerá –decía la Tía Miseria con mucha tristeza.

—No se preocupe Tía Miseria, si pasa eso, usted viene a vivir con nosotros y formará parte de nuestro cuento —le dijo Cenisosa.

—¡Jovencita, mi cuento es mi cuento y no lo abandonaré jamás! ¡Jamás! ¡Nunca me iré a otro cuento! —contestó muy molesta la Tía Miseria.

—¡Era una broma, Tía Miseria! ¡Ríase un ratito que se va a arrugar más de lo que está! Cuando yo era pequeña, mi madrina, me enseñó a espantar el miedo, el hambre y la tristeza. Ella gritaba con mucha fuerza: ¡Zape, zape,zape,zapatón! ¡Gritemos con mucha fuerza! ¡Repitan conmigo! ¡Zape, zape, zape, zapatón! ¡Zape! —exclamó su amiga.

— ¡Zape!, ¡Zape, zape! ¡Zapatón! —repitió la Tía Miseria.

—Tía Miseria, puede estar segura de que todos la cuidaremos Vamos a cantar rondas para que se anime. ¡Usted no está sola! Somos una familia muy grande —le dijo Cenisosa mientras la abrazaba y cantaba alegremente:

A la limón, a la limón
que se rompió la fuente.
A la limón, a la limón
mandadla a componer.

Urí, urí, urá,
la reina va a pasar.
Urí, urí, urá
la reina va a pasar.

Mientras tanto...las nubes borrascosas iban arropando el cielo que se veía " entorunao" y de repente apareció El pájaro que habla. Venía volando desde Jayuya. Estaba muy, muy nervioso y gritaba:

—¡El huracán es gigantesco! ¡Descomunal! Lo vi desde Cerro Punta.¡Está que mete miedo! ¡Ese huracán viene arrasando! ¡Es el diantre! ¡Vayamos al refugio ahora!¡No podemos esperar más! Aceleren el paso, que para luego es tarde!

—¡Avisemos a todos! ¡Miren el cielo! ¡Esto se está poniendo pelú! Tenemos que buscar a los que viven jalda arriba: La abuela Zapatona, al Vendedor de Sombreros y a El Pavero. Vamos antes de que la cosa se ponga apretá —exclamó Catilanguá Lantemué.

—¡Qué no se nos olviden Juan Periquito, La Carbonerita y a San Serení! Todavía tenemos chance de buscarlos —les recordó El Principe Negro.

—El cielo está encancaranublado
¿Quién lo encancaranublaría?
El que lo encancaranubló,
buen encancaranublador sería
¡Nuestro cielo está bien encancaranublado!
—repetía una y otra vez, Catilanguá Lantemué,
mientras aceleraban el paso para avisar a los demás.

—¡Vamos al refugio! ¡El terrible huracán está cerquita! ¡El viento nos puede llevar! —gritaba con fuerza El Esclavo.

3.

¡Más vale tarde que nunca!

El Príncipe Negro, El Esclavo
y Catilanguá Lantemué
le explicaron a los demás lo que
El Pájaro que habla les había contado.
Entonces decidieron buscar un refugio
enseguida para protegerse
del terrible huracán.

—Traigan los recuerdos valiosos que tengan. Si el río sube causará inundaciones —les recordó La Cucarachita Martina y sin pensarlo dos veces corrieron a sus hogares para sacar todo aquello que tenía valor.

¡Taca tán! ¡Taca Tán!
¡Por ahí viene el huracán!

¡No olviden los plátanos, ni la banasta
y llenen bien la canasta!
¡Ayuden al chivo, al grillo, a la changa,
y también a la hormiguita!

¡Taca tán! ¡Taca Tán!
¡Por ahí viene el huracán!

¡Traigan el güiro y el cemí de la abuela!
¡El trompo de higüera y el palito de hinojo!
¡Los mosquiteros y el pandero de piojo!
¡Y el arroz con habichuela!

¡Taca tán! ¡Taca Tán!
¡Por ahí viene el huracán!

¡Dúndere-dúndere,
péndere-péndere,
périli-périli!
Veo, veo que ya viene
me lo dijo San Serení:
¡Esto no es una peregrina,
ni el chequi morena chequi!

¡Taca tán! ¡Taca Tán!
¡Por ahí viene el huracán!
¡Taca tán! ¡Taca Tán!
¡Por ahí viene el huracán!

La marcha para el refugio comenzó en un santiamén. Todos los habitantes de aquella comunidad se ayudaban y comentaban sobre las pertenencias valiosas que se llevaban en aquel éxodo forzoso. Mercedes guardó su sortija. El Caballo de siete colores buscó la llave. La Cucarachita Martina buscó el polvo, la guitarra, el abanico de mano y el libro de recetas.

—¡Me acompaña el amuleto que me regaló mi abuelo Anansi —exclamó el maravilloso Compay Araña.

—¡Ay Santa Barbara Bendita! Nosotros llevaremos el caldero lleno de viandas —explicaba Juan Bobo quien estaba muy nervioso.

—Traigo mi machete y mi cuatro. Uno para abrir el camino y el otro para abrir las puertas a la música —decía El Ratoncito Pérez.

—Adornaré la cueva con las rosas, los claveles, flores del guayacán y las miramelindas. La convertiré en un hermoso jardín —decía Doña Ana mientras recordaba con tristeza de su querido vergel.

—¡Vamos a buscar a papá! ¡Papá! ¡Papá! ¡Queremos ver a papá! —gritaban Los dos hermanitos.

—Su papá viene hacia acá. Se reunirá con nosotros ya mismo. Me lo dijo el gato de trapo —les dijo con cariño Doña Ana.

Todos los personajes caminaban hacia la cueva mientras cantaban:

¡San Isidro Labrador
quita el agua y pon el sol!
¡San Isidro Labrador
quita el agua y pon el sol!

La travesía hacia el refugio fue lenta porque el fuerte viento los empujaba, pero nada los detenía. Tenían que llegar a la cueva antes de que el tiempo empeorara y el huracán los azotara.

—¡SSS! ¡SSS! ¡SSS! —sonaba el viento huracanado mientras sacudía las ramas de los árboles de un lado a otro y algunas se quebraban cuando chocaban entre sí.

A lo lejos se podía divisar un espectáculo aterrador. El cielo estaba oscuro, como la barriga de un burro. El sonido de los truenos y el resplandor de los relámpagos asustaba a cualquiera, El viento era fuerte y arrancaba las hojas de los árboles y plantas. Unos ayudaban a los otros en aquella caminata tan difícil, pero no se detenían. Ya se sentía la presencia del terrible huracán en aquella isla tropical.

—¡Aceleren el paso! ¡Aceleren! ¡Tenemos que llegar a la cueva antes de que nos atrape un remolino! —ordenaba El Príncipe Negro.

—¡Ya la vi! ¡Es la cueva María de la Cruz! ¡Llegamos! ¡Llegamos a la cueva! —gritó muy emocionado El esclavo y todos comenzaron a caminar con rapidez.

Ya se sentían los vientos huracanados. El refugio era un lugar perfecto. Todos estarían bien protegidos. Todos estarían a salvo.

4.

A mal tiempo, buena cara.

Al llegar a la cueva se encontraron
con el coquí, el inrirí, el cucubano,
el sapo concho, y el San Pedrito.
Allí estaba Julián Chiví con
Pepito Palito, el lagartijo jardinero,
el comeñame, la cotorra,
la boa, el murciélago
y la mariposa Arlequín,
entre muchos otros

Aquella cueva era el refugio ideal.
Poco a poco se fueron acomodando
para esperar a que el huracán saliera
de la isla. Compartieron el agua,
los alimentos, las canciones,
los juegos y sus cuentos.

—¡Vengan todos, toditos! Ratoncito Pérez, siéntate a mi lado. ¡Vamos a contar cuentos! —explicó Martina con voz clara y melodiosa.

Mientras el huracán atravesaba la isla, en la cueva todos escucharon encantados aquella frase que los unía como comunidad:

Había una vez y dos serían tres...

Como de costumbre, todos quedaron encantados con el cuento de su querida amiga Martina. Luego le tocó el turno al maravilloso Compay Araña y al Compay Conejillo, quienes hicieron reír a todos con sus cuentos.

Catilangua Lantemué encantó tanto a sus amigos con su fascinante narración, que le hicieron coro para cantar su canción:

—Juey, juey, juey,
juey, esperanza de mué
¿has dicho que yo me llamo
Catilanguá Lantemué?

Juan Gandules, el de los ojos azules, repitió su cuento tres veces hasta que los demás lo contaron junto a el:

—Pues señores, este es el cuento
de Juan Gandules
que tenía los ojos azules
y los zapatos al revés.
¿Quieres que te lo cuente otra vez?

Más tarde jugaron con Antón Pirulero y a La Vibora. Los niños jugaron a San Sereñí y a la Gallinita Ciega. A pesar de todo, fue una noche inolvidable y se fueron quedando dormidos cantando:
Una, do, li, tra
elelé mengua,
un sofete, carolete.

Afuera, el terrible huracán traía un repertorio de sonidos aterradores y estridentes que no cesaban.

—¡Grrrrr! ¡Sss Sss Sss! ¡Craaac! ¡Zis! ¡Zas! ¡Ploc! ¡Ploc! ¡Brum- mmmm! ¡Ssss Ssss Ssss! ¡Brummmm! ¡Clang! —se escuchaba el crujido de las ramas de los árboles. Las planchas de zinc chocaban contra las piedras de la cueva y el sonido constante de la lluvia y de los truenos no cesaban. A medida que pasaba el tiempo, algunos cantaron lindas nanas y poquito a poquito se durmieron. Dentro de la cueva el coquí y los grillos cantaban. El tímido Múcaro ululaba suavemente y las palomas los arrullaban.

Al día siguiente la lluvia continuaba azotando la isla, sin embargo todos se llenaron de paciencia. Volvieron a cantar, a jugar, y a con- tar sus cuentos. Prepararon un caldo con viandas riquísimo y una deliciosa ensalada de frutas. Todos y todas compartieron en paz como de costumbre.

¡Por fin el huracán salió de la isla y regresó la calma! El Pájaro que habla fue el primero en salir de la cueva y cuando volvió a entrar estaba desesperado.

—¡Despierten! ¡Salgan de la cueva! ¡Salgan! ¡Todo está destruido! ¡Quiero llorar! —se lamentaba mientras sacudía sus alas alrededor de sus amigos.

A medida que iban saliendo del refugio, las expresiones de dolor y pena llenaban aquel espacio destrozado. El paisaje era triste y desgarrador. A lo lejos se podían divisar las casitas destruidas sin techos y sin paredes. El lodo cubría los muebles rotos y la ropa que estaba regada por todas partes. Había ventanas, tablones de madera y planchas de zinc a diestra y siniestra. Cientos de árboles se amontonaban sobre los escombros. Parecía como si un enorme incendio los hubiera quemado.

—¡Lo perdimos todo!—gritó Juan Calalú mientras su madre lloraba a lágrima viva porque habían perdido su bohío.

—¡Nuestro bohío ya no está! ¡Lo hemos perdido todo!—repetía doña Juana mientras se unía al llanto de los demás.

—Cálmate querida Juana. Tenemos que calmarnos. Entre todos reconstruiremos nuestra querida comunidad. ¡Lo haremos! Tenemos que desahogarnos, pero recuerden que hemos enfrentado un huracán más terrible que este y hablo del huracán del olvido. Ya no cuentan nuestros cuentos y no recuerdan nuestros nombres. ¡Estamos a punto de desaparecer para siempre ¡Aún así, nos hemos levantado y hemos resistido! ¡Somos fuertes! ¡Sacaremos los estorbos y levantaremos nuestra querida comunidad! ¡A trabajar! —les dijo Martina con fuerza y entusiasmo.

—Estamos unidos y nada nos separará. Nada nos vencerá. Es cierto lo que dice Martina. No podemos temer —dijo muy emocionado el maravilloso Compay Araña.

—"No permitas que el miedo te eñangote". Eso me lo decía mi querida abuela doña Juana Agripina, quien recorrió muchas millas para luchar por su libertad —les recordó El Esclavo.

—Volveremos a renacer, como renacerá nuestra isla con sus bellos paisajes y su poderosa cultura ¡Vamos, levántense! ¡Busquen sus machetes! El sol nos ilumina. Volveremos a levantar nuestra comunidad —exclamó La Cucarachita Martina y todos se pusieron a trabajar.

—¡Pa' atrás, ni pa' coger impulso! ¡A trabajar sin tregua! —exclamó el Ratoncito Pérez mientras levantaba la bandera de Puerto Rico y todos empezaron a cantar el himno de su comunidad:

La Folclorriqueña
comunidad de bienestar.
Aquí todos vivimos
rodeados de mucha paz
y juntos celebramos con orgullo
y defendemos con valor
nuestro amado folclor.

Meses más tarde La Cucarachita Martina
escribió una carta a sus familiares y les explicó
lo que había sucedido en la isla:

—Queridos tíos: Espero que se encuentren bien.
Ya arreglamos algunos techos. Tuvimos que construír
muchas casas porque el huracán las destruyó.
¡Por fin está llegando la luz y el agua potable!
Les cuento que no ha sido una tarea fácil.
Recogimos los escombros, organizamos comedores sociales,
cosimos mosquiteros, colocamos en nuestra comunidad filtros
de agua potable,compartimos todo lo que teníamos
y recibimos ayuda del mundo entero.
Con paciencia, afán y empeño todos nos enfrentamos
al huracán María y salimos adelante.
Ustedes saben que somos un pueblo de gente valiente,
luchadora y agradecida que no se rinde ante ningún huracán.
Tal vez pueda ir a visitarlos el verano próximo,
pero si quieren venir a la isla,
ya saben que mi casa es su casa.
¡Siempre serán bienvenidos!
Los quiero mucho y los extraño.
Reciban todo mi cariño,
su sobrina que los extraña,

Martina

Y se acabó el cuento con ají y pimiento
y como me lo contaron te lo cuento
y te lo vuelvo a contar.
Cuando escuches:
¡Por ahí viene un huracán!
Siéntate y escucha
el cuento una vez más.

Lo que aprendimos con el paso
del huracán María

"Entonces por un agujerito que había en la ventana vi, por primera vez en mi vida, cómo los aguacates volaban". Así me contó un estudiante de 5to grado de la escuela Las Mareas Bilingual School de Salinas, sobre su experiencia con el huracán María. Los huracanes Irma y María nos dejaron muchas historias que tenemos que contar, escuchar, recopilar y guardar. De esa forma, las generaciones futuras aprenderán de estas experiencias. No podemos permitir que el huracán del olvido desaparezca nuestros cuentos.

Lo que me enseñó el huracán María

Narrar nuestros cuentos, nos convierte en personajes activos de la historia de nuestro país. El cuento Martina y el huracán, es producto de las vivencias que tuve en diferentes comunidades donde narré cuentos y ofrecí talleres creativos. Hay diferentes tipos de huracanes y uno de ellos es el del olvido. Para mi asombro, cuando contaba el cuento de La Cucarachita Martina, la mayoría de los niños y las niñas no lo conocían. Entonces nació Martina y el huracán.

El 19 de septiembre por la noche, me encontraba en el refugio Pedrín Zorrilla ofreciendo un taller de cuentos y títeres a las niñas y los niños que estaban junto a sus familias, refugiándose del huracán María. Esa noche un amigo que me había encontrado allí me dijo que "la historia de Puerto Rico se va a escribir antes de María y después de María."

A pesar de que el 5 de septiembre el huracán Irma nos había azotado causando mucho daño, el huracán María venía con una fuerza y un tamaño descomunal. El 20 de septiembre de 2017 el huracán María entró a la isla de Puerto Rico. Este era un huracán gigantesco y poderoso que traía consigo tornados que fueron destrozando todo a su paso.

El jueves por la mañana regresé al refugio. Era difícil conducir por las carreteras porque la gran cantidad de árboles, letreros, postes de energía eléctrica, techos de madera y aluminio, planchas de zinc, cables, postes y todo tipo de objetos estaban regados por todas partes y entorpecían el libre acceso. El paisaje era desolador.

Cuando llegué al refugio volví a contar cuentos. Las niñas y los niños, al igual que los adultos estaban nerviosos y tristes, pero el arte sana y reconforta. Al igual que yo había otros artistas, como los miembros del grupo Agitarte, Y No Había Luz e Israel Lugo, que salieron a ofrecer su talento y ayuda a los damnificados. Nuestra amada isla estaba herida y maltrecha. No había luz, ni agua potable en la mayoría de los pueblos, ciudades y comunidades. Se habían caído puentes y había inundaciones por todas partes.

Los medios de comunicación también se afectaron. Fueron muchas las familias que lo perdieron todo. Las brigadas de rescate no cesaban de trabajar. Todo el mundo ponía de su parte y Puerto Rico se transformó en una comunidad gigantesca. Una sola, como la estrella de nuestra bandera.

Éramos una comunidad trabajando mano a mano para ponerse de pie y salir adelante como lo habían hecho nuestros antepasados con los huracanes San Ciriaco y San Felipe y como ya lo habíamos hecho cuando pasaron los huracanes Hugo y George, los que también hicieron mucho daño a nuestra patria.

Por desgracia muchos puertorriqueños emigraron por diferentes razones. Algunos lo habían perdido todo y tenían familia en Estados Unidos, otros perdieron sus trabajos, otros estaban enfermos o necesitaban terapias. Una gran cantidad de boricuas emigró buscando alternativas para enfrentar la situación. Otros desaparecieron entre el lodo, los derrumbes, las corrientes de agua y otros murieron por falta de luz, de medicinas, de cuidados, de transportación, aislamiento y depresiones.

La mayoría de los artistas y artesanos quedamos en el limbo, al igual que muchísimos trabajadores de diferentes profesiones. Todas las actividades culturales cesaron. Por otro lado, el turismo se detuvo. San Juan, la capital, parecía un pueblo fantasma.

A pesar de todo renacía el compañerismo y aprendimos que la solidaridad mueve montañas. Del mundo entero comenzó a llegar la ayuda que necesitábamos para resistir y levantarnos. Miles de seres humanos comenzaron a contribuir de forma desinteresada y a pesar de que siempre hay individuos y compañías que solo piensan en el lucro y la ganancia, yo prefiero recordar a la gente y las organizaciones sin fines de lucro que nos ayudaron y apoyaron.

Las compañías de teatro Agitarte, Pregones y Teatro Yerbabruja fueron de los grupos que le dieron la mano a la clase artística y a muchas comunidades. Agitarte Inc. creó comedores sociales y generó un movimiento cultural que todavía al día de hoy sigue promoviendo el quehacer artístico y la defensa de nuestra cultura. Gracias a su apoyo pude pintar la manta para el cuento afropuertorriqueño Catilanguá Lantemué. Con el apoyo solidario de miles de personas han levantado fondos para seguir apoyando el trabajo artístico de muchos artistas. Miles de personas se han beneficiado con la labor social y cultural de esta compañía. Gracias a ellos muchos artistas pudimos ofrecer talleres en diferentes comunidades. Teatro Yerbabruja ayudó económicamente, trajo alimentos, medicinas y todo tipo de productos que necesitabamos en la isla. Teatro Pregones ayudó económicamente a muchos artistas y El Dramatist Guild Foundation fue muy solidario y generoso con la ayuda económica que le brindó a las dramaturgas y dramaturgos.

Durante el tiempo que estuve viajando por la isla, escribí el cuento de *La Cucarachita Martina y el huracán*. Ver tanta gente luchando por salir adelante, tanta gente ayudando a otros, unos creando, otros organizando, abrazando, martillando, sembrando, cosiendo o cocinando me llenaba de ánimo porque en la unión está la fuerza. El espíritu de lucha nos daba el empuje para seguir adelante.

A medida que fui visitando refugios y comunidades contando cuentos, me di cuenta de que la mayoría de los niños y jóvenes no conocían nuestros cuentos folclóricos. ¿Por qué se habían dejado de contar estos cuentos? ¿Por qué los habíamos dejado a un lado? Por otro lado contar sus historias, sus anécdotas era sanador y es que el ser humano necesita compartir y contar sus experiencias. Contar en voz alta es un acto de sanación. ¡Es un acto de liberación y solidaridad!

La Cucarachita Martina y el huracán es un cuento dedicado a todos los niños y las niñas de nuestra amada patria. Durante este proceso, todos fueron muy valientes. En especial a los estudiantes de la escuela Las Mareas Bilingual School de Salinas y al profesor Orlando Valentin León, quien ya no está entre nosotros. El profesor Valentín era un ser humano exepcional. Estaba siempre de buen humor y dispuesto a compartir, apoyar y animar a sus queridos estudiantes. Nunca lo olvidaremos.

Tengo que agradecer a la líder y presidenta de la Legislatura Municipal de Salinas, la Sra. Jacqueline Vázquez Suárez quien me animó para que comenzara el proyecto de kamishibai y a la directora de la escuela la Directora de la escuela, la Sra. Aurora Figueroa Rosario, educadora de excelencia, quien respaldó el proyecto en todo momento. Durante el 2018 y el 2019 se ofreció nuevamente el taller de kamishibai impactando otros grupos de estudiantes.

de kamishibai impactando otros grupos de estudiantes. Los estudiantes de Las Mareas Bilingual School nos dejaron cuentos sobre sus experiencias con el huracán María. Estos son testimonios muy importantes que debemos conservar y dar a conocer. Todos tenemos el poder de contar nuestras experiencias y contar los cuentos que forman parte de nuestra cultura. El compañero Fernando Silva consiguió que la organización CIVITAS Club, nos donara el dinero para comprar los materiales de arte y un butai (teatro de madera japonés de tres puertas) para la escuela. Comenzamos a escribir y dibujar sobre las experiencias que recordábamos sobre el paso del huracán. Fue una experiencia sanadora. De esta forma comenzó el Proyecto: Letraverde, Te cuento con el kamishibai en la escuela Elemental Bilingüe Las Mareas, comunidad localizada en Salinas. Más tarde recibí el Premio en Reciclaje y Reutilización otorgado por los Fondos Ambientales Ford. Gracias a este reconocimiento pudimos filmar un documental sobre el trabajo realizado por los estudiantes en este proyecto. El mismo fue realizado por el Sr. Eduardo Aguiar, reconocido director y documentarista. Pueden ver el video en : https://vimeo.com/265133581.

No permitamos que el huracán del olvido desaparezca nuestros juegos, cuentos y canciones folclóricas. ¡Fomentemos la lectura y la narración de nuestros cuentos! ¡Volvamos a cantar y a jugar en nuestras escuelas y comunidades!¡Celebremos nuestra maravillosa cultura puertorriqueña!

Agradecimientos:
Agitarte Inc.
Donativos Ambientales de la Fundación Ford
Dramatist Guild Foundation
Teatro Yerbabruja
Margarita Espada
Teatro Pregones
Fernando Silva
CIVITAS Club
Poli Marichal, Ricardo Méndez Matta,
Familia Marichal-Lugo
Rosa Janer,
Editorial SM
Hector Aparicio
Perla Sofía

Gracias a su solidaridad y ayuda
he podido seguir ofreciendo talleres
en diferentes comunidades,
crear cuentos y obras de teatro
para aportar al desarrollo
y fomentar el respeto hacia
nuestra cultura puertorriqueña

¡Viva nuestra cultura! ¡Viva nuestro folclor!

Huracanes y tormentas en Puerto Rico en los siglos XX y XXI

San Zacarías: 11-12 de septiembre de 1910

San Hipólito: 22 de agosto de 1916

San Liborio: 23-24 de julio de 1926

San Felipe: 13 de septiembre de 1928 (huracán)

San Nicolás: 10-11 de septiembre de 1931

San Ciprián: 26-27 de septiembre de 1932 (huracán)

San Calixto II: 14 de octubre de 1943

Santa Clara: 12 de agosto de 1956 (huracán)

San Lorenzo: 6 de septiembre de 1960 (huracán)

Eloísa: 15-16 de septiembre de 1975 (tormenta)

David: 30 de agosto de 1979 (huracán)

Federico: 4 de septiembre de 1979 (huracán)

Klaus: 7 de noviembre de 1984 (tormenta)

Hugo: 18 de septiembre de 1989 (huracán)

Luis: 6 de septiembre de 1995 (huracán)

Marilyn: 16 de septiembre de 1995

Berta: 8 de julio de 1996

Hortensia: 9-10 de septiembre de 1996

Georges: 21 de septiembre de 1998 (huracán)

Irma: 5 de septiembre de 2017 (huracán)

María: 20 de septiembre de 2017 (huracán)

Ellos contaron, estudiaron, recopilaron, protegieron, investigaron, escribieron, grabaron, publicaron y dieron a conocer nuestra cultura y folclor:

John Alden Mason(1885-1967)
Antropólogo y lingüista estadounidense que grabó, entre 1914 y 1915, música y canciones folclóricas puertorriqueñas, luego de la invasión norteamericana en 1898.
(http://muse.jhu.edu/article/263522)

Ricardo Alegría (1921-2011)
Historiador, escritor, gestor cultural y antropólogo puertorriqueño. Defensor y promotor de la cultura puertorriqueña. Escribió *Historia de nuestros indios* (1952), *La fiesta de Santiago Apóstol en Loíza Aldea* (1955), *Cuentos Folclóricos de Puerto Rico* (1968), entre muchos otros. Fue director del Instituto de Cultura Puertorriqueña y ocupó otros cargos relacionados con todo el quehacer cultural de Puerto Rico.
(http://www.miradero.org/uploads/4/3/1/4/4314859/folclorstica_puertorriquea.pdf)

Pura Belpré (1899-1982)
Contadora de cuentos, bibliotecaria, titiritera, educadora y defensora de los cuentos folclóricos de P.R. Fue la primera bibliotecaria puertorriqueña en ser contratada por el sistema de la Biblioteca Pública de Nueva York. En su biblioteca contaba cuentos y en muchas ocasiones utilizaba el teatro de títeres para acompañar la narración, por lo tanto se cree que ella fue una de las primeras titiriteras boricuas. Ante la necesidad de contar cuentos para los niños puertorriqueños, se dio a la tarea de rescatar cuentos del folclor puertorriqueño. Esa fue la razón por la cual publicó en 1932 en cuento de *La Cucarachita Martina y al Ratoncito Pérez, El caballo de siete colores*, entre otros.
(https://centropr.hunter.cuny.edu/sites/default/files/faids/pdf/Belpre%2C%20Pura%20 Jan%202015.pdf)

María Cadilla de Martínez (1886-1951)
Cuentista, poeta y folclorista puertorriqueña. En 1933 escribe su tesis doctoral sobre La poesía popular en Puerto Rico. Trabajó incansablemente en definir y aclarar nuestra identidad cultural e hispánica. Recopiló, investigó el folclor puertorriqueño.
Escribió: *Rememorando el pasado heroico, Hitos de la raza, Raíces de la tierra, Juegos y canciones infantiles de Puerto Rico*, entre otros.
(http://www.encaribe.org/es/article/maria-cadilla-de-martinez/1110)

Marcelino Canino Salgado: (1947)
Profesor universitario, crítico, defensor de la cultura puertorriqueña y folclorista. Escribe *La copla y el romance populares en la tradición oral de Puerto Rico, La canción de cuna en la tradición de Puerto Rico* y *El cantar folclórico de Puerto Rico*.

Cayetano Coll y Toste (1850-1930)
Poeta, narrador, ensayista, historiador, periodista, político y médico, En 1893 es nombrado Médico Forense de la Real Audiencia Territorial de Puerto Rico. En 1913 es nombrado

Historiador Oficial de Puerto Rico, comenzando a publicar su "Boletín Histórico". Recopiló las tradiciones y leyendas puertorriqueñas que cubren tres siglos y medio de vida colonial y las publica en 1924.

Monserrate Deliz (1896-1969)
Profesora universitaria que recopiló un gran caudal de música puertorriqueña. Mientras ejerció la profesión de maestra en las escuelas públicas recopiló una gran cantidad de canciones infantiles. Su libro *Renadío Del Cantar Folklorico de Puerto Rico* se publica en 1985.(http://bibliotecademusicapr.blogspot.com/p/coleccion-monserrate-deliz.html)

Elsa Escabí
Tecnóloga médica, investigadora de campo y colaboradora del proyecto de la Décima puertorriqueña del Centro de Investigaciones Sociales de la Universidad de Puerto Rico(1970) Edita la nueva versión del libro *El rosario popular de Puerto Rico* escrito en su función de colaboradora de investigación de su hermano Pedro Escabí.

Pedro C. Escabí
Profesor universitario, investigador, folclorista y escritor. Autor de *La décima: Vista parcial del folclor* (Estudio etnográfico de la cultura popular de Puerto Rico)

Aurelio Macedonio Espinosa (1880–1958), profesor en la Universidad de Stanford, fue un erudito conocido internacionalmente por sus estudios en folklore y filología hispanoamericanos. Era especialmente conocido por su promoción del estudio de la lengua y la literatura españolas.

Roberto Fernández Valledor
Nació y estudió en La Habana donde se graduó de maestro normalista; pero en 1961 se trasladó a Puerto Rico obteniendo el doctorado en filosofía y letras en 1986 en la Universidad de Puerto Rico. Ha publicado una veintena de libros, la mayoría investigaciones de la literatura y el arte antillanos, pero especialmente de la cubana y la boricua. Estudia la figura del pirata Cofresí, tanto en la literatura como en el folclor.

Yvette Jiménez de Báez (1934-)
Profesora e investigadora puertorriqueña. Su tesis doctoral *La décima popular en Puerto Rico* es uno de los trabajos pioneros sobre el tema.

Francisco López Cruz
Músico, investigador, profesor, conferenciante, folclorista y escritor puertorriqueño. Se le llama el Padre del Cuatro Puertorriqueño. Escribió: *El Aguinaldo y el Villancico en el Folklor Puertorriqueño, La Música Folklórica de Puerto Rico, El Aguinaldo en Puerto Rico, Método para la Enseñanza del Cuatro Puertorriqueño*, entre otros.

Walter Murray Chiesa (1923 - 2014),

Gran defensor y gestor de nuestra cultura. dedicó su vida a la educación y la gestión cultural. Fue el creador del concepto de Promotor Artesanal de P.R. Publica la primera edición del *Mapa Artesanal de P.R.* e inicia la Serie de Carteles Conmemorativos honrando al Maestro Artesano. Fue el primer conferenciante itinerante, que visitó cientos de escuelas de Puerto Rico, universidades e instituciones educativas fuera de P.R. para compartir con los estudiantes y maestros sus conocimientos sobre el tema indígena y artesanal.

Nestor Murray Irizarry (1946-)

Educador, conferenciante, ensayista y editor. Ha dedicado su vida a promover estimular y enriquecer la cultura puertorriqueña. Es Coordinador general del Programa de Promoción del Centro de Investigaciones Folklóricas de Puerto Rico; presidente y fundador de la Casa Paoli.Cofundador de la Revista Miradero, primera revista del ciberespacio puertorriqueño. Escribe: *El caballo de los siete colores y otras narraciones tradicionales de Puerto Rico.* (http://www.angelfire.com/ny/conexion/murray_irizarry_nestor.html)

Julia Cristina Ortiz Lugo

Nació en Mayagüez. Es profesora retirada del Departamento de Estudios Hispánicos del Recinto Universitario de Mayagüez. Ha dedicado su vida profesional a la enseñanza e investigación en lectura y escritura y en literatura oral afropuertorriqueña. Creó y enseñó en el RUM los cursos de Cuento folclórico puertorriqueño y Mujer y folclor. Entre sus publicaciones sobre literatura oral se incluyen: *De arañas, conejos y tortugas. Presencia de África en la cuentística de tradición oral en Puerto Rico* (CEA, 1995); *Saben más que las arañas. Ensayos sobre narrativa oral afropuertorriqueña* (FPH/Casa Paoli, 2004); *Cuentos populares puertorriqueños de ayer para la juventud de hoy. Leo, escribo, pienso e investigo.* (Gaviota/ Casa Paoli, 2013). Es editora cofundadora de la primera revista de folclor en el ciberespacio puertorriqueño, Revista Miradero.
(http://academic.uprm.edu/jcortiz/)

Ángeles Pastor (1905 - 1997)

Educadora inigualable, poeta, autora de libros infantiles y ensayista. En el año 2000 se le dedicó La Semana de la Lengua, reconociendo de esta forma la inmensa aportación y el legado que nos dejó. Entre sus libros se encuentran: *A Jugar y a Gozar* (1960), *A la Escuela* (1961), *Aventuras Maravillosas* (1971), *Camino de la Escuela* (1961), *Campanillas Folklóricas, Decires y Cantares* (1960), entre muchos otros.
(http://www.angelfire.com/ny/conexion/pastor_angeles_3.html)

Flor Piñero de Rivera

Catedrática, bibliotecaria, educadora, investigadora, escritora y misionera. Nos dejó un libro muy importante: *Un siglo de Literatura Infantil Puertorriqueña.*

Rafael W. Ramírez de Arellano(1884-1974)

Profesor universitario, investigador y folclorista. Fue propulsor de investigaciones históricas de P,R. Fundó y dirigió la revista El Mes histórico. Más tarde publicó el libro *Folklore portorriqueño:cuentos y adivinanzas recogidas en la tradición oral*(1926);

54

Calixta Vélez Adorno

Profesora de historia, investigadora y folclorista nacida en Bayamón.
Autora de los libros: *Juegos Infantiles de Puerto Rico* y *Juguetes tradicionales de Puerto Rico.*
(http://www.primerahora.com/estilos-de-vida/cultura/nota/artesaniasparajugar-255230/)

Teodoro Vidal(1923-2015)

Dicen que desde que don Teodoro Vidal era pequeño comenzó a coleccionar objetos. Conocía muy bien el arte popular,y era experto en tradiciones puertorriqueñas. Dedicó una gran parte de su vida a proteger y estudiar el folclor de Puerto Rico. Llegó a coleccionar 6,000 piezas de artesanía y arte puertorriqueño. Escribió *Tradiciones en la brujería puertorriqueña,* entre otros.
(https://issuu.com/revistamiradero/docs/revista_miradero_numero_9_-_2017_v3)

Libros y documentos que recomendamos:

- *El Folklore Portorriqueño*, de Rafael Ramirez de Arellano
- *De arañas, conejos y tortugas. Presencia de África en la cuentística de tradición oral en Puerto Rico y Cuentos populares puertorriqueños de ayer para la juventud de hoy, Araña y el buey y Cenisosa* de Julia Cristina Ortiz Lugo
- *Juegos tradicionales de Puerto Rico,* de Calixta Velez Adorno
- *Cuentos folclóricos de Puerto Rico,* de Ricardo Alegría
- *El cantar folclórico de Puerto Rico,* de Marcelino Canino
- *Tradiciones en la brujería puertorriqueña,* de Teodoro Vidal
- *La Cucarachita Martina y al Ratoncito Pérez, El caballo de siete colores* de Pura Belpré
- *Un siglo de Literatura Infantil Puertorriqueña,* de Flor Piñero de Rivera
- *El Aguinaldo y el Villancico en el Folklor Puertorriqueño, La Música Folklórica de Puerto Rico,* de Francisco López Cruz
- *Juegos y canciones infantiles de Puerto Rico,* de María Cadilla de Martínez
- *La décima popular en Puerto Rico,* de Yvette Jiménez de Báez
- *Cofresí, La flecha, Otoquí, Mamá Toa, La muñeca, La vasija, Coabey, Colibrí, Homenaje, Cinco llagas, y Cuentas del collar artesanal,* de Walter Murray Chiesa
- *El caballo de los siete colores y otras narraciones tradicionales de Puerto Rico,* de Nestor Murray Irizarry
- *El pirata Cofresí mitificado por la tradición oral puertorriqueña,* de Roberto Fernandez Valledor
- *Renadío del cantar folclórico de Puerto Rico,* de Monserrate Deliz
- *Chanda Candela te cuenta el Compay Araña y las habichuelas, La vaca de Juan Gandules,* de Tere Marichal-Lugo
- *Refranero,* de Eliseo Echevarría Santos
- *La colección John Alden Mason (1914-1915): Una documentación sonora para el estudio de la historia cultural y musical puertorriqueña,* de Hugo René Viera Vargas
(https://musike.cmpr.edu/la-coleccion-john-alden-mason-1914-1915-una-documentacion-sonora-para-el-estudio-de-la-historia-cultural-y-musical-puertriquena/)

Frases y refranes que decimos en Puerto Rico

Un refrán es una frase popular que enseña o nos da un consejo.

Encuentra los refranes que hay en el cuento.

1. **¡Ay bendito!**: Expresión que expresa lástima, pena y queja.

2. **Pa' luego es tarde**: Los problemas hay que resolverlos inmediatamente.

3. **Es mejor prevenir que tener que lamentar**: Hay que ocuparse de hacer nuestras tareas para no tener que lamentarnos después.

4. **Hablaban hasta por los codos**: Hablaban muchísimo.

5. **Lo que viene no es un mamey:** Lo que viene no es cosa facil.

6. **¡Qué nadie se ponga kikirimiao y salga pitao que no hay por que tener miedo!** : Enfrentar lo que venga sin miedo alguno.

7. **No dejes para mañana lo que puedas hacer hoy**: No atrases tus obligaciones.

8. **Camarón que se duerme se lo lleva la corriente**: Si te despistas y no estás atento,puedes tener un mal rato o perder algo.

9. **Cuando el río suena, es porque agua trae**: Cuando se está escuchando un rumor sobre algo, es porque puede ser verdad.

10. **Acelera el paso, que pa' luego es tarde**: No lo tomes con calma que se nos hace tarde.

11. **Esto no es un mamey**: No es facil ni sencillo.

12. **Esto se está poniendo pelú**: La situación se está complicando.

13. **Antes de que la cosa se ponga apretá**: Hacer las cosas antes de que se compliquen.

14. **Más rápido que ligero**: Hacer las cosas inmediatamente, sin perder tiempo.

16. **A mal tiempo, buena cara:** Aunque la situación esté difícil tenemos que hacer lo mejor que podamos y con ánimo.

17. **Me canso hasta de arroparme**: La persona está tan cansada que no puede hacer nada.

18. **El que más, más y el que menos, sabe martillar**: Todos sabemos hacer algo productivo.

19. **¡Mientras más pronto mejor!** : Las cosas hay que hacerlas con prontitud.

20. **¡Vamos a meterle el diente!** : Vamos a ponernos a trabajar

21. **¡Pa' atrás, ni pa'coger impulso!**: Ir siempre hacia adelante y no mirar atrás.

22. **De bobo no tiene ni un pelo**: No tiene nada de tonto.

23. **No dejen que se los coma el moho**: No se queden impotentes. No se queden tiesos.

24. **No me pierden ni pie ni pisá**: Lo sigue para todas partes y está pendiente a todo lo que hace.

25. **En la unión está la fuerza**: Cuando estamos unidos podemos más.

¿Dónde encontrar información sobre nuestra historia y folclor?

Puedes visitar **El Archivo General de Puerto Rico** donde podrás encontrar el Patrimonio Histórico Documental de Puerto Rico (conjunto de documentos de valor permanente que forma parte del patrimonio cultural del país). Estos se conservan en los archivos públicos y privados y sirven como fuente de información para la investigación de los aspectos históricos, sociales, económicos, políticos, culturales y legales. Está adscrito al Instituto de Cultura Puertorriqueña. Su misión es recoger, custodiar, conservar y divulgar el patrimonio histórico documental de Puerto Rico.
El Archivo General de Puerto Rico está localizado en Avenida de la Constitución (antes Ponce de León) #500 Puerta de Tierra,San Juan, Puerto Rico

Vocabulario

1. **acerola**: Fruta

2. **algarrobas**: Fruto del algarrobo.

3. **anafre**: Hornillo portátil.

4. **baldes**: Cubo de cuero, lona o madera usado en las embarcaciones.

5. **carambolas**: Fruta tropical.

6. **cimarrón**: Esclavo que escapaba a los montes para ser libre.

7. **chance**: Oportunidad

8. **chipichipi**: Lluvia menuda o llovizna.

8. **drones**: Tambor de acero o plástico para guardar líquidos.

9. **entorunao**: De mal humor.

10. **folclor**: Es el conjunto de costumbres, tradiciones, historia oral, cuentos, juegos, bailes, canciones, entre otras, de un pueblo, una región o de un país. El folclor, también denominado como folklore o folclore, es la expresión de la cultura de un pueblo determinado y lo distingue de los demás países.

11. **higüera**: Fruto del higüero.

12. **huaco**: Planta medicinal.

13. **inrirí**: Nombre que daban los taínos al pájaro carpintero.

14. **jaibería**: Habilidad, astucia.

15. **jacha**: Hacha.

16. **jacho**: Especie de antorcha rústica.

17. **jamaquearnos**: Moverse agitadamente. Sacudida.

18. **mamey**: Árbol y fruto americano. La pulpa del fruto es roja y dulce.

19. **parcha**: Planta que crece en forma de enredadera. Produce una fruta redonde que contiene semillas envueltas en una capa gelatinosa. Con esta se prepara un jugo muy rico.

20. **pomarrosa**: Fruto del yambo,semejante en su forma a una manzana pequeña,de color amarillento con partes rosadas,sabor dulce,olor de rosa y una sola semilla.

21. **Julian Chiví**: Pájaro de las Antillas. También se conoce con el nombre de Juan Chiví. Es el símbolo del Bosque Escuela de Casa Pueblo en Adjuntas. 20. **lerenes**: Tubérculo pequeño parecido a la papa.

22. **palangana**:Recipiente circular que se utiliza para lavar la cara y las manos.

23. **pilón**: Utensilio de cocina hecho de madera que se utiliza para machacar los ingredientes.

24. **quinqué**: Farol que se utiliza en Puerto Rico para alumbrar los hogares.

25. **yagrumo**: El árbol es nativo de México, Centroamérica, las Antillas, el norte de Sudamérica, Brasil y Colombia

26. **yagua** (Tigüero): Base de la rama de la palma real.Con esta se prepara un juguete con el que los niños se deslizan por las lomas.

Aprende más sobre nuestro folclor...

Revista sobre el folclor puertorriqueño:
Revista Miradero: revista de la Casa Paoli, la primera y única revista de folclor en el ciberespacio puertorriqueño. En la revista se encuentran enlaces de artículos sobre temas de folclor, repositorios de cuentos, videos y podcasts.
miradero.org

Artículo sobre los juegos tradicionales:
Calixta Vélez Adorno habla de su colección de juguetes tradicionales
https://www.elnuevodia.com/noticias/locales/nota/juegosdeantanoquesirvenparaeducaralosninos-1158107/

No dejes para mañana
lo que puedas hacer hoy.

Aprende y comparte
los juegos, los refranes,
las canciones, las adivinanzas
y los cuentos folclóricos
de Puerto Rico.
¡No permitas que
el huracán del olvido
los desaparezca!

¡Viva la cultura
puertorriqueña!

Made in the USA
Monee, IL
29 May 2022

97025662R00038